# THE
# PARADOX
# OF POWER

# THE PARADOX OF POWER

## A TRANSFORMING VIEW OF LEADERSHIP

# PAT WILLIAMS

*with* JIM DENNEY

Warner Faith

**WARNER BOOKS**

An AOL Time Warner Company

An AOL Time Warner Company

Printed in the United States of America
First Warner Books printing: November 2002

10 9 8 7 6 5 4 3 2 1

ISBN: 0-446-52938-9
LCCN: 2002108166

To my son, Richie

*"Now, my son, the Lord be with you,
and may you have success."*

1 CHRONICLES 22:11

# Contents

# A Word of Tribute

*by Bobby Bowden*
Head Football Coach,
Florida State University

When I was thirteen years old, America was in the middle of the most deadly war in human history—World War II. I spent my thirteenth year flat on my back with rheumatic fever. My two pastimes during that year were radio and reading. I studied military history—particularly the history of bold military leaders, people who accomplished amazing, audacious things through the people they led. That began a lifelong fascination with the subject of leadership that has carried me through a fifty-season coaching career.

I have found that virtually all the lessons and principles of leadership that apply to war also apply to football—and to life. The leadership principles that achieve great results on the battlefield also achieve great results in a church, in an office, in a classroom, on a football field or basketball court, or anywhere else a leader seeks to reach a goal through people. As author Tim LaHaye wrote, "All of us are vulnerable to leadership."

Coaching is leadership. Successful coaching is winning through other people. As a coach, if you don't know how to motivate and inspire other people to win, you lose. My success as a coach, then, is directly proportional to my ability to understand and apply the principles of leadership in everyday situations. The same is true for you in your leadership arena. And that's why you need to read *The Paradox of Power* by Pat Williams.

Having been a fan of Pat's books for many years, I know he and I are alike in a lot of ways. As senior vice president of the Orlando Magic, Pat is a tough competitor. Like me, this fellow Floridian hates to lose. Like me, he is a student of leadership and a student of history. In his new book you'll read stories of all my longtime heroes: Washington, Lee, Lincoln, Eisenhower, MacArthur, Patton, and many more.

Flipping through the pages of Pat Williams's new book, I get a tingle of *déjà vu*, a sense of recognition: These are the principles I have lived and coached by for half a century! This stuff is real! This is gritty, realistic, transforming truth!

Like Pat Williams, I have made a lifelong study of leadership. That is what motivated me to write my own book, *The Bowden Way*. The book you hold in your hands is the culmination of Pat's lifelong study and experience with leadership—but you'll notice he doesn't call it *The Williams Way*. He calls it *The Paradox of Power*. An equally valid title might be *The Jesus Way*. Here again, I see a great affinity between myself and Pat Williams, because the seven paradoxes of leadership he teaches in this book come from the words and example of the person I regard as The Greatest Leader Who Ever Lived—Jesus of Nazareth.

Understand, this is not a religious book. It's not a book just for Christians (though Christians can certainly learn a lot from it). This is a book for leaders—*all* leaders, in any and all leadership arenas.

If you want to be a great leader, shouldn't you learn leadership from the Master? And what else would you call Jesus—the leader who used twelve unschooled and completely unexceptional men to transform the world? Imagine how your team or organization might be transformed if you could learn and apply the leadership secrets of Jesus of Nazareth!

I do a lot of speaking on the subject of leadership, and in my speaking I regularly use stories and principles that come from Pat's many books. This new book on leadership is going to be a rich source of ideas for me, and a rich source of insight and inspiration for you.

Pat writes with a teacher's heart and a motivator's spirit. He loves to tell stories to illustrate his points. Having read all his books, I can assure you that this is his best one yet. Whether you lead on a playing field or a battlefield, in a church sanctuary or in a corner office, you have picked up the right book to enhance your leadership skills.

I'm a big Pat Williams fan. After reading this instant classic on leadership, you will be, too.

Tallahassee, Florida
November 2002

# Foreword

*by John C. Maxwell*

Leadership Coach and
Bestselling Author

One of the great paradoxes of leadership is that authentic leaders are also learners, great coaches are also coachable, and great teachers are willing to be taught. Pat Williams is all of the above.

I have read every book on leadership, teamwork, and success that Pat Williams has ever written—and he has read all of mine. Pat constantly tells me I am his "leadership coach." You can imagine how honored I feel to hear that, because I constantly draw inspiration and insight from his writings and example.

As a general manager in the NBA, Pat has served with the Chicago Bulls, the Atlanta Hawks, and the Philadelphia 76ers (who won an NBA championship under his management). Then he became the founding general manager of the Orlando Magic. It can truly be said that the Magic would not exist today without the extraordinary leadership of Pat Williams. So when Pat talks about leadership, leaders listen!

His new book, *The Paradox of Power*, is clearly the result not only of intensive research, but intense experience in the leadership arena. Pat Williams has not only *studied* leadership and *observed* leadership, he has *lived* it. Through stories, inspirational quotes, and hard-won insights from the depths of his experience, he has given us a book that nails down the issue of leadership.

This book is not a textbook. It's a *life* book. Pat has drawn seven paradoxical principles of leadership from the ultimate leadership model, Jesus Christ. Yet there is nothing preachy or proselytizing about this book. Whether you are a person of faith or not, the insights in this book will transform your leadership style and enhance your leadership skills.

If you're like me, you've probably read a lot of books on leadership and you've found many were lightweight, filled with obvious platitudes and padded to fill out the space between the covers. Not this book. It is full of meaning and truth. As you read it you quickly realize that Pat Williams doesn't waste a single word—he crams as much insight and knowledge between these covers as will possibly fit. That's why this book continually yields fresh insights with each reading.

So turn the page and begin your journey. Read it and reread it. Build its paradoxical principles into your life. *Live* in this book—then *lead*.

Atlanta, Georgia
November 2002

# THE
# PARADOX
# OF POWER

# The Power of Paradox

Curly Lambeau was the original Green Bay Packer.

He was in the editorial offices of the Green Bay *Press-Gazette* on August 11, 1919, when the team was founded. He played halfback for the Packers from 1919 through 1929. As head coach, he led the Packers to six world championships.

One incident from Lambeau's coaching career illustrates just how important a leader can be.

On December 11, 1938, the four-time world champion Packers had advanced to the NFL title game in New York. The first half of the game between the Packers and the New York Giants was a close, hard-fought contest. When Lambeau's Packers went into the locker room at halftime, they trailed 16–14. The team counted on Coach Lambeau to come up with a second-half game plan to give them an edge.

Unfortunately, Coach Lambeau never got to the locker room.

Unfamiliar with the layout of the Giants' stadium, he took a wrong turn and walked through the wrong door. He realized his error as the door slammed shut behind him—and he was locked out of the stadium.

Coach Lambeau pounded on the door, but no one heard. He ran around to a public gate and told the security guard, "I'm Curly Lambeau of the Green Bay Packers! You've gotta let me in!"

"Forget it, bub," said the guard. "No one gets in without a ticket."

"But I'm the coach!" said Lambeau.

"Yeah, and I'm the king of England," the guard sneered. "Beat it before I call the cops."

Meanwhile, in the locker room, the Packers waited for their coach to show up. They needed some new Xs and Os, some inspiration, some leadership! Where was Coach Lambeau? Soon, halftime was over. The bewildered Packers returned to the field and proceeded to play the second half leaderless and directionless.

At the gate, Coach Lambeau got red in the face, yelling at the security guard. The commotion attracted a crowd, including some sports writers who recognized the coach. "Hey," they said, "it's Curly Lambeau! Let him in!"

By the time Lambeau made it to the sidelines, the third quarter was almost over, and the Giants had scored another touchdown. By the end of the game, the Packers had fumbled away the championship, 23–17. Football historians chalk up that loss to Curly Lambeau's wrong turn.[1] Every team, company, club, organization, military unit, church, nation, and family needs leadership. Wherever even two or three people gather together around a task or a purpose, there must be direction. If not, the task won't get done and the people will fail.

Even nature shows us the importance of leadership. A French naturalist from the nineteenth century, Jean-Henri Fabre, once conducted an experiment with a species called processionary caterpillars. These caterpillars get their name from the fact that they link to one another in a long procession when they go looking for food. The one caterpillar in front—the leader—does all the searching, while the rest are hooked together like boxcars in a freight train.

This arrangement works just fine as long as there is a leader. But Fabre wondered what would happen if he eliminated the leader from the procession. He placed the caterpillars inside the rim of a large dirt-filled flower pot. He arranged the caterpillars so that they were linked all the way around the pot—a continuous circle without a leader. In the center of the pot he placed the processionary caterpillars' favorite food—a pile of pine needles. The caterpillars inched their way around and around the pot, each one following the one ahead. For a full week they followed each other around the pot until they all died of starvation. An abundance of food was just inches away—but they never found it because they had no leader.

So how do we lead? Is leadership an inherited trait? Or is it something that can be taught and learned?

I'm convinced that leadership is nothing more than a skill—and a skill can be acquired and passed on to others. Every year, the Chamber of Commerce in my hometown of Orlando, Florida, offers a course called "Leadership Orlando." It's a twelve-month course that meets a couple of times a month. The people who run these courses must believe that leadership is a skill that can be taught and learned, because that's what they do: They teach leadership skills. Hardly a week goes by that I don't get another brochure, mailing, or e-mail about some leadership seminar. And then there are the books on leadership! Look in the business section of any bookstore and you'll see dozens of books on the subject. (And you know what? I've just written *another*—and you're reading it!)

All of those speakers and authors clearly believe that leadership can be taught and learned. I believe it, too. And you must believe it, as well—or you wouldn't still be reading.

Well, I've read all the books—all of 'em. I've gone to all the seminars and workshops—well, a lot of 'em, anyway. I've studied leadership principles from biblical times to medieval times, the Civil War era to the Great Depression, World War II to the Gulf War, and beyond. I've studied the leadership principles that come out of the military, the sports world, the business world, and church ministry. The striking thing I've seen, again and again, is that all the great principles of leadership in all of these arenas of life can be distilled down to seven essential points. These seven characteristics of outstanding leaders never change. They are constant, like pillars of granite in the sands of time.

I've designed this book to be a fun journey through those seven vital qualities. In these pages, you will meet all sorts of great leaders from history. I'll tell their stories and share with you the words they used to explain their own leadership abilities. As you journey through these seven principles with me, you'll acquire insights into the essence of leadership—principles you can begin applying in your own life right now!

And let's face it: The issue of leadership has never been more important than it is right now, in these uncertain times in which we live.

## THE GREATEST LEADER OF ALL

Over the years, I have worked with great leaders in sports and business. I have served in leadership roles as general manager of the Philadelphia 76ers, the Chicago Bulls, the Atlanta Hawks, and the Orlando Magic. As I have said, I have made a lifetime study of the issue of leadership. I have concluded that the greatest leadership model of all time was Jesus of Nazareth.

Let me put my cards on the table: I am a Christian. I want to make my personal biases clear at the outset. But having said that, I want to emphasize that you don't have to be a Christian to admire Jesus, or to emulate his leadership principles.

H. G. Wells, the English historian and novelist, was a socialist, an atheist, and one of Christendom's harshest critics. But he was the first to state his admiration for Jesus as a leader. "I am an historian, I am not a believer," he once said, "but I must confess as an historian that this penniless preacher from Nazareth is irrevocably the very center of history. Jesus Christ is easily the most dominant figure in all history."[2] Other historians have come to the same conclusions. "I find the name of Jesus Christ written on the top of every page of modern history," said George Bancroft.[3] The apex of history, wrote Will Durant, was "the three years that Jesus of Nazareth walked the earth."[4]

There has never been another leader like Jesus. No one in human history has accomplished so much, using nothing more than the power of his personality and his innate leadership skills. His leadership model was the most effective and compelling model ever demonstrated. Yet—amazingly!—the leadership model of Jesus is almost universally ignored.

Oh, we pay lip service to the way Jesus led, especially in churches and religious organizations. But look closely at any organization that is "Christian" in name, and you will almost certainly find that it is run on a traditional, hard-headed, secular business model—not the counterintuitive leadership model of Jesus. Churches are generally corporations operating on corporate management principles with corporate flow charts. The pastor is the CEO, and you might have a deacon or an associate pastor who functions as a COO or CFO. The church board is virtually indistinguishable from the board of directors in any secular corporation. So even Christians, who revere the leadership model of Jesus in theory, tend to ignore it in practice.

Why is Jesus' way of leading so widely praised but so universally ignored? In part, I think it's because it's rife with *paradox*.

A paradox is a truth embodied in a seemingly contradictory statement. It violates common sense and confounds reason. The paradoxes of Jesus are many. For instance, listen to a few of his paradoxical statements:

- "For whoever wants to save his life will lose it" (Luke 9:24).
- "If anyone wants to be first, he must be the very last, and the servant of all" (Mark 9:35).
- "Blessed are the meek, for they will inherit the earth" (Matthew 5:5).

Common sense tells us that we must look out for Number One; that we must get there early if we want to be first; and that only the strong survive. Reason tells us that the paradoxes of Jesus are absurd. Given a choice between common sense and paradox, we'll choose common sense every time.

I'm convinced, however, that if we would just have the courage to take the leadership model of Jesus seriously—to put it into daily practice and to live by the paradoxical truths he exemplified—we would revolutionize our companies, our organizations, our families, and our society. Who knows? We might even revolutionize our churches.

A well-known work entitled "One Solitary Life"[5] has been repeated over the years because its words are so amazingly powerful—and so profoundly paradoxical.

[Jesus] was born in an obscure village, the child of a peasant woman. He grew up in another obscure village. He worked in a carpenter shop until he was thirty, and then for three years was an itinerant preacher.

He never wrote a book. He never held an office. He never owned a home. He never had a family. He never went to college . . . He never did one of the things that usually accompany greatness. He had no credentials but himself . . .

While still a young man the tide of popular opinion turned against him. His friends ran away. One of them denied him. Another betrayed him. He was turned over to his enemies. He went through the mockery of a trial. He was nailed upon the cross between two thieves . . . When he was dead, he was taken down and laid in a borrowed grave through the pity of a friend.

Nineteen wide centuries have come and gone and today he is the center of the human race and the leader of the column of progress. I am far within the mark when I say that all the armies that ever marched, and all the navies that were ever built, and all the parliaments that ever sat and all the kings that ever reigned, put together, have not affected the life of man upon the earth as powerfully as has this one solitary life.

Others have made similar observations. English social critic Malcolm Muggeridge noted that everything Jesus accomplished, he did with "no organization, no headed notepaper, no funds, no registered premises, no distinguished patrons or officers, except only a treasurer—the ill-famed Judas Iscariot."[6] And one of the greatest military leaders of all time, Napoleon Bonaparte, once compared Jesus to other great leaders in history, including himself:

You speak of Caesar, of Alexander, of their conquests and of the enthusiasm which they enkindled in the hearts of their soldiers; but can you conceive of a dead man making conquests, with an army faithful and entirely devoted to his memory? My armies have forgotten me even while living, as the Carthaginian army forgot Hannibal. Such is our power.

I know men and I tell you, Jesus Christ is no mere man. Between him and every other person in the world there is no possible term of comparison. Alexander, Caesar, Charlemagne, and I have founded empires. But on what did we rest the creations of our genius? Upon force. Jesus Christ founded his empire upon love; and at this hour, millions would die for him.[7]

There has never been a leader like Jesus—not before, not since. Beginning with just eleven faithful men (plus a twelfth who betrayed him), he began a movement that has endured for two thousand years and has grown to include over two billion followers—one-third of the population of this planet. Yet he accomplished it all by employing leadership principles that defy logic and common sense. Through his leadership style, Jesus demonstrated both the *power of paradox* and the *paradox of power.*

A leader is a person who achieves goals through people. A leader moves and motivates people. A leader challenges and inspires people. A leader energizes people to do what they don't want to do so that they can achieve what they all want to achieve. The ability to do all that is not just leadership—it's power. Jesus had that kind of power, and he used it in a positive and enormously constructive way.

He also showed that the power of leadership rightfully belongs only in the hands of the humble, the gracious, those he called *the meek.* As we look at the leadership model of Jesus Christ, we see a leader whose power derives from powerlessness. We see a leader whose strength derives from his willingness to be weak. We see a leader who wins by losing, who is great by serving, whose genius is foolishness, and who lives by dying. That is the paradox of power.

## THE HIDDEN LESSONS OF LEADERSHIP

You may be thinking, *Whoa, there! Winning by losing? Living by dying? That's nonsense! I want to be a leader in the real world of business or the military or government. If this book is going to be full of a lot of pseudo-spiritual platitudes, I'm going to toss it right out the window.*

Don't worry. I guarantee this book is practical and real. I begin each chapter with a principle drawn from the leadership model of Jesus. Then I support every point with real-life stories of leaders in all situations, from all walks of life—leaders just like *you*.

When you finish this book, you'll believe in paradox. You'll find out that common sense isn't all it's cracked up to be, especially in the leadership realm. Real life is rich in paradox, overflowing with enigma. In fact, once you open your eyes to the wonderful paradoxes all around you, amazing things begin to happen. Paradox often opens the door to new insights, wonderful discoveries, and great intuitive leaps.

We see the power of paradox not only in the spiritual realm, where so many of Jesus' paradoxes are found, but in the realm of nature and science. In fact, physical reality is riddled with paradox.

For example, common sense tells us that time passes at the same rate in every corner of the universe. Einstein's theory of relativity, however, tells us that time passes more slowly when you are subjected to high rates of speed or an intense pull of gravity. This is paradoxical; it violates reason and common sense. But experiments have shown that Einstein is right and common sense is wrong.

Einstein's theory gave us the famous "Twins Paradox." In this paradox, you take a set of twins and separate them. One twin leaves earth in a spaceship that travels at speeds approaching the speed of light. The other twin stays home on earth. When the first twin returns to earth, he is much younger than his earthbound twin, because time passes more slowly the faster you travel.

In 1975 Professor Carol Allie of the University of Maryland tested this paradox. She used two synchronized atomic clocks—one which remained on the ground and another which was flown around on a jet aircraft for a number of hours. The airborne clock was slightly slower than the earthbound clock.

Experiments have also shown that subatomic particles, such as photons (light particles) and electrons, have a dual nature. If you measure them one way, they behave as particles. If you measure them another way, they behave as waves. This so-called "wave-particle duality" of photons and electrons violates common sense. Subatomic particles should be either waves or particles—not both! And their behavior should not depend on the kind of experiment you perform on them—that makes no sense at all! Yet experiments have shown that subatomic particles are paradoxical—they do not obey common sense. In fact, it was the discovery of wave-particle duality that led to the development of the entire field of quantum physics.

That is what paradox does: It points us in the direction of new discoveries. When something is clearly true but seems to defy logic and common sense, our tendency is to retreat in confusion. But that is just the moment when we need to advance in confidence, knowing that a profound and exciting discovery is just around the corner. Paradox is the gateway to insight and change. When everything we thought was true is suddenly stood on its head, we are ready to take an intuitive leap to the next level of growth and understanding.

That is the power of paradox.

But of course this book is not about the power of paradox, but the paradox of power. It's not about the logical, commonsense lessons you will find in most books on leadership. This book is about the *hidden* lessons embedded in the life and teaching of the greatest leader of all time. After reading this book, I believe you will have a transformed view of your leadership role, and of life itself.

Every year, I crisscross the country, speaking to groups and meeting with business and community leaders. Everywhere I go, I see a hunger for a new understanding of leadership. People are no longer content to compartmentalize their lives into professional versus spiritual; there is an increasing focus in the business world on the importance of spirituality and the soul, on using one's leadership ability not merely to maximize profits and return on investment, but to humanize the business landscape and to make the world a better, more compassionate place.

Appropriately—and paradoxically—the new understanding of leadership that people seek is actually one of the oldest leadership models around. The leadership model of Jesus bridges the gap between Western technology and Eastern spirituality (Jesus was an Eastern teacher, remember), between new information and ancient wisdom, between sacred and secular, between intellect and soul.

You may have bought this book merely to pick up a few tips on how to be a better coach or supervisor or CEO. But as we walk through these pages together, I hope you will find not just information but transformation.

Are you ready to begin? Good.

Let go of your logic. Loosen your grip on common sense. Plunge into the realm of paradox with me. Here we go . . .

# A Visionary Leader Sees What Is Not There

Ted W. Engstrom, president emeritus of World Vision, tells the story of a friend who took his little daughter on a cruise to Catalina Island, off the coast of Southern California. It was a beautiful, clear day, and the air was as transparent as crystal all the way to the horizon. As the little girl looked out over the blue Pacific, she called out, "Daddy! I can look farther than my eyes can see!"

That little girl didn't know it, but she was describing a paradoxical quality every great leader has. Vision is the ability to see farther than the eye can see, the ability to see what isn't there. Only by seeing what is not there can you bring something new, creative, and exciting into existence. One of former senator Bill Bradley's heroes was President Woodrow Wilson. Bradley felt Wilson had this ability to see around the corners, to see the future before it came into being.

George Bush—the first President Bush—learned the importance of vision, and he learned it the hard way. President Bush was very good at his job. He expertly assembled the international coalition to fight the Gulf War. The Allied victory over Iraq earned him a whopping 85 percent approval rating as of March 1991. With the 1992 election only a year and a half away, Bush's re-election seemed a foregone conclusion. But we all know what happened on the second Tuesday in November 1992: America rejected Bush and elected Bill Clinton. Where did George Bush go wrong? Well, the faltering economy was one thing—but it wasn't bad enough by itself to explain Bush's steep fall in the polls.

My own assessment: President George Bush lacked vision.

During the '92 campaign, he admitted that he didn't handle "the vision thing" very well. Yep, that's what he called it: the vision thing. And the problem wasn't just that he was uncomfortable with the word *vision*. More to the point, voters could tell he really didn't have one. After the victory of the Gulf War, he could have proposed a bold agenda for America and the American people would have embraced it. He could have said something like, "My fellow Americans, we have just won an astounding military victory. We have seen what we are capable of. Now let me suggest to you an exciting new vision for America." Instead, he settled for the role of caretaker rather than visionary. An 85 percent approval rating is an enormous surplus of political capital—and President Bush squandered it for want of a vision. (Mr. Bush forgot the advice of Ronald Reagan: "To grasp and hold a vision is the very essence of leadership.")

Conversely, Walt Disney was a leader who spent his life seeing what was not there—and then turning his vision into reality. The Disney entertainment empire is a tribute to that vision. Soon after his Disneyland theme park opened in 1955, a woman who worked for the Disney Studio was walking through Disneyland and noticed Walt on a bench between Fantasyland and Tomorrowland, staring off into the sky. She stopped and asked, "What are you looking at, Walt?"

"My mountain," he said, pointing to an expanse of empty air.

A few years later, in June 1959, the Matterhorn Bobsleds attraction opened to the public—a scale model of the famed Alpine peak. Today, Walt's mountain still defines the skyline of Disneyland.

Disneyland itself began as a vision that only Walt Disney himself could see. When the project was still in the planning stages, Walt took his friend, TV host Art Linkletter, for a ride out to Orange County. Linkletter recalls:

> We went and went and went and went and went, down through the orange groves. And finally we came to the place where it was going to be, and I couldn't believe my eyes—

because it was so far from downtown Los Angeles. And it was so small—the communities in those days were so straggly. And I thought, "My gosh, to put up a bunch of merry-go-rounds out in the middle of a cow pasture is ridiculous!"[1]

As they walked around the property, Walt described in glowing detail the various lands of his park: Fantasyland, Adventureland, Tomorrowland, and more. Then Disney advised Linkletter to buy property around the park and sell it to developers. "You'll make a fortune," said Disney.

But Art Linkletter failed to grasp Walt Disney's vision. He said thanks but no thanks. Looking back on that decision, Linkletter calculates that each step he took on that property was worth about $3 million—money that could have gone into his pocket but didn't.

A few years later, Walt Disney envisioned another and even larger Disney theme park. He laid the groundwork, but died in 1966, almost five years before the opening of Walt Disney World in Orlando, Florida. On the day the new park opened, a visitor commented to Mike Vance, Creative Director of Walt Disney Studios, "Isn't it too bad Walt Disney didn't live to see this?"

"Oh, but he did see it," Vance replied. "That's why it's here."[2]

## A VISION OF A TRANSFORMED LIFE

True visionaries are paradoxical people. You might even call them oddballs. The imaginary world of their vision is more real to them than the solid reality all around them. People talk to them, but they don't hear a word. They walk into walls or stumble over chairs because they don't see the walls or the chairs. Their minds are not in the here and now but in the there and then. Their vision is their reality; it's where they live and what they see, hear, touch, taste, and smell.

Most people are focused on the everyday, practical, mundane reality—and that's fine. We need people like that. Most managers are good, practical, salt-of-the-earth people—the kind of people who would say, "I believe in what I can see." But we also need that rare oddball visionary who says, "I see what I believe in." Visionaries are people of paradox who see what is not there. They are the ones who truly deserve to be called leaders because they are the ones who truly change the world. The greatest leaders live in the present but focus intently on the future.

Can you look beyond the present and see things that do not exist? If so, then you have the wonderful, paradoxical gift of vision. Without vision, the future would look just like the past. Without vision, there would be no innovation, no transformation, no progress. Vision is a *magical* ability—the next best thing to time travel. With vision, you can actually look into the future. Then, with that vision as your blueprint, you can build a brighter tomorrow out of the raw materials of today.

Jesus was a master visionary. He started with nothing. He chose twelve men from varied backgrounds, mostly "working class stiffs." A few were social outcasts. Four—Peter, Andrew, James, and John—were fishermen, and there were probably other trades represented as well. Most of the twelve were illiterate; they are called "unschooled, ordinary men" in Acts 4:13. At least one of them, Simon the Zealot, was an agitator in an extremist organization. Jesus only chose two men with any real financial experience—Matthew, who was a despised tax collector and a collaborator with the Roman occupation; and Judas Iscariot, who was the treasurer among the twelve, and later found to be an embezzler and a traitor. There wasn't one impressive résumé in the lot.

Would you have chosen these twelve as your means of changing the world? A bunch of uneducated fishermen? A tax collector? A crook? An extremist? Probably not.

But Jesus was a visionary. He saw what was not there—and he built it. He looked into the souls of these twelve underachievers, and he envisioned a group of overachievers who one day would turn the world upside down.

The best example of how Jesus envisioned the future through these men is found in the life of Peter. When Jesus first met him, his name was Simon. In John 1, Simon's brother, Andrew, brought him to Jesus and introduced them. Jesus looked at Simon and said, "You are Simon son of John. You will be called Cephas" (John 1:42). *Cephas* is an Aramaic name that in Greek is *Peter*—or in English, *rock*. At the time Jesus met this man, Simon Peter was anything but rocklike! He was unstable, impetuous, and unreliable. On several occasions, Jesus reprimanded Peter for his impulsiveness. Ultimately, though, Peter lived up to the paradoxical name Jesus gave him and became a stable and dependable man and one of the foundational leaders of the church.

But first, Jesus had to see something in Peter that wasn't there. Jesus had to look at Peter and see "The Rock" when all there was in Peter's personality was shifting sand. Jesus projected that vision onto Peter in a powerful way by changing his name from Simon to Cephas. In so doing, Jesus imparted to him a vision of his *future* life, his *transformed* life.

Jesus didn't settle for what people *were*. He focused on what they could *become*. He looked into human souls, saw what wasn't there, and invested himself in people so that his *vision* for their lives ultimately became the *reality* of their lives.

## A VISION OF HOPE

Jesus communicated a vision of spiritual liberation and reconciliation between God and humanity. His vision came to be called the gospel, from the Old English *godspel* (*god* = good; *spel* = news).

A true vision is always good news; it is always optimistic. Can you name one great leader who was a pessimist? There has never been one. A visionary leader can be honest about obstacles and problems, but he or she places them in a hopeful and positive framework. That is the way Jesus taught. He predicted problems and persecution for his followers, and he even predicted his own death. But he always framed obstacles and problems as challenges and opportunities for blessing.

At the beginning of his public ministry, he made this visionary announcement of hope:

> The Spirit of the Lord is on me, because he has anointed me
> to preach good news to the poor. He has sent me to proclaim
> freedom for the prisoners and recovery of sight for the blind, to

release the oppressed, to proclaim the year of the Lord's favor. (Luke 4:17–18)

It is a message other great leaders, following in his footsteps, have adopted as their own.

Martin Luther King Jr. had a vision of a society that did not yet exist. He described it in his famous "I Have a Dream" speech on the steps of the Lincoln Memorial on August 28, 1963:

> I have a dream that one day this nation will rise up and live out the true meaning of its creed: "We hold these truths to be self-evident: that all men are created equal."
>
> I have a dream that one day on the red hills of Georgia the sons of former slaves and the sons of former slaveowners will be able to sit down together at a table of brotherhood . . .
>
> I have a dream that my four children will one day live in a nation where they will not be judged by the color of their skin but by the content of their character.

Like the vision Jesus proclaimed, Dr. King's vision was an optimistic image of a better tomorrow. He did not ignore the reality of obstacles, frustration, pain, and sacrifice. But he placed the present-day problems within a hopeful context, framing them as challenges and opportunities for blessing.

Dr. Billy Graham is another visionary leader who follows the paradoxical pattern of Jesus of Nazareth. In the days immediately following the terrorist attacks on the World Trade Center and the Pentagon on September 11, 2001, the entire nation was reeling in shock and grief. At a National Day of Prayer and Remembrance service three days later at the National Cathedral in Washington, D. C., Dr. Graham shared his vision of hope:

> I have hope, not just for this life, but for heaven and the life to come. And many of those people who died this past week are in heaven right now, and they wouldn't want to come back. It's

so glorious and so wonderful. And that's the hope for all of us who put our faith in God. I pray that you will have this hope in your heart.

Dr. Graham's words are the epitome of hope. A visionary leader calls people to expect more of their world, to take bold steps of faith, to venture out with risk-taking courage, to dare to hope for something beyond themselves. In the Bible, we find a classic illustration of a visionary leader who called his people to hope. It is the story of Jesus and Peter on the lake (Matthew 14). The disciples took their boat out onto the Sea of Galilee, where they encountered a terrible storm. In the middle of the storm, they saw Jesus coming out to them, walking on the water. Peter, ever the impulsive disciple, said, "Lord, if it's you, tell me to come to you on the water."

Peter wanted to follow in Jesus' footsteps—even if those footsteps led across the surface of a lake. That kind of eager *followership* warms the heart of anyone in leadership. So Jesus said, "Come." Peter climbed out of the boat and started walking to Jesus across the water—and, amazingly, he didn't sink! Jesus, the parodoxical, visionary leader, had called forth the impossible from one of his followers.

But after a few steps, Peter became aware of the insanity of what he was attempting. He saw the wind and waves and thought, *What am I doing out here on the water?* He took his eyes off of Jesus and focused on his circumstances—and he started to sink. On the way down he cried out, "Lord, save me!" Jesus caught him and helped him back into the boat. "You of little faith," said Jesus, "why did you doubt?"

I think Jesus' chiding of Peter was gentle, not harsh—and I'm sure Jesus was pleased by the fact that Peter even dared the impossible for a few steps out on the lake. After all, Peter was the only one of the twelve who even risked getting out of the boat!

The point is that Jesus expressed a vision of hope in his words and he exemplified a vision of hope in his actions. His vision of hope inspired Peter to step out in the belief he could transcend everyday existence and achieve the impossible. That is a powerful object lesson for every leader of vision.

## ACHIEVING THE IMPOSSIBLE

When a leader can see the invisible, his followers can do the impossible. A leader with a powerful, optimistic vision can get his people to walk on water. Ask Fred Smith, the founder and CEO of Federal Express.

In 1965, while a student at Yale, Smith came up with his innovative airfreight concept and wrote it up as a term paper in his economics class. His professor read the paper, then took his red pen and wrote a big C at the top, adding this note: "The concept is interesting and well-formed, but in order to earn better than a C, the idea must be feasible."

Fred Smith had envisioned what was not there—and his Yale economics professor couldn't see it. But Smith didn't care. What mattered was that Smith could see it—and he refused to lose sight of it. After graduation, he joined the Marines and went to Vietnam, first as a platoon leader on the ground (wounded several times) and later as a pilot of over two hundred ground-support missions (winning the Bronze and Silver Stars).

After the war, Smith inherited $4 million when his father died. He invested it in Federal Express and raised $72 million in loans and equity investments. The company suffered heavy losses during the first few years (the first profitable year was 1975, when FedEx was a paltry $20,000 in the black).

But Fred Smith's vision of a successful overnight express company seized the imaginations of his employees. In its early days, FedEx and its employees walked on water, performing the miracle of staying afloat. Today, Smith's visionary company operates in 210 countries, employs 140,000 people, delivers 3 million packages per day, and is valued at $7 billion. It happened because a visionary leader saw what wasn't there, went forward with hope and belief, and achieved the impossible.

## WHEN VISION FAILS

Some people mistake vision for the ability to see. In reality, vision has nothing to do with eyesight. In fact, some of the most visionary people in the world are those who can see nothing at all. As blind-deaf author Helen Keller once noted, "The most pathetic person in the world is someone who has sight but no vision."

In 1998, Dr. David K. Winter, then president of Westmont College in Santa Barbara, California, and his wife, Helene, were getting ready to leave on vacation when he noticed some gray spots in his eyesight. Over the next few days, the dots grew into large blind patches. Within weeks, he had lost almost 90 percent of his sight. The diagnosis: nonarthritic ischemic optic neuropathy—an incurable condition. Although he could see shapes in sufficiently bright light, he was essentially blind for life.

Despite his blindness, Dr. Winter continued to serve as president until 2001. Even without his eyesight, Dr. Winter is a visionary leader. He says that blindness has made him a better person. Telling Winter's story, authors Bruce Bickel and Stan Jantz made this observation:

> We noticed that people are very careful with their use of certain terminology at Westmont College. They make a distinction between words like *sight*, *seeing*, *vision*, and *outlook*. To us, those words seemed fairly interchangeable. But at Westmont, their meaning is quite different. David Winter sees primarily darkness, but his outlook is bright. While his sight is obscured, he has tremendous vision.[3]

The leadership landscape is littered with those who have 20–20 eyesight but are sadly lacking in vision. Case in point: In 1870, a church denomination held its annual conference on a college campus in Indiana. In the course of the meeting, the president of the college remarked on the times they were living in: "I think we live in an exciting age," he said, "an age of wonders and discoveries."

The presiding bishop gave the college president a dour look. "Whatever do you mean?" he asked.

"Well," said the college president, "we are approaching a time of great inventions. For example, I believe the day is not far off when men will fly through the air like birds."

"Heresy!" snorted the bishop. "The Bible tells us that the gift of flight is reserved for the angels!"

After the conference, that bishop—his name was Milton Wright—returned to his family home in Ohio. Three decades later, Bishop Wright's two sons, Wilbur and Orville, made the first successful powered flight at Kitty Hawk, North Carolina. So much for the bishop's vision!

Alexander Graham Bell was another who struggled with those who lacked vision. He invented the telephone in 1876, but it was slow to catch on because people just didn't see it as practical. A member of the British Parliament once said that there was no need for telephones because "we have enough messengers here." And Western Union, the telegraph company, declined to invest in the device. "This 'telephone' has too many shortcomings to be seriously considered as a means of communication," said a Western Union internal memo. Imagine if Bell had listened to his pessimistic contemporaries!

The list goes on and on. In 1899, Charles H. Duell, director of the U. S. Patent Office, assured President McKinley, "Everything that can be invented has already been invented." In 1921, a *New York Times* editorial scoffed at the ideas of rocket pioneer Robert Goddard, who predicted the future of rocket-powered space exploration. In 1977, Digital Equipment Corporation turned its back on the home computing market. Said Digital's founder-president, Ken Olson, "There is no reason anyone would want a computer in their home."

What causes such a failure of vision? In each example you see a common thread: Someone decided that a vision had limits. Someone said, "This will never happen" or "That will never be possible." As soon as some "expert" puts any limit or restriction on the future, a visionary leader is bound to come along and prove the expert wrong.

Naysayers are pessimists; visionaries are optimists. If you want to be a leader, you have to be an optimist. You have to say yes to a future of limitless possibilities. Senator Joseph R. Biden Jr., that battle-scarred political veteran from my home state of Delaware, put it this way: "I am an optimist by occupational requirement." And communications executive Sumner Redstone said, "I believe optimism is the only philosophy of life that's compatible with sustained success and sanity." You have to be an optimist to survive as a national leader—or as a leader in any arena, great or small. You have to believe that anything's possible, that the future is wide open and boundless, that tomorrow is a blank check just waiting for your endorsement. There's no future in naysaying. When it comes to vision, the ayes have it.

## THE COMPONENTS OF A VISION

Jesus lived in Palestine under the harsh, repressive rule of the Roman empire—a cruel, murderous, racist regime. Yet Jesus had a vision that was completely at odds with the world in which he lived. In contrast to the kingdom of Rome, he envisioned a kingdom of God—of love, of compassion. He envisioned a world of equality and justice without racial division and wars. Though the vision of Jesus has yet to be realized in full, the world is a better, more civilized place wherever that vision has been shared and implemented. Christians around the world continue working to bring about his vision of the kingdom of heaven.

As I have studied the paradoxical vision of Jesus, I have come to the conclusion that an effective vision is made up of at least ten essential qualities or components. Let's take a look at each one.

*1. A vision should be clear and simple.*

Habakkuk 2:2 suggests that a vision should be written plainly, in such large letters that even a man running past can easily read it. A vision must be simple enough to be grasped by everyone at every level of the organization. It must be simple enough that it can be passed from one person to the next without distortion or ambiguity. It must be simple enough to be memorable. It must be simple enough to be understood and implemented. "Great leaders," observes Colin Powell, "are almost always great simplifiers."

*2. A vision should be visual and imaginable.*

Every member of the organization should be able to picture what the vision will look like when it's achieved. Use word pictures, metaphors, and stories to paint the image in the minds of your followers. Images are like mental Velcro; they stick in the mind and won't let go. Make sure your people can *see* the brighter future you want them to achieve. Your job is, first, to see what is not there, and second, to make sure everybody around you sees it, too. "Vision," says Christian leadership expert Dr. Leighton Ford, "is the very stuff of leadership: the ability to see in a way that compels others to pay attention."

### 3. A vision should be focused on change.

The purpose of a vision is to take you and your organization from where you are to where you dream of being. This implies positive change, progress, growth, expansion, and improvement. A vision is a picture of a brighter future. It focuses everyone's attention on completing today's tasks in order to achieve tomorrow's promise. White House correspondent Helen Thomas covered nine presidential administrations for United Press International. She was once asked which president she personally liked best. Her answer: John F. Kennedy. Asked why, she replied, "His vision—launching the Peace Corps, and promising to put a man on the moon."

### 4. A vision should demand sacrifice.

"If your vision doesn't cost you something," says John C. Maxwell, "it's only a daydream." A leader must be willing to pay the price to achieve his or her vision—and willing to ask the members of the organization to pay the price as well. When the people see their leader is committed, body and soul, to a vision, they are inspired to commit themselves as well.

### 5. A vision should be communicated with contagious optimism.

A vision is a picture of a coming celebration. People should associate your vision with confetti, the popping of champagne corks—whatever you choose as symbols of celebration. The image should be fun, elevating, exhilarating, and upbeat. "You have to be so excited about your vision that people can't wait to come and try to achieve it with you," says Carol Bartz, CEO of AutoDesk. "You have to have people excited about what you are doing, because going to work is not just about getting paid."

## 6. A vision should be personal.

Achievement of the vision should make everyone's life better—not just the leader's or the organization's. The shared accomplishment should produce individual benefits for every member of the team. Each person's desire for a better life should be bound up in the organization's dream of a brighter future. The more personal stake each individual has in the vision, the greater the collective desire and effort to achieve that vision—and the greater your chances of success as a leader.

## 7. A vision should be relentlessly stated and restated.

"A vision of the future is not offered once and for all by the leader, then allowed to fade away," says management expert Warren Bennis. "It must be incorporated in the organization's culture, and reinforced through the strategy and decision-making process."

Never tire of restating your vision. Celebrate it, underscore it, put it up in lights for everyone to see. Make sure that everyone in the organization, from the leader in the corner office to the guy in the mailroom, adheres to that vision.

## 8. A vision should be personified by the leader.

People should not be able to see the leader walking down the hall without being reminded of the vision. And people should not hear of the vision without picturing the leader. The leader is the walking embodiment of the vision. Don Shula, the winningest coach in NFL history, was a walking example of his vision for the Miami Dolphins. "My vision has always been a vision of perfection," he once said. "I wanted to have perfect practices, and I wanted to do the best job in preparation and just make sure that everything was done the right way. I was always demanding—do it the right way!"

### 9. A vision should be a broad vista, not a detailed plan.

Plans tend to be rigid and confining; a vision is boundless and liberating. A vision is flexible enough to withstand changing conditions within the organization and in the marketplace. Jack Welch, former CEO of General Electric, put it this way:

> Trying to define what will happen three to five years out, in specific, qualitative terms, is a futile exercise. The world is moving too fast for that. What should a company do instead? First of all, define its vision and its destiny in broad but clear terms. Second, maximize its own productivity. Finally, be organizationally and culturally flexible enough to meet massive change.

### 10. A vision should be difficult—even seemingly impossible—to achieve.

A *vision* that is easily within an organization's grasp is not a vision. It's just a goal. A true vision should be daunting in its scope—and breathtaking in its audacity. I'm not saying a vision should be unrealistic—but it should be so big, so grand that it is only possible if *everyone* pulls together. To truly be a vision, your image of success should lift people's eyes from the ground at their feet, and even above the horizon, to the limitless skies of possibility.

## THE EXHILARATION OF VISION

In their book *Built to Last*, James Collins and Jerry Porras coined the term BHAG (pronounced "bee-hag") to describe a bold, well-nigh-impossible vision. BHAG stands for Big Hairy Audacious Goal. Common sense would tell you that a BHAG would intimidate people and discourage them from trying. But BHAGs are paradoxical. The idea of attempting the impossible is so exciting and energizing that organizations usually experience an upsurge of motivation when a leader presents a BHAG to his people.

A great example of a BHAG is the vision announced by President John F. Kennedy in a speech on May 25, 1961:

> I believe that this nation should commit itself to achieving the goal, before this decade is out, of landing a man on the moon and returning him safely to the earth. No single space project in this period will be more impressive to mankind, or more important for the long-range exploration of space; and none will be so difficult or expensive to accomplish.[4]

Now, that's vision! Many people who heard those words in 1961 thought President Kennedy had lost his mind. But on July 20, 1969, at 10:56 P.M. EDT, astronaut Neil Armstrong stepped out of the lunar module of Apollo 11 and made the first human footprints on the moon. His words—"That's one small step for a man, one giant leap for mankind"—fulfilled the vision of President Kennedy. Even though the leader who proposed that vision didn't live to see it fulfilled, the vision itself became a historic reality.

What kind of history do you dream of making? What is the audacious vision that burns a hole in your soul right now, yearning to get out and become a grand reality? Whatever it is, define it, refine it, personify it. Make it simple and memorable. Make it a vision worth sacrificing for. Make it a vision full of optimism and excitement.

Then watch in amazement as your people boldly, enthusiastically hammer it into reality.

## THE RESULTS OF A VISION

An effective vision produces a number of powerful, transforming results in the life of an organization.

*A vision provides a sense of direction and an impetus for growth.*

A vision is like a treasure map with "X marks the spot" clearly identified. Vision marks the path to victory, so that everyone can move in
the same direction together. "The world makes way for the man who
knows where he is going," said Ralph Waldo Emerson. Football great
Joe Namath put it in different words: "Nobody wants to follow somebody who doesn't know where he's going."

There's a saying that those who rest on their laurels are wearing
them on the wrong end. Our natural human tendency is to dwell on
past glories rather than focus on future possibilities. Nostalgia comes
more easily to us than foresight. But organizations must grow, change,
expand, and conquer new challenges—or they will die. A sense of
vision gives an organization a forward lean that keeps the organization
alive and thriving.

*A vision gives everyone in the organization a sense*
*of involvement, purpose, and significance.*

John C. Maxwell tells the story of how Winston Churchill inspired the
English people with a vision during the darkest days of World War II.
England was having a hard time keeping workers in the coal mines
because so many miners were volunteering for military service. Serving on the front lines was dangerous but glorious duty, compared with
the mundane job of digging coal out of the ground. Yet the war effort
needed coal.

So Churchill, Britain's prime minister, went to the mines and gave a
speech. In it he gave his countrymen a vision of the future. He pictured for them what would take place when the Nazis were beaten and
the war was over. Churchill said there would be a great parade honoring all who sacrificed for victory. First, there would be the Royal Navy
sailors who had battled Hitler on the sea. Then would come the Royal
Air Force pilots who had fought the Luftwaffe in the skies. Then
would come the Army soldiers who had fought at Dunkirk. Last of all
would come the working men in miner's hard hats, covered with coal
dust. And when people would ask, "Where were these men during the

dark days of the war?" ten thousand voices would answer, "We were deep in the earth, with our faces to the coal."

As Churchill shared his vision with the miners, tears streaked their blackened faces. They returned to the mines with a renewed sense of purpose, knowing that every ton of coal they took from the earth served the goal of defending their beloved England.

Churchill knew it well: Leaders *must* make everyone on the team feel like an integral, indispensable part of the total effort. Those who aren't rowing are dragging their oars in the water—and a dragging oar pulls the entire boat off course. Everybody's oar must be in the water, everybody must be rowing in sync, and no one should ever feel excluded or unimportant. Those who don't feel they matter tend to be unmotivated and frustrated. Those negative emotions eventually poison the entire organization. So a leader *must* create a sense of total involvement and shared significance from top to bottom.

### A vision clarifies decision making.

A clear vision of the future is a benchmark. Every decision we make should be measured against our vision. If that decision takes us closer to achieving the vision, it's a good decision. If it doesn't, it isn't. In this way, a clear vision defines what we should and shouldn't be doing as a leader, and as an organization. It keeps us focused. A vision should be flexible enough to allow for creativity, inspiration, and response to new circumstances. But it should be clear enough and strong enough to keep us from squandering energy in wasted motion and fruitless directions.

I see this principle at work in our own Orlando Magic organization—and every NBA team I've been associated with. On every NBA ballclub there is a healthy, creative tension between the coach and the general manager. They can be great friends and they can work well together, but a certain tension is always present. The tension is this:

The coach is always looking at the present situation and asking, "How can I win tonight?" I've heard hundreds of coaches say, "I'm not looking at winning the championship or winning any game down the road. I'm focused on winning this game, period. Nothing else matters. You have to take your season one game at a time."

Now, that's the coach's job, and there's nothing wrong with it. But the general manager has a different focus. He's not just looking at one game or even one season. He is looking three, four, five years down the road. He's not just building a team, he's building a franchise—a *dynasty*. Sure, he wants to win tonight—but he's also focused on the horizon.

So there is an ongoing tension, and that tension affects decisions that are made on a daily basis. The coach will go to the general manager and say, "We need this or that in order to win tonight." The general manager will counter with, "We need that or this in order to build a long-term winning franchise." For the general manager, it's all about "the vision thing."

The coach may say to the general manager, "Okay, we've got this twenty-two-year-old phenom, but he's not ready yet, and I can't win with this guy. I need you to deal him to some other team and bring in this other thirty-five-year-old veteran with the skills and experience to help us win right now!"

The general manager may counter, "Okay, your thirty-five-year-old veteran can help you win tonight, but his knees and ankles are aging, and he's going to be out of the game in a year. I've got to think about the future, about our vision for this team. So the twenty-two-year-old stays here, and we can't bring in the veteran. Sorry, Coach, but you're going to have to find some other way to win tonight."

Your vision is your lens on the future. It brings clarity and focus to every decision you make as you build toward the future you have envisioned for your organization.

*A vision keeps the focus on what's important.*

It's easy to lose your concentration, to major on the minors. You can't afford to waste resources or effort—especially in turbulent economic times. Everything must be focused on making your vision a reality. Your vision of the future clarifies what is important and what is not.

Some years ago, ten whales beached themselves on the Baja Peninsula and died. Marine biologists were alarmed. They rushed to study the whales and discover the reason for this massive loss of life. A few weeks later, a newspaper reported their conclusions with this headline: "Giants perish while chasing minnows." The whales had lost their focus and beached themselves while chasing tiny little fish into the shallows.

A clear vision can keep the same fate from befalling you. That's what Andy Stanley meant when he said, "To focus on what's around you diminishes your ability to focus on what's before you."

### A vision motivates people over the long haul.

A vision calls us toward a brighter future, even through tough times and obstacles. It provides momentum and velocity. It gives us the courage to take risks. It gives us energy to maintain our momentum. A clear and optimistic vision enables an organization to persevere and remain focused through both good times and bad.

In 1855 engineer John Roebling proposed that a suspension bridge be built over the East River. Roebling envisioned a bridge suspended by a web of steel wires from four massive steel cables, supported by a pair of giant granite towers.

His project was fraught with hardships. Roebling himself died just days after the Army Corps of Engineers approved his plans. His son, Washington, took over the project. While overseeing work in one of the huge metal cylinders that had been sunk into the riverbed, Washington Roebling was paralyzed by decompression sickness ("the bends"). The bends, as well as fires and explosions, killed a number of workers. But everyone involved with the project refused to give up. And on May 23, 1883, President Chester Arthur and Governor Grover Cleveland dedicated the bridge. This bridge—the Brooklyn Bridge—stands today as proof of one man's motivating vision.[5]

### A vision empowers people.

The most effective organizations push decision making down from the top of the organizational pyramid and out to the people on the front lines. Leaders cannot lead effectively by micromanaging their people. Decision making must be decentralized so the organization can respond quickly to changes and needs. You want people in the trenches—those out on the floor and those meeting the public—to have the information and authority to make good decisions on their own. If your organization has a clear, strong vision, and that vision is communicated to every member of the organization, you can afford to invest more authority and autonomy in your rank-and-file. You can be assured that they will make good decisions, because every decision they make will be measured against the organizational vision.

## A vision calls people to attempt the impossible.

Our natural tendency is to settle into a comfort zone. But a grand vision calls forth a grand effort that reaches beyond "good enough" and sometimes carries us all the way to "the impossible." We are capable of far more than we think. Jesus knew that and he continually called his followers to attempt the impossible. Sometimes they failed. When they did, he encouraged them to go out and try again. Eventually, the impossible became a reality in the lives of his disciples. The impossible can become a reality in your life and the life of your organization as well.

## A vision evokes emotion and spreads enthusiasm.

Emotion and enthusiasm are infectious. If you, as a leader, project a vision that generates excitement, your organization will be energized and motivated to go out and make that vision a reality. People will get caught up in the spirit of a great movement—and you will see miracles happen.

"Vision evokes emotion," says Andy Stanley, founding pastor of Atlanta's North Point Community Church:

> There is no such thing as an emotionless vision. Think about your daydreams. The thing that makes daydreaming so enjoyable is the emotion that piggybacks on those mind's-eye images. When we allow our thoughts to wander outside the walls of reality, our feelings are quick to follow . . . Through the avenue of vision, the feelings reserved for tomorrow are channeled back

into our present reality. Vision is always accompanied by strong emotion, and the clearer the vision, the stronger the emotion.

*A vision keeps the leader fueled, fired up, and focused.*

My wife, Ruth, teaches for the FranklinCovey Company and is qualified to teach Stephen Covey's three-day "Seven Habits of Highly Effective People" course, based on the book of the same name. I must confess that I don't fully grasp all seven Habits, but I have Habit Two nailed: "Begin with the end in mind." Once it is clear in the leader's mind what the end is going to be, getting there is simple. It's just a matter of working backwards and putting all the pieces in place. John Maxwell put it this way: "Show me a leader without vision, and I'll show you someone who isn't going anywhere. At best, he is traveling in circles." Professor George F. Custem said of Hollywood agent Lew Wasserman, "He was the kind of visionary who always saw a few squares ahead on the board. That was his greatest gift."

So define your vision, set it in front of you like a beacon, and let it draw you in a straight, unswerving path toward that brighter tomorrow that burns in your soul.

## THE PARADOXICAL POWER OF A VISION

My hometown of Orlando, Florida, is the Home of the Attractions. And every one of those attractions, from Walt Disney World to the Orlando Magic organization (of which I am a part), had its genesis in a vision. I vividly recall a drive I took to the Orlando airport in September 1985. I was in my twelfth year as general manager of the Philadelphia 76ers and had come to Orlando to give a talk at the First Presbyterian Church. About to return home to Philly, I was being driven to the airport by Pastor John Tolson and one of Orlando's leading businessmen, Jimmy Hewitt.

"You know," I said offhandedly, "the NBA is thinking of expanding, and Florida could get one of the teams. If you guys were in charge, where would you put the team—Miami or Tampa?"

"Neither one!" said John Tolson.

"Just look around you, Bubba," said Jimmy Hewitt (to whom everyone is Bubba). "Ever see a cleaner, more exciting city than Orlando?"

"Sure," said John. "And with Walt Disney World, Orlando's already the entertainment capital of the world. NBA basketball would fit this city like a glove!"

I thought about that conversation all the way home. The more I thought about it, the more excited I became about this vision of a shining new sports arena rising in central Florida. In the days that followed, I put Jimmy Hewitt in touch with NBA commissioner David Stern, and things began to gather momentum. Long story short, Jimmy put an ownership group together, then called me in Philadelphia and said, "Hey, Bubba, we're putting an NBA franchise together! This thing is rolling down the tracks and picking up speed. You'd better hop on quick." I agreed to come aboard as general manager.

In June 1986 I left the 76ers and moved to Orlando. From the moment I arrived, every day was a high-intensity adventure. Even though the NBA had not yet committed to awarding Orlando a franchise, I was running all around central Florida, telling people, "When Larry Bird and Magic Johnson come to town, folks, you've got to have your tickets!" People thought I was nuts! But I had a clear picture in my mind: I could see the arena, I could see the players on the floor, I could see the uniform colors, I could see Bird and Magic on our floor. None of it existed, but I saw it all. Then I simply worked backwards from that vision to make it all happen.

Finally, in April 1987, the NBA board of governors added four new teams, including the Orlando Magic. We played our first game in the fall of 1989. Jimmy Hewitt, John Tolson, Pat Williams, and a lot of other people had caught sight of something that didn't exist, and together we made the dream a reality. A leader is a person who sees the invisible before anyone else sees the reality. A leader hears the inaudible, thinks the unthinkable, believes the unbelievable, attempts the impossible, and achieves the supernatural.

That's the paradoxical power of this magical thing called *vision*.

# A Wise Leader Dares to Be a Fool
## (AND OTHER PARADOXES OF COMMUNICATION)

One of the wisest leaders I've ever known was Mr. R. E. Littlejohn. Everyone called him "Mr. R. E.," even his wife. I met Mr. R. E. in 1965 when I took over as general manager of a minor league baseball team in South Carolina, the Spartanburg Phillies. Mr. R. E. was one of the team owners, as well as the owner of a prosperous petroleum tanker company (they called him "The Tanker Tycoon").

Mr. R. E. was a southern gentleman, charming and soft-spoken. A Christian, he modeled his life and leadership style after that of Jesus Christ. He was a walking paradox: A hard bargainer and a hardheaded businessman, he had the softest, warmest heart of any man I ever knew. Serious about his business, he also knew how to make a workday fun. He was shrewd and skilled at making money, but he didn't have a greedy bone in his body; in fact, he was one of the most generous people I've ever known.

A lot of leadership "experts" will tell you that a wise leader should keep a margin of detachment between himself and his subordinates. After all, the employee who is a friend today might be a candidate for firing tomorrow—and you don't want personal feelings to interfere with what's best for the bottom line. Those leadership "experts" would have said Mr. R. E. was just plain foolish—because he violated this maxim and many others. Mr. R. E. Littlejohn dared to be a fool (at least in their eyes)—and that's what made him such a wise leader.

I first learned the importance of foolishness from Mr. R. E. During my years in Spartanburg, he and I had a New Year's Day ritual. He and his wife, "Sam," would invite me over for a traditional southern New Year's supper. There was roast pork to signify good health, black-eyed peas to represent coins, and turnip greens for dollar bills.

After the meal, Mr. R. E. and I would sit down and watch the bowl games on TV. Then would come our annual round of salary negotiations. Mr. R. E. had an unusual approach to these negotiations. He called it a "paper swap." He would have me write the pay I wanted on a piece of paper. He would write his figure on another piece of paper. Then we'd swap papers. It was an amazingly simple process, because his number was always higher than mine!

Foolish on Mr. R. E.'s part? Sure it was. Most would say "Why pay someone more than they're asking for?" But consider this: Mr. R. E. probably had the highest productivity and the lowest employee turnover rate of any business leader you'd ever meet. He knew how to cultivate his people—and secure their loyalty. There was a wisdom in his foolishness that reminded me of the wisdom of another leader: Jesus Christ.

## THE SEVEN COMMUNICATION PARADOXES OF JESUS

Two thousand years ago, Jesus demonstrated profound insight into the nature of human communication in the way he conveyed his vision of "the kingdom of heaven." For instance, he talked about his vision frequently, using a variety of imaginative metaphors. Here's a sampling (all taken from the Gospel of Matthew): "The kingdom of heaven is like a man who sowed good seed in his field" (13:24). "The kingdom of heaven is like a mustard seed" (13:31). "The kingdom of heaven is like yeast" (13:33). The kingdom of heaven is like "a net" (13:47), "a king" (18:23), and "a landowner" (20:1). He presented a multidimensional vision through a series of rich, imaginative word-pictures.

In this chapter, I have to depart from the usual format of building my theme around a single paradox of Jesus. Why? Because, as I looked at the communication model of Jesus, I found not just *one* but *six* paradoxes. Those six paradoxes of communication are:

1. The wise leader dares to be a fool.
2. The great leader leads from the middle, not the top.
3. The prudent leader welcomes conflict.
4. The leader's most powerful tools are words.
5. The effective leader communicates without words.
6. The influential leader persuades by listening.

By means of these six paradoxical approaches to communication, Jesus presented his vision in such a powerful way that his vision continues to shape our world some twenty centuries later. Let's begin with the first of these six paradoxes: The wise leader dares to be a fool.

## COMMUNICATION PARADOX 1:

### The Wise Leader Dares to Be a Fool

It's a paradox as old as the Bible: "But God chose the foolish things of the world to shame the wise" (1 Corinthians 1:27). If you want to be truly wise, dare to be a fool.

Well, what do I mean by a fool?

Some would say a fool is someone deficient in judgment. Others would say a fool is someone who appears ridiculous or absurd. But I say a fool is someone who defies conventional thinking to communicate truth—that's the kind of fool every great leader should be.

This is the kind of ultra-wise foolishness Jesus exemplified for us all. Knowledge, Jesus said, is much overrated. Real truth is paradoxical and unruly. It is considered foolishness by conventional minds. Real truth often comes disguised in a foolish package, so that the "wise" and the "learned" cannot recognize it, though it is readily embraced by the simple, the childlike, the "foolish."

Recall that in Luke 10:21 Jesus prayed, "I praise you, Father, Lord of heaven and earth, because you have hidden these things from the wise and learned, and revealed them to little children." The so-called wise and learned live by conventional wisdom, but true truth is often found by fools and children in the realm of unconventional wisdom.

Too many leaders, whether in business, government, sports, or ministry, take themselves too seriously. They jealously guard their dignity. They demand respect. Some even want to be feared by their subordinates. Thinking themselves wise, they foolishly maintain a stiff dignity that communicates coldness and creates resentment and distrust.

But a wise leader is not afraid to sacrifice dignity in order to make a personal connection with the people in the organization. This leader knows that a willingness to play the fool pays off in motivation, enthusiasm, and contagious energy. If taking a pie in the face will help make a point and build an atmosphere of healthy fun in the workplace, why not?

When John Amerman took over as CEO of Mattel Toys in 1987, the company was reeling from a $113-million one-year loss. Several of the toy lines had fizzled. Morale had plunged. His first day on the job, Amerman wandered around the company headquarters and made a startling discovery: It was as if Santa's workshop had become a Soviet gulag! The company's products were fun—but nobody at Mattel was having any fun.

On his second day at Mattel, John Amerman announced a new policy: Henceforth, people at Mattel were expected to have fun. And to make sure that the lines of communication were open at Mattel, Amerman took a walk through the Mattel facility every day. He ate in the cafeteria and talked to all the workers. Morale began to soar. Profits climbed. In just three short years, Mattel rebounded to a record $91 million profit in 1990.[1]

Foolish behavior, right? Outrageous. Undignified. Shocking. Maybe so. But that kind of wise foolishness saved a lot of employee jobs and shareholders' equity at Mattel.

It's paradoxical, but true: A wise leader is a fool.

# A FOOL IS A STORYTELLER

In William Shakespeare's time, fools were entertainers whose job it was to keep kings and queens happy. They used any and all tricks in the book to amuse: puns, jokes, pratfalls, anything to entertain. As Dave and Tom Gardner explain on their Motley Fool website, "Fools were, in fact, the only members of their societies who could tell the truth to the king or queen without having their heads rather unpleasantly removed from their shoulders."[2]

Shakespeare—great storyteller and entertainer that he was—saw fools as the epitome of wisdom. In his plays, the wisest characters are usually fools—and fools are almost always storytellers. You've no doubt heard the phrase, used to introduce many a story: "And thereby hangs a tale." This phrase occurs in many of Shakespeare's plays, and it is usually spoken by one of his beloved "wise fools." It is said by the fool Touchstone in *As You Like It* (Act 2, Scene 7), by the fool known simply as Clown in *Othello* (Act 3, Scene 1), and by the servant Grumio in *The Taming of the Shrew* (Act 4, Scene 1).

Shakespeare was right: Wise leaders are fools. In other words, they are entertainers who will do anything to hold their audience's attention. Wise fools can, as Motley Fools' Dave and Tom Gardner observed, use entertainment as a vehicle for telling the truth without the consequences another might suffer. So the wise leader is not only a fool, but a storytelling fool. He uses entertainment as the medium for imparting truth to the people around him.

Jesus was a storyteller. He conveyed most of his lessons and principles through stories—stories that are as relevant now as they were when he first told them on the hillsides of Judea and in the streets of Jerusalem. They are disarmingly simple on the surface, yet they contain complexity that continues to challenge our thinking.

Jesus usually left it up to his hearers to figure out the meaning of the stories he told. Rarely did he explain what they meant. Sometimes the meaning of his stories was as obvious as the nose on your face. At other times, there was a sense of mystery surrounding them; they did not have just one interpretation but many. It is easy to imagine people pricking up their ears, moving in a little closer, and listening even more attentively when Jesus said the Aramaic equivalent of, "And thereby hangs a tale . . ."

Jesus used characters and settings that were familiar to his listeners. And his stories often gave two sides of an issue by presenting characters from contrasting points of view. There were parables of tenant farmers and landowners, a generous employer and a dishonest employee, a rich man and a beggar, a master and a servant, a loving father and a wandering son. He challenged his listeners to identify with one side or the other, and to choose one.

Most important, the lessons embedded in Jesus' storytelling stick in the mind. As leadership guru Ken Blanchard observed:

> The best way to learn is through stories. I know that because of the way people respond to my stories in my lectures. Stories permit the audience and readers to identify and get into the characters and learn right along with the characters. It makes learning effortless and enjoyable.

Management expert Tom Peters agrees. "The best leaders," he says, "are master users of stories and symbols . . . Numbers are numbing. Stories are personal, passionate, and purposeful." Adds pastor-author-storyteller Charles Swindoll: "Stories transport us into another world. They hold our attention. They become remarkable vehicles for the communication of truth and meaningful lessons that cannot be easily forgotten. If a picture is better than a thousand words, a story is better than a million!"

It's true. Whenever I am speaking, I watch the audience members closely. If I see any eyes glaze over, if I see someone begin to yawn, I use a phrase that is guaranteed to get them awake and attentive once more: *Now, let me tell you a story* . . . (Shades of "Thereby hangs a tale . . ."). It never fails to stir the crowd.

In 1995, I agreed to play in a celebrity golf tournament in Orlando. I'm not a great golfer by any means, and when I accepted, it seemed like the tourney was a long way off. But months passed and the event snuck up on me. One of our secretaries, Barb Jones, reminded me of the tournament, and I groaned. "Oh, I don't want to do it!" I said. "I'll be out there with all those celebrity golfers and I'll make a fool of myself!"

"Well," Barb said, "you promised to be there, so I guess you'll just have to play golf."

"Oh-ho-ho-no I'm not!" I said. "I've done for golf what the *Titanic* did for the winter cruise business!"

"But you have to," she said. "For one thing, it's for a good cause. And for another thing, you're not out there to play golf anyway!"

"I'm not?"

"No," she said. "You're out there to collect stories."

I thought, *Whoa! I never looked at it that way. But she's right! I may make a complete fool of myself, but I'm bound to get some good stories.*

So I went. And wouldn'tcha know it? The celebrity golfer in our group was Ken "Hawk" Harrelson, the longtime American League home-run hitter and just about the best golfer of any ex-athlete in the country—good enough to go on the Senior Tour. What's worse, Hawk is one of the most merciless kidders you'll ever meet on a fairway. He didn't let me get away with a thing.

But I did collect some great stories from a lot of celebrities and fellow duffers that day.

The world of sports is a world of stories. This is especially true of pro baseball players. Whenever I'm around a bunch of old ballplayers, I am in story-lover's heaven. I tell you, these old players remember *everything*, and the stories they tell and the way they tell them is nothing short of spellbinding. I recently heard eighty-five-year-old Enos Slaughter, a Hall of Famer, speaking at a baseball convention. He remembered the count, the pitch, the weather, every detail of games that were played fifty or sixty years ago. After hearing those stories, I told my son Bobby, who's just begun a coaching career in the Cincinnati Reds system, "Save your stories, Bobby. Store 'em up—you'll be telling those stories fifty years from now." He said, "You bet I am!"

Sports players aren't the only good storytellers. Abraham Lincoln was one of the best storytellers ever to inhabit the White House. Most of his stories were parables that contained a powerful lesson or point.

"They say I tell a great many stories," he once said, "and I reckon I do. But I have learned from long experience that plain people are more easily influenced through the medium of a broad and humorous illustration than in any other way."

It has been said that stories are windows to the truth. It has been said that the universe is made of stories, not atoms. I believe that's all true. Why are the *Chicken Soup for the Soul* books approaching the hundred-million mark in total sales? Because people can't get enough of stories! Stories entertain, enthrall, instruct, and stick forever in the heart and soul. Stories define who we are as leaders, and they define the meaning and history of an organization. The greatest leaders of all are the leaders who tell stories.

Senator John McCain says that he learned the power of stories while he was imprisoned in Hanoi during the Vietnam War. He had been raised on stories of the sea told by his father and grandfather, who were both admirals in the Navy. So, as a prisoner of war, it was only natural that McCain became the storyteller of the group. He would retell his favorite movies to the other men, scene by scene. At Christmastime, his captors allowed him ten minutes with a Bible to reread the Christmas story, then he retold that story to the men.

In 1974, then governor of California Ronald Reagan—a gifted storyteller in his own right—invited McCain to speak at the governor's prayer breakfast in Sacramento. Though not a particularly religious man, McCain had a story to tell. He talked about being in solitary confinement in a hole in the ground. His entire world was squeezed down to a space six feet wide by nine feet long. On the stone wall of that hole, an earlier prisoner had scratched a message: *I believe in God, the Father Almighty*. Those words, said McCain, sustained him through two and a half years in the dreaded "Hanoi Hilton."

When he had finished telling his story, the entire audience, including Governor Reagan, was in tears. "I realized," McCain later recalled, "that it wasn't really me that moved them. It was the story that did it."[3]

So if you want to be a leader, be an entertainer. Be a storyteller. Be a fool—in the Shakespearean sense. You can't go wrong if you remember that wonderful, foolish phrase, "Thereby hangs a tale . . ."

# COMMUNICATION PARADOX 2:

## The Great Leader Leads from the Middle, Not the Top

The legendary retail baron James Cash Penney once evaluated a clerk at one of his stores. The young clerk, he said, "wouldn't have much of a future in the retail business." The name of that employee? Sam Walton, who would later found the Wal-Mart retail chain. Today, with its three thousand outlets, Wal-Mart is the largest retail company in the world, with revenues over four times that of JC Penney's.

Walton opened his first Wal-Mart store in Rogers, Arkansas, in the summer of 1962. The theme of his store was discount prices: Squeeze profit margins to the bone and pass the savings on to the consumer. Walton carved out an ingenious niche. To compensate for smaller margins, the company had to sell merchandise in high volumes. Walton would fly his private airplane over farmland, looking for locations between three or four small towns. Then he'd build a Wal-Mart store there that could serve not just one but several communities at the same time.

Walton was not only a retail wizard, he was probably the first corporate leader to practice a twenty-first-century management style. His method appeared as absolute foolishness compared to traditional models. And the result of his foolishness? Phenomenal success. By 1985, the value of Wal-Mart stock had made him the wealthiest man in America; by 1991, his company had eclipsed Sears as the biggest retailer in America.

"Walton may have been the first true information-age CEO," said John Huey, managing editor of *Fortune* and collaborator on Walton's autobiography.[4]

What was Walton's secret? Well, unlike the business leaders he first learned from, Walton didn't lead from the top of the organization. He led from the middle. The old leadership model was a pyramid, with the leader at the top. Walton understood that in order to communicate best, information shouldn't flow in just one direction, from the boss to the troops, but in every direction—up, down, and sideways.

Information is power, and Walton believed in decentralizing that power and distributing information throughout the organization.

And he lived that belief. He was a charismatic man of the people who drove an old pickup, spent time on the retail floor, and earned his employees' trust and loyalty. He viewed his employees not as subordinates or underlings, but as associates and partners. Shortly before his death in 1992, he said: "Communicate everything you possibly can to your partners. The more they know, the more they'll understand. The more they understand, the more they'll care. Once they care, there's no stopping them."

Where did Sam Walton learn that approach to communication? He once said, "I learned early on that one of the secrets of campus leadership was the simplest thing of all: Speak to people coming down the sidewalk before they speak to you. I would always look ahead and speak to the person coming toward me. If I knew them I would call them by name, but even if I didn't I would still speak to them."

## HOW TO LEAD FROM THE MIDDLE

Here, then, are nine principles of communication for wise, effective leaders who want to lead from the middle, not from the top of some corporate ivory tower:

### 1. Dispense information freely in order to build esprit de corps.

When people feel informed, they feel important and included. This sense of being valued and trusted builds team loyalty. It motivates people to give their best effort to the entire organization. Ivory-tower leaders tend to hoard information. As a result, morale breaks down and people feel they are not trusted—or worse, that the boss is not to be trusted. But leaders who lead from the middle share information freely, and that builds trust. Author Fred Smith wrote: "Vision, policies, and plans are more or less useless unless they are known to all who may be concerned with them. Lord Montgomery, commander of the Eighth Army, made it a rule that the plan of campaign should be known to every soldier."

Once a decision is made, announce it early. Take your people into your confidence, and they will have confidence in you. Sure, there are some matters that should be kept secret. But make sure that any "top secret" information in your organization really deserves that designation. Everything else, be quick to declassify and disclose. Retired U.S. Air Force General William A. Cohen puts it this way:

> When you are a leader, it is those who follow you that make you look smart—or not, as the case may be. If those who follow you make errors and look bad because they are missing information that you could have given them, you will ultimately suffer far more than they. This is because it is you who are responsible for everything your organization does or fails to do, and no one else.

Author Max Depree wrote, "I learned that if you are a leader and are not sick and tired of communicating, you probably aren't doing a good enough job."

## 2. *Go out of your way to solicit ideas and suggestions.*

Good ideas can be found everywhere, from the janitors and secretarial pool to the corner office. Bosses insist only *their* ideas deserve any credit. But leaders invite ideas from the entire organization—and they receive credit for recognizing people with good ideas! Even if an idea is impractical or unworkable, always thank that person for thinking and speaking up. After all, the next idea could be worth millions.

One of my mentors, early in my sports management career, was the great Bill Veeck, who began his executive career with the Milwaukee Brewers and later owned the Cleveland Indians, the St. Louis Browns, and the Chicago White Sox. Bill was famous for crowd-pleasing stunts like exploding scoreboards, contests, and giveaways. He told me that some of his best ideas came from fans. For example, he got a lot of complaints about vendors walking through the stands, selling products and blocking the view of the game. In response, Bill hired a concession crew made up of "little people"—people who were literally, physically short—so that fans could buy from the vendors and still see the game.

You never know where a great idea will come from, so make sure your people know that you welcome ideas. In fact, ask for them! Get out on the floor of your company, in the middle of your organization, and make sure everyone knows you are approachable and interested in their suggestions.

### 3. Don't just give orders—explain them.

The people in your organization will be better motivated and better empowered to carry out their jobs if they know *why* they are doing it. If the members don't understand the how and the why of their task, they may fail to appreciate the importance of doing it the right way— and that could be expensive for your organization. You don't want people to simply comply with your orders; you want them to be enthusiastic about carrying out your vision.

Former Miami Dolphins head coach Don Shula, the win-ningest coach in NFL history, said this about his relationship with his players:

> The word I stress is communication. I try to always keep the doors of communication open. Then when you do make a decision, players will accept it more readily than they would if you were dogmatic.

### 4. Rip out the office grapevine by its roots.

"The vacuum created by a failure to communicate," observes historian C. Northcote Parkinson, "will quickly be filled with rumor, misrepre-sentation, drivel, and poison." It's true. Rumors spring up whenever there is an information vacuum—and no office grapevine ever pro-duced anything but sour grapes.

When people don't know, they speculate—and those speculations are usually contaminated with resentment and distrust. When you provide timely, accurate, complete, trustworthy information to the people in your organization, you pull the grapevine out by its roots. Good communication kills rumors while building trust and loyalty.

## 5. *Talk to those who will be directly affected by your decisions.*

The success of your decisions depends on the people who will have to implement them. Talk to them, inform them of your thinking, ask them for their input. In doing so, you'll avoid hurt feelings and gain useful insight and information—and you'll win supporters to your cause.

I have found in over three decades as a general manager of NBA teams that it is vitally important to keep everybody in the decision-making loop—both those who are above me (such as the owners) and the people who work for me (such as the players). I've never had an owner who worked in the office full time. Our owners have always had other companies to run and other offices to work in. So I've had to expend a little extra effort to keep the owners informed. If the owner feels he's been cut out of loop, I've got problems on my hands. If the owner finds out about major decisions from the media or the neighbors instead of from me, the general manager, then I'm building an atmosphere of suspicion and distrust.

It is equally important to keep employees and associates in the loop so they know what's going on at all times. For example, players in sports franchises often don't know that they are being traded to another team until they get a call from reporters. There are few things more humiliating in life than to find out you are the last one to know about changes in your own career! So it's important to be open with employees and associates. Whenever a tough decision must be made that affects their lives, that decision should be communicated honestly and face to face, not in a cowardly fashion through intermediaries or back-channel communication. Players and associates who get this kind of news secondhand tend to hold grudges for years.

In 1974, when I was general manager of the Atlanta Hawks, I took part in a decision to trade the great Pistol Pete Maravich to the New Orleans Jazz. In exchange for Maravich, we got players, cash, future draft picks, trading stamps, and a big pot of crawdad gumbo—it was a very sweet deal from our point of view. I knew it was not going to be easy to break the news to Maravich, but I also knew this was not the kind of news to convey over the phone. I had to go talk to Pete in person.

I'll never forget that day because it was my birthday—May 3. I was plenty nervous as I drove to Pete's apartment. I arrived and got right to the point: "Pete," I said, "we've decided to trade you to New Orleans. We've just concluded the deal and I wanted to tell you right away, before you heard it from anyone else." Then I laid out the deal we had made while Pete listened, frowning. He resisted at first—and he could have put his foot down and killed the deal since he had a no-trade clause in his contract. But he respected the fact that I had come to tell him about it in person and he agreed to go along with it. Honest, straightforward communication won his trust so the trade could go forward without a hitch.

When you level with people, they know you're on the level.

## 6. Maintain an informal atmosphere.

Communication flows more freely and ideas are generated more spontaneously when people are at ease and free to be themselves. Avoid rigid agendas or emphasis on roles, status, or authority.

Texas oilman, entrepreneur, and philanthropist T. Boone Pickens once said:

> Keep things informal. Talking is the natural way to do business. Writing is great for keeping records and putting down details, but talk generates ideas. Great things come from our luncheon meetings which consist of a sandwich, a cup of soup, and a good idea or two—no martinis.

## 7. Communicate with simplicity, clarity, and a strong point of view.

Remember what Colin Powell said about leaders? "Great leaders are almost always great simplifiers, who can cut through argument, debate and doubt, to offer a solution everybody can understand." Insecure leaders hedge and hem and haw, often cluttering their statements with ambiguity and buzzwords. Great leaders speak clearly and simply and can state their point of view in a few words.

Former Chrysler chairman Lee Iacocca tells the story of reading a fifteen-page paper that was tough to understand. He called in the author and asked him to clarify what he had written.

> He did it in two minutes flat. He identified what we were doing wrong, what we could do to fix it, and what he recommended. When he finished, I asked him why he didn't write that in the paper the way he had just said it to me. All he said was, "I was taught that way," and he was an MBA to boot. Write the way you talk. If you don't talk that way, don't write that way.

## 8. Be accessible to the people in your organization.

Bill Veeck was way ahead of the curve. Whenever he bought a ballclub, his first act was to remove the door from his office. In fact, when he returned to the White Sox ballclub in 1976, he not only removed the door, but he removed the walls as well! Veeck always answered his own phone, opened his own mail, roamed the ballpark, visited with the fans, stood at the gate, and shook hands with people as they left. I've modeled my own leadership style after his, and to this day I always shake hands with the fans as they are leaving the arena and I'm always accessible to people who work with me.

## 9. Encourage personal relationships and personal connections.

We sometimes forget that the world is not just a place of deadlines, bottom lines, meetings, agendas, strategies, and competition. The world is also a place of personal relationships, emotions, and spiritual yearnings. As leaders, we need to reconcile these two worlds, the public world of the organization and the private world of the human heart and soul. Herb Kelleher, CEO Southwest Airlines, expressed this perfectly when he observed:

> There's a lot being said about the importance of communication, but it can't be rigid, it can't be formal. It has to proceed

directly from the heart. It has to be spontaneous. Communication is not about getting up and giving formal speeches. It's saying, "Hey, Dave, how are you doing? Heard your wife is sick—is she okay?" That sort of thing.

We need to show the people around us we care about them not just as cogs in the organizational machine, but as *people*.

## THE MOTIVATOR IN THE MIDDLE

I have nineteen kids: four birth children, fourteen by international adoption, and one by remarriage. At one point in my life, sixteen of my children were teenagers at the same time. Our breakfast table was sixteen feet long—one foot longer than the free-throw line on a basketball court. We always had breakfast at 6:30, before the whole herd rushed off to school. Now, that's awfully early in the morning to try and engage a teenager's brain. But I always gave it a try, usually by posing a Question of the Day.

On one particular morning, I asked my mob of teens, "Twenty years from now, what will you remember most about your old dad?" As you can imagine, that's a risky question; you never know what will come back. Well, my kids broke up into buzz groups and discussed the question. Then sixteen-year-old David, who is now a United States Marine, said, "Dad, we decided that the one thing we'll remember is that you were always motivating us."

That nailed it. That's what I did. And do. I was constantly trying to motivate my teens to do their homework, to work hard in school, to keep their rooms neat, to stay out of trouble, and on and on. Now most of my kids are scattered around the country, though some are still at home. But to this day, I send out newspaper clippings and letters to them, still encouraging and motivating them. It's sort of a family tradition. My eighty-eight-year-old mother is still doing the same thing with me, sending me things from her nursing home in Wilmington, Delaware. And news anchor Diane Sawyer's eighty-two-year-old mother is no different than mine. At age fifty-six Diane said, "To this day I get messages about clothes that didn't look good or how I didn't sit in a ladylike position. She thinks if she just says the right thing, one day I'll get it right."[5]

Bob Collings, president of The Collings Foundation, says, "When people are highly motivated, it's easy to accomplish the impossible. And when they're not, it's impossible to accomplish the easy."

In my forty years in sports, I'm still waiting for the ultimate—a team that is self-motivated. It hasn't happened yet. What about your team, your company, your church, your organization, your family? Is everybody motivated? Until that happens, a big piece of your job description as a leader is to be a motivator. To be effective, you can't motivate from the top of the organization, from an ivory tower. You must lead and motivate from the middle. The motivator in the middle is the motivator who truly inspires people to do and be their best. John Quincy Adams challenged all managers when he wrote, "If your actions inspire others to dream more, learn more, do more, and become more, you are a leader."

There are a number of facets or components to motivation. People tend to be motivated when one or more of these facets is communicated to them in a powerful way. Here's a rundown:

## Motivate through optimism.

People who feel positive are motivated to be productive. Optimism sells; gloom kills. If you want to keep the people around you motivated, then you've got to be a tireless cheerleader. Optimism radiates, it spreads, it increases across the ranks. As Colin Powell has said, "Optimism is a force multiplier. I don't like wallowing with pessimists." Optimism is an intellectual choice.

When Tommy Lasorda retired after twenty years as the manager of the Dodgers, I called him up and asked, "Tommy, what was the most important thing you did every day as a manager?" I thought he would talk to me about the strategic side of the game—the lineup card, getting the right matchups, and so forth.

But no. He said, "The most important thing I did was walk into the clubhouse the right way."

"What do you mean?" I asked.

"It's real simple," he replied. "It didn't matter whether we had won eight in a row or lost eight in a row. Whether things were great at home or not so great, I had to walk into the clubhouse the right way. The minute I came in, my players had to see an upbeat, positive manager. I had to walk straight, have a smile on my face, and an optimistic gleam in my eye. If my players had seen my chin at my belt buckle, the gloom would have spread like wildfire. It would have destroyed the ballclub. You have to be optimistic all the time. That's a manager's most important job."

*Motivate through hope.*

This facet is derived from optimism. Napoleon once said, "A leader is a dealer in hope." As long as we have hope, we can keep going, keep battling, keep striving. Only when there is no more hope is there no reason to live. Former Chicago Bears owner George Halas said, "Hope, hope, what can be accomplished without hope?" How true!

In 1630 John Winthrop sold everything he had and moved his family from England to the New World, where he would serve as the first governor of the Massachusetts Bay Colony. Before disembarking and setting foot on the soil of America, Winthrop stood on the deck of the *Arabella* and spoke to pilgrims of the life they would have in the New World. It was a motivational message of *hope*. "We shall be as a city on a hill," he said. "The eyes of all people are upon us."

Arriving on land, Winthrop and his fellow pilgrims found themselves in a wilderness clearing, where their "city on a hill" consisted of a few rude huts. Many were already sick and malnourished from the journey, and a lot of the provisions they had brought with them had spoiled. A few days after their arrival, Winthrop's son drowned in the river. But Winthrop and his people worked hard, built shelters, and planted crops. The colony suffered through a terrible winter; of the thousand colonists who had come on the first few ships, two hundred died. When spring came, another two hundred gave up and returned to England.

But over the next decade, Winthrop governed his people and motivated them with the same message of hope he had given them from the deck of the *Arabella:* "We shall be as a city on a hill. The eyes of all

people are upon us." Under his leadership, the Massachusetts Bay
Colony eventually grew to a population of 20,000. Hope pulled the
colony through a terrible winter, hope sustained their lives, and hope
laid the foundation for a dream that would energize generations of
Americans for centuries to come.

Congresswoman and diplomat Clare Booth Luce was right when
she said, "There are no hopeless situations; there are only men who
have grown hopeless about them."

## Motivate through self-esteem.

People who feel important and significant are empowered to do their
best. Let people know they are valued and that their contribution
counts. Management consultant John Baldoni says:

> Recognition is critical to self-esteem. Money is nice, sure,
> but once you establish a basis of monetary rewards without the
> accompanying verbal and social affirmation, the employee will
> quickly become disgruntled and ask for more. Eventually, more
> will never be enough.

## Motivate through personal connection and caring.

When their leader knows them, acknowledges them, and roots them
on, people feel they can achieve anything.

Though Jim Leyland never played baseball in the majors, he was
considered one of the best managers in Major League Baseball. Leyland was your typical baseball guy—a high school graduate who went
right into pro ball, with stubble on his chin and a wad of tobacco in
his mouth. I asked Frank Wren, assistant general manager of the
Florida Marlins, what made Leyland so good at his job. Frank thought
for a moment, then said:

> From the first day of spring training to the last day of the
> season, every single day, Jim goes one on one with every player.
> It may be just a few minutes, and it may not be about baseball.

It could be about family or the news or just joking and kidding, but he takes time with each player, every day. We've got twenty-five ballplayers, so if he just spent three minutes with each one, that's an hour and a quarter right there. But he does it, and that's why he's so good.

### Motivate through inspiration.

Communicate with the people around you to animate and enliven their energy and enthusiasm. Donald T. Phillips, the mayor of Fairview, Texas, and author of *Lincoln on Leadership* and *Martin Luther King, Jr., on Leadership,* says, "When people really care about a cause, they will not only act on their own initiative, they will move mountains to get the job done."

I know from personal experience how true those words are. Every leader I have ever been involved with or watched from afar or talked to others about had this quality: They inspired people to perform beyond their normal capabilities. Inspirational leaders touch human souls and ignite human spirits. Inspiration is the most powerful kind of motivation in the world.

I'll always remember my baseball coach from my freshman year in high school. His name was Peanuts Riley (I'm sure it didn't say "Peanuts" on his birth certificate—but I never heard him called anything but Coach or Peanuts). He was a former pro ball player, and he was a great teacher of the game. My teammates and I would gladly do anything he asked of us because we were so captured and inspired by this man. I didn't see it at time, but now I know what this man had: the gift of *inspiration*. He inspired us and motivated us, and his inspirational example is still etched in my memory after all these years. That's the kind of leader I want to be.

### Motivate through a sense of urgency.

A motivated person knows he or she must do the job and do it now—there is no time to waste. NBA coach Pat Riley is a master communicator. He is great at firing up his players with a sense of urgency. Here's an excerpt from one of his pregame speeches:

> Do you realize that each of us spends no more than thirty thousand days on this planet? That's two and a half billion seconds. And do you realize that tonight you're going to be on the court for forty-eight minutes, and that's only 2,880 seconds. And the only thing you have the power to do today is to go out and play your best for 2,880 seconds? That's a very small part of your two and a half billion seconds. So let's make it your very best!

*Motivate through excitement.*

Michael S. Dell founded his computer company in 1984 with one thousand dollars of start-up capital. Today, Dell Computer Corporation is the number one personal computer company in the world, with over $30 billion in sales per year and more than thirty-four thousand employees worldwide. "The real challenge," he says, "is to get people excited about what you're doing. A lot of businesses get off-track because they don't communicate an excitement about being part of a winning team that can achieve big goals."

So lead from the middle and motivate from the middle. Hone your skills as a communicator so you can inspire and motivate your people. An organization of highly motivated members is an unstoppable force.

## COMMUNICATION PARADOX 3:

### The Prudent Leader Welcomes Conflict

Jesus modeled for us another crucial function of a leader: A leader uses communication to manage conflict. Jesus never avoided conflict, nor did he go out of his way to create conflict. But he always used conflict as a teaching opportunity, a growth opportunity, a tool for generating positive change and building stronger relationships. A key example of Jesus' approach to conflict management is found in Luke 22:24–27:

> Also a dispute arose among them as to which of them was considered to be greatest. Jesus said to them, "The kings of the Gentiles lord it over them; and those who exercise authority over them call themselves Benefactors. But you are not to be like that. Instead, the greatest among you should be like the youngest, and the one who rules like the one who serves. For who is greater, the one who is at the table or the one who serves? Is it not the one who is at the table? But I am among you as one who serves."

Human nature hasn't changed much in two thousand years. People still compete with each other, jockey for position, and bump their oversized egos against one another. The twelve men who followed Jesus were no better or worse than the people in your organization. Just as Jesus did then, you still have to settle disputes and deal with human pride and vanity on a daily basis in order to keep your organization functioning smoothly.

Jesus managed the conflict in his twelve-member organization in exactly the same way you need to deal with conflict in your organization. He *communicated*. He faced the issues squarely, brought the hidden conflicts out into the open, laid down principles for resolving conflict, and modeled a healthy conflict resolution style.

Jesus also taught in a direct way that it is important to settle disputes quickly:

> Therefore, if you are offering your gift at the altar and there remember that your brother has something against you, leave your gift there in front of the altar. First go and be reconciled to your brother; then come and offer your gift. Settle matters quickly with your adversary (Matthew 5:23–25a).

Managing conflict is a big part of the job description of any leader. Notice I said *managing* conflict, not avoiding, squelching, or suppressing conflict. Conflict is inevitable. Is conflict good or bad? It's *both*. Conflict can generate change and growth if handled in a healthy way—and that kind of conflict is good. But conflict can also be bad. If we duck it, avoid it, deny it, or mismanage it, conflict can actually destroy an organization.

In the 1950 film *Harvey*, the kindly Elwood P. Dowd (played by Jimmy Stewart) shows us the attitude we should have toward conflict: "An element of conflict in every discussion is a very good thing," he said. "It shows that everyone is taking part and no one is left out." Here are some keys to managing conflict in a healthy and productive way:

## Welcome disagreements.

Remember that disagreements are a stimulus for change and a corrective for error. Robert Townsend, author of *Up the Organization*, put it this way: "A good manager doesn't try to eliminate conflict; he tries to keep it from wasting the energies of his people. If you're the boss and your people fight you openly when they think that you are wrong— that's healthy."

## Listen carefully.

When disagreements arise, resist the natural impulse to leap to your own defense. Hear the other person out. Let him or her know that you have heard the complaint or disagreement. Mirror it back in your own words so that the other person knows you've absorbed it accurately. One of the reasons people fail to see eye-to-eye is that they don't take the time and trouble to hear ear-to-ear. In his book *How to Attend a Conference*, Dr. S. I. Hayakawa put it this way: "Few people have had much training in listening. Living in a competitive culture, most of us are most of the time chiefly concerned with getting our own view across, and we tend to find other people's speeches a tedious interruption of our own ideas."

*Whatever you do, keep your cool.*

Distrust your own initial reaction—it is probably defensive, not objective or constructive. Don't lose your temper. Instead, take time to reflect and consider: Is there merit in this complaint? Should I change? What can I learn from this situation of conflict?

I have gotten to know a wonderful counselor in Orlando, Dr. Debbie Day. She is interviewed and quoted often in the media, and I have spent time with her in counseling sessions. (Believe me, with nineteen children in our family, we have needed some family counseling!) If there is one central thread in her professional counseling, it is this: "Whatever you do, don't blow up. Once your temper flares, you are not going to make any progress and your meeting is over. So take a walk, count to ten or a hundred, do whatever you have to do, but don't lose your cool." That advice has been a real anchor to our family.

*Focus first on areas of agreement.*

If you honestly feel that the other person's complaint is in error, look for things you can affirm before launching into your counter-arguments. It will help dispel a negative atmosphere and open the door to better communication.

I have learned the hard way, both in family situations and in professional settings, that you've got to cut through all the accusations and unrest and get to one issue: What do we agree on? In many cases, once you get all the emotion out of the way, you find there is much more common ground than you realized. That common ground, that area of agreement—no matter how seemingly small—is the beachhead. That's that starting point. Seize it, build on it, and I guarantee you will be able to make progress in managing and resolving that conflict.

Whenever you are in conflict with someone, there are always things that you agree on. You may disagree on short-term methods, but you agree on long-term goals. You may be mad at each other about the in-laws or the harsh words that were said, but you agree on your long-term love for each other and your commitment to the relationship.

Whatever it is, take that little patch of common ground and use it as a starting point for resolving the problem.

## When you're wrong, admit it.

Many people feel it diminishes them to say, "I was wrong." The truth is we increase our stature when we are big enough to admit mistakes. Leaders who can honestly admit they were wrong are the most respected and admired leaders of all. People who can't admit mistakes are seen as pathetically insecure—especially when their mistakes are painfully obvious to everyone around them.

The most frustrating man I've ever known was an NBA owner I worked for some years ago. He not only couldn't admit he was wrong, but he couldn't admit he was even *capable* of making a mistake. No matter what happened, it was always somebody else's fault. People like that think they look powerful and strong by pretending to be infallible. In fact, others immediately spot these people for what they are—insecure souls with weak, fragile egos.

A man once went into a blacksmith shop. The blacksmith warned him, "Don't touch those horseshoes; they're very hot." Well, the man couldn't resist. He picked up a horseshoe—and as the skin of his hand began to sizzle, he flung that horseshoe away from him. The blacksmith said, "I told you those horseshoes were hot!" But the man said, "It wasn't hot; it just doesn't take me long to look at a horseshoe."

Friend, if you make a mistake, own up to it. Life is a lot easier for people who are strong enough to say, "I was wrong."

## Weigh concerns and criticism of others honestly, objectively, and fairly.

After all, these people just might be right.

## Praise in public, reprimand in private.

Nobody likes to be shown they are wrong—and it is a hundred times worse to have your mistakes exposed in front of your peers. It is not only embarrassing to be reprimanded in public, it is embarrassing to watch it happen to someone else. If you humiliate a member of your organization in front of his or her peers, you will not make one enemy, you'll make a roomful. But if you praise one member publicly, you'll make not just one friend but many.

I only had one encounter with Bobby Knight, the infamous former head basketball coach at Indiana University. I was general manager of the Philadelphia 76ers at the time, and I was in Bloomington for the Olympic trials. Some bleachers had been set up courtside for NBA executives and scouts. I happened to be standing a few feet from the end of the bleachers, talking with a friend of Knight's, Wayne Embry of the Milwaukee Bucks. Suddenly, here came Bobby Knight. His face was red and there was smoke shooting out his ears. He looked me right in the eye and screamed at me, "Who do you think you are! Get up in those bleachers!"

I don't recall ever being publicly screamed at like that before—and certainly not for something so minor. It was embarrassing at the time, and twenty years later the memory still has power to sting.

Sometimes leaders are called upon to correct people in the organization—but a wise leader never sets out to humiliate others. The purpose of correction is to build up, not tear down.

### Absorb the gripes and grievances of your organization.

The noted psychologist and author Dr. George W. Crane once said, "It's healthy for employees to air their gripes. Accumulated irritations build up pressure in people and, if not released, may burst with major consequences." Great leaders encourage and accept criticism.

If a leader says there are no gripes in his or her organization, it only means that the leader is out of touch. There are gripes in *all* organizations. Listening to those gripes can often produce a harvest of crucial information and useful ideas. Look at it this way: Absorbing and dealing with complaints is part of a leader's job description. It comes with the turf. It's not the most pleasant part of the job, but that's why you get the big bucks, right? You have to keep grievance channels open or complaints will fester into resentment and discontent—and you and your organization will pay the price.

## COMMUNICATION PARADOX 4:

### The Leader's Most Powerful Tools Are Words

Aram Bakshian Jr., a speechwriter for Ronald Reagan, wrote, "To rise to the top in any field you must be an outstanding public speaker." I can't think of a single great leader who was not also a great speaker. Dynamic leaders are always dynamic communicators. They communicate effectively one-on-one, and they communicate effectively before groups. Jesus himself was a leader who continually communicated through public speaking, and though no film or video record of his speeches were made, those who were there remembered his words and preserved them. As a result, the world has been shaped by the words of Jesus.

Leadership involves being out in front of people and being an example to people. Leadership involves inspiring people, sharing your vision with them, and leading them where you want them to go. So it naturally follows that if you are comfortable speaking in front of people, you will be comfortable leading in front of people. The ability to speak in public is an enormous asset to have in your leadership portfolio.

Whatever it takes to gain experience and mastery as a speaker, do it! Join Toastmasters International. Watch your speeches and rehearsals on video so you can see ways to improve. Hire a speech coach. Practice, practice, practice! When you gain experience as a speaker, you gain confidence and expertise.

Poll after poll has shown that the number one fear we face in life is not the fear of death or snakes or the dark. No, the number one fear in the world is fear of public speaking. Most people would literally rather die than speak in front of an audience! Perhaps that is one reason great leaders are so rare: Leaders are people who have overcome their fear of public speaking and who have taken the time to develop their public speaking skills. Leaders have the ability to move and influence people by their words.

History has been shaped by talkers. The inspiring words of Winston Churchill kept Great Britain upbeat and energized through the dark days of World War II; when a later British prime minister, Anthony Eden, was asked Churchill's greatest contribution to the war effort, Eden replied, "He talked about it." John Kennedy once said that "Churchill mobilized the English language and sent it into battle." In the opinion of historian Arnold Toynbee, "Churchill's speeches spelled the difference between survival and defeat."

In America during WWII, Franklin Delano Roosevelt kept America inspired and battle-ready through his stirring speeches—"December 7, 1941: a date which will live in infamy!"—and his Fireside Chat radio broadcasts. John F. Kennedy gave Americans a vision of their own place in history with his powerful words, "Ask not what your country can do for you; ask what you can do for your country." And another president, Ronald Reagan, went to Berlin in 1987 and delivered a powerful speech with a seemingly impossible demand: "Mr. Gorbachev, tear down this wall!" And two years later, the wall came down.

People forget that when Margaret Thatcher became prime minister of Great Britain in 1979, her nation was on the brink of economic collapse and Soviet-style communism was advancing around the globe. Her vibrant speeches in favor of a free-market economy and her defiance of tyranny and totalitarianism (she was "Reaganesque" a full eighteen months before Reagan became president!) were a major factor in saving Britain from collapse and in defeating global communism.

Prior to the terrorist attacks of September 11, 2001, President George W. Bush was pounded in the media for his mangling of the English language and his mediocre speaking skills. But his Churchillian speeches in the aftermath of the attacks changed the minds of Bush's critics. Again and again, those who had disparaged Bush repeated the phrase, "The president has found his voice." In other words, "Dub-byah" was talkin' good. Jack Valenti, a former aid to Lyndon B. Johnson, observed: "As governor of Texas Mr. Bush was an awful speaker. He has improved mightily and is a master now."

In the business realm, the Amway Corporation would have never reached the astounding multibillion-dollar heights it reached without the inspirational, motivational cheerleading of cofounder Rich

DeVos—a truly gifted speaker and leader. And in the realm of spirituality, Dr. Billy Graham has a great message to deliver, and no one has delivered it more powerfully and to more people than he has. In his sixty years of ministry, it is estimated that he has spoken (both by personal appearance and by radio and television) to over a billion people! By his well-chosen words, his gestures and inflection, and his podium skills, he is recognized as a master of public speaking—and he has used those skills in the service of his Master for an entire lifetime.

I have already mentioned the powerful influence Bill Veeck had on my life when I was a young sports executive. Veeck owned ballclubs in Milwaukee, Cleveland, St. Louis, and Chicago, and in each of these cities, he was continually on the stump, speaking at business meetings, clubs, commencements, anyplace people needed a speaker. His argument was, "What better way to sell my team than to go out in the community and talk about it?"

I bought into that philosophy and made public speaking part of my job description wherever I went in an effort to promote the team, sell tickets, and make our franchise more visible. I also found that if people had met you and felt that they knew you, they quickly became enthusiastic fans of the team. In the process, I kept improving my skills, honing my delivery, and increasing my confidence. Little did I realize it would lead to a whole new career as a professional speaker years later.

Now, I'm not suggesting you need to launch a career as a professional speaker. But I know this to be true: The ability to verbalize your vision and inspire people is a powerful asset for any leader. This ability is a learned skill.

Long before he became president, Ronald Reagan spent years learning and improving his speaking skills. During the years after he left Hollywood and before he went into politics, Reagan served as a goodwill ambassador for the General Electric company. He traveled the country, speaking to groups of G.E. employees, sometimes giving three or four speeches a day. In a period of just three or four years, he gave thousands of speeches. Today, history fittingly remembers him as "The Great Communicator."

Conversely, former president Gerald Ford was not a great speaker as president—and that is probably one of the principal reasons he never won election to a full term after gaining the office upon Richard Nixon's resignation. He once said, "If I went back to college again, I would concentrate on two areas: learning to write and learning to speak before an audience. Nothing in life is more important than the ability to communicate effectively." I once heard Ford speak at a Peter Lowe Success Day in Tampa, Florida, and the then-eighty-six-year-old former president was a witty, energetic, engaging speaker. Somewhere along the line, he had acquired the communicating skills he once lacked as president, and those skills serve him well today. Winston Churchill put it this way: "Of all the talents bestowed upon men, none is so precious as the gift of oratory. He who enjoys it wields a power more durable than that of a great king. He is an independent force in the world." Churchill knew. Leader, your most powerful leadership tools are not your capable staff or your computer, cell phone, or fax machine. Your most powerful tools are simply your words.

# COMMUNICATION PARADOX 5:

## The Effective Leader Communicates Without Words

History has always been shaped by leaders and their words—and sometimes by abilities that go beyond words. In 1940 England was a nation under siege. German bombs had destroyed much of London, killing nearly fifty thousand people. Winston Churchill went on the radio and stirred the nation with a message of courage and defiance. As soon as each air raid ended, he would walk through the rubble of bombed-out neighborhoods, joking with survivors, weeping with the bereaved, and offering encouragement wherever he went. He rallied the British people and buoyed their morale by summoning a sense of England's past grandeur and future destiny. The British people were so inspired and bolstered by Churchill's words that they didn't even know they'd been licked—so they kept right on fighting until they had won.

Did Winston Churchill have a natural gift for public speaking? Certainly. But even more important, he had a gift for nonverbal communication. NBC newscaster David Brinkley reflected on hearing Churchill give a speech some years earlier:

> I thought at the time that I was seeing more than a statesman. I was seeing an actor who did not make a speech or deliver a speech. He acted a speech. He threw his whole body into it, but somehow managed to do so without excessive gestures or histrionics . . . The audience sat still, quiet, entranced, eager to applaud, but afraid to. The clapping of hands would have somehow seemed vulgar.

Leaders move the world with words. But words are not the only form of communication at our disposal. In fact, words are not necessarily the best and most powerful way to communicate. The wise leader knows that words are only half (at most!) of a spoken message. As the French author La Rochefoucauld once observed, "Tone of voice, look, and manner can prove no less eloquent than choice of words."

Nonverbal cues convey as much or more information as the words themselves. Does the leader fumble with papers or wring his hands as he speaks? Does he avoid eye contact with his audience? Does his voice quaver? His words may be as stirring as the Gettysburg Address—but the nonverbal cues will fatally undermine the audience's confidence in that leader. If he appears unsure or fearful, who will follow him?

Here's another example: Does the leader have a warm smile, a strong and pleasing voice, and an interesting range of facial expressions and physical gestures? Does she move confidently around the stage? Does she make eye contact with people around the room? If so, she could be reciting from the phone book, and people would hang on every word.

Communications expert Bert Decker describes the nonverbal dimension of speaking this way:

> An enormous amount of communication is taking place as these thousands of multi-channel impressions are carried to

your brain. Most of these impressions register at a preconscious level. As a result of these impressions, your brain forms a continuous stream of emotional judgments and assessments: Do I trust this person? Is he or she honest? Evasive? Friendly? Threatening? Interesting? Boring? Warm? Cold? Anxious? Confident? Insecure? Hiding something?[6]

These nonverbal cues have a profound impact on whether we trust the speaker or not—and whether or not we would follow the speaker as a leader. If the trust is not there, the words will not get through—and the speaker will not be able to lead. Therefore, be aware of how your tone of voice, your expression, your eyes, and your gestures shape your message. Don't neglect the nonverbal dimension of your communication. A wise leader knows how to move and motivate people—with and without words.

# COMMUNICATION PARADOX 6:

## The Influential Leader Persuades by Listening

In the realm of communication, we tend to focus on achieving our own goals and communicating our own message to others. We think that the best way to persuade others to our point of view and motivate them to action is by talking. But Jesus showed us that, paradoxically, one of the most persuasive things we can do as communicators is close our mouths, open our ears, and *listen*.

Jesus was a talker, no question. But it's instructive to see how much time he spent listening before speaking. He was the first interactive leader. In his time there were lots of leaders—caesars, Roman governors, Roman generals, and Jewish high priests. All of these leaders made speeches and issued decrees. They gave commands and people obeyed.

But Jesus was different. He *listened*.

He didn't merely broadcast his vision. He talked to people, asked questions, listened to their hopes, fears, and confessions of failure. He didn't merely preach, he had conversations. He listened to the rich young ruler, the woman at the well, the Roman centurion, the woman afflicted with chronic bleeding, Nicodemus the Pharisee, the blind beggar by the road. Above all, he spent countless hours with his followers, questioning them, talking with them, getting to know them, listening to them.

Even today, listening is not a skill highly regarded among leaders. The ability to speak, to command, to issue orders—no one questions that these are necessary qualifications for leadership. But the ability to listen? That's for followers, not leaders. Again and again, I have seen leaders with an attitude that says, "I'm the boss! I don't have to listen! People have to listen to me!" To them, the idea that a good leader is a good listener sounds like foolishness.

How many times have you heard the complaint, "Oh, he talks too much!" I've heard that said many times of many leaders. But I've never heard this complaint about any leader: "Oh, he listens too much!" Listening is an art—a lost art, it sometimes seems. Yet one of the great paradoxes of communication is that when we listen to people, we become much more persuasive communicators. People like to follow leaders who listen.

University of Louisville head basketball coach Rick Pitino (and former coach of the national champion Kentucky Wildcats, as well as the New York Knicks and Boston Celtics) said:

> The art of communication is about relating to people, and you do that by *listening* to them. There are other things to pay attention to: looking at people when they speak; concentrating on what people are saying instead of thinking about what you're going to say; trying to understand where people are coming from and what their concerns are. These things make people feel comfortable, make them feel that you're talking to them, not just talking *at* them.

Our tendency as leaders is to generate an idea, call in the troops, tell them that idea, and send them out to implement it. The problem with that approach is that it's *our* idea, not theirs. The troops don't have a vested interest in making our idea succeed. But what if the troops were

asked to offer *their* ideas—and were then sent out to implement the
ideas they came up with? Would that make a difference in how
enthused and motivated they would be? You bet it would! NFL coach
Marty Schottenheimer puts it this way:

> The more people have a sense of ownership and leadership
> in a project, the higher the level of motivation. It is when
> people feel disconnected from the whole that they question
> whether their efforts matter. That's when they start going
> through the motions.

This is not to say you shouldn't generate and promote ideas of your
own—you should. That's what leaders are for. But at the same time,
you want to make sure there is a healthy influx of ideas from all over,
and a healthy sense of ownership and stewardship of the vision among
all the members of your organization.

Leaders who are good listeners create an environment of imagination and enthusiasm throughout the organization. Here, then, are
some keys to becoming a better listener:

*Pay attention.*

Make a conscious decision that you will listen twice as much as you
talk. No one ever learned anything by talking. Focus on what the
other person says as if you were going to be tested on it. In a very real
sense, you may be. The survival of your organization could hinge on
your ability to receive, grasp, and act upon what the people around
you are telling you. Celebrated journalist and broadcast interviewer
Diane Sawyer has made a career out of giving focused attention to
other people. "I think the one lesson I have learned," she said, "is that
there is no substitute for paying attention."

*Keep your mouth shut.*

Let other people speak first. If you speak first, you may miss hearing
some great ideas. Don't fall prey to the misconception that you're the
only one who has something important to say. "The first principle of

listening," author-educator Howard Hendricks once said, "is to develop a big ear rather than a big mouth."

*Ask questions.*

Ask intelligent questions. Focus on open-ended questions: the *why* questions, the *how* questions, and the *what* questions. These questions will encourage the other person to speak out—and to give you the information you need. Likewise, asking questions not only makes you appear more interested, but also more interesting. People who ask good questions are more likeable, and more likely to be liked.

Before he ran for president of the United States, Calvin Coolidge was invited to a dinner hosted by an influential industrialist, Dwight Morrow, father of Anne Morrow Lindbergh. At the time Anne was only six years old. After the dinner, when Coolidge had left, Dwight Morrow said he thought Coolidge would make a good president. Others at the dinner disagreed. "He's too quiet," said one. "No charisma," said another.

Then six-year-old Anne piped up. "I like him," she said. Then she raised her bandaged finger. "He was the only one here," she said, "who asked me about my hurt finger. That's why he would make a good president."

*Show interest.*

As you give verbal feedback, use the other person's name. This establishes a personal connection and helps to fix that person's name in your mind. Listen with your whole head, not just your ears; make eye contact, nod, and show empathy with your facial expressions.

I was in a Dallas TV station to do an interview for my book *Unsinkable*. The makeup lady, Jules Hoffman, had an interesting story about Sarah Ferguson. "I was doing her makeup early in the morning," Jules told me, "before she went on the air to promote her new line of china. One of our employees, Sally, came in to meet Fergie and tell her she'd be bringing in a tray to the store that night where Fergie would be signing her china. Hours later, Sally arrived at the store and Fergie greeted her—'Sally, it's good to see you! Where's that tray for me to sign?' That was amazing! Sarah Ferguson had met hundreds of people that day, but she remembered Sally's name."

When you call people by name, they feel valued—and are ready to listen to anything you have to say!

*Be objective.*

Listen to all sides of every issue before you make a decision. Agree heartily; disagree gently. And as you listen, *learn* from what you hear. Let the things you learn guide your decisions.

M. Scott Peck, author of *The Road Less Traveled*, once observed:

> An essential part of true listening is . . . the temporary giving up or setting aside of one's own prejudices, frames of reference and desires so as to experience as far as possible the speaker's world from the inside. You step inside his or her shoes. This unification of speaker and listener is actually an extension and enlargement of ourselves, and new knowledge is always gained from this.

Leadership expert Warren Blank, author of *The Nine Natural Laws of Leadership*, says that few people are good listeners. On average, people hear only about 50 percent of what is said to them. They only pay attention to about 25 percent of what is said. They only understand 12 percent, only believe 6 percent, and only remember 3 percent.

Three percent! Anyone can do that. Anyone can do *better* than that. So if you exert *any* real effort at listening to the people around you, they will be amazed at your incredible skills as a listener! As former secretary of state Dean Rusk said, "One of the best ways to persuade others is by listening to them."

## THE WISE FOOLISHNESS OF GOOD LEADERSHIP

These, then, are the six paradoxes of communication, as found in the example of Jesus himself:

1.  The wise leader dares to be a fool.
2.  The great leader leads from the middle, not the top.
3.  The prudent leader welcomes conflict.
4.  The leader's most powerful tools are words.
5.  The effective leader communicates without words.
6.  The influential leader persuades by listening.

A church leader must communicate his vision of what the church can become—the future reach of its ministry, what the congregation can achieve, how the community and the world will be impacted for the better. A military leader must communicate his vision of what his forces will achieve, the objective that will be reached, how the battlefield will be tilted in favor of the good guys. A business leader must communicate his vision of how his organization will saturate and dominate the marketplace, how his company's products or services will become household words, and how the lives of everyone in the organization will be transformed and improved by the company's success.

Communication is the process of moving information, emotion, meaning, and vision from one human mind to another. Through the power of paradox, Jesus communicated his vision to the people around him, and each generation of followers has passed that vision down from mind to mind, from generation to generation, century after century after century. That vision is still alive and powerful today.

The transmission of a vision is the goal of every great leader. To lead, you must master the paradoxes of communication.

# The Strong Leader Dares to Be Weak

I didn't dare be weak. I had to prove I could do it all.

I was in my mid-twenties, just starting out in pro sports, eager to succeed, eager to show others (and myself) that I could make it. I had been hired by Mr. R. E. Littlejohn to run the Spartanburg Phillies, a Philadelphia Phillies farm club in South Carolina. I had enough in the budget to hire some help, but I didn't trust anyone else to do the job the way I wanted it done.

So I did *everything*.

I labored from dawn to dusk, cutting the grass, painting the outfield walls, refurbishing the rest rooms. I met with the town council to drum up support from the city. I sold every ad in the game program and got the tickets printed. I organized all the game night promotions and handled all the publicity. I got the brooms out for the cleanup crew and drove the gate receipts to the night deposit at the bank. I ran myself into the ground—and paid a price for it in stomach lining.

I had a lot to learn about being a leader.

In my mind, a leader was a guy who could do it all. If I couldn't do it all, people would think I was weak. The fear of failure was like a bullwhip at my back, driving me through eighteen-hour days, seven days a week. I had no social life. I didn't date. The ballpark was my home, my life, my reason for living.

Finally, it dawned on me that the job was too big, and I was only one person. I wouldn't get the job done without some help. I advertised for a secretary but I didn't get one nibble. Two days before the season was to open, we held an open house for our fans at the ballpark. While I was walking through the stands, a woman reached out and grabbed my arm.

"Mr. Williams," she said, "I'm Claire Johns. I understand you need a secretary. I'm interested in the job."

"Terrific," I said. "How fast do you type?"

"I don't know," she said. "I've never used a typewriter before."

"Ever do any filing?"

"Nope."

"What kind of experience do you have?"

"None. I've never worked in an office before."

"Can you show up at eight in the morning?"

"Sure!"

"Congratulations. You've got the job."

She turned out to be a great assistant—I couldn't have run the ballclub without her. She took care of a lot of detail work, leaving me free to promote. I began to learn some important lessons about leadership. Effective leaders know they can't do it all themselves. Successful leaders know that their success—and the success of the organization—depends upon other people.

The strong leader dares to delegate. The strong leader dares to be weak.

## THE MASTER DELEGATOR

Delegation is the essence of leadership. The leader who cannot delegate cannot lead. Retailer James Cash Penney stated: "The surest way for an executive to kill himself is to refuse to learn how, when, and to whom to delegate work."

Jesus set the example for all leaders in how he related to people and achieved his goals and his vision through people. His leadership model has never been surpassed. He was a master recruiter, a master teacher-trainer-mentor, and a master delegator. He didn't need anybody to achieve his goals. He could have done it all himself, without any help. Yet he chose to work through other people. The strongest leader the world has ever known dared to be weak, dared to entrust his vision to others, dared to stand back and let others take over the work of his kingdom. His leadership model is the most revolutionary and trans-forming approach to leadership this world has ever seen.

Jesus put a great deal of time and thought into the selection and recruitment of the twelve. He spent an entire night in prayer before he chose the twelve people he wanted on his team (Luke 6:12–13). This was a crucial decision, and he not only deliberated within himself, but he consulted extensively with his Father before making his choices.

Jesus recruited for diversity, not conformity. He didn't want people who had been stamped out with a cookie-cutter. He wanted a team of individuals, with unique gifts, personalities, strengths, and back-grounds. His team was a spectrum of people ranging from the out-spoken to the reserved, from extroverts to introverts, from conservatives to liberals, from a government bureaucrat like Matthew to an anti-government radical, Simon the Zealot.

Jesus didn't start delegating right off the bat. He used one-on-one mentoring, group teaching, small group dynamics, and on-the-job training as tools to shape his followers into a unified force for change.

First, he laid down serious conditions and requirements. "I am the vine; you are the branches. If a man remains in me and I in him, he will bear much fruit; apart from me you can do nothing" (John 15:5). The mission he gave his twelve followers was a demanding one, and no half-hearted effort or slacker attitude would do; each disciple would have to follow Jesus closely—or the disciple's efforts would pro-duce nothing.

Jesus then put the twelve through intensive training sessions. He taught the twelve, and they questioned him about his teaching. With each new challenge or experience they faced, he gave them deeper and more thorough instruction. Sometimes Jesus even tossed them into situations where they were clearly over their heads—and that's where they learned the most, and learned it very quickly.

As the disciples grew in their understanding and experience, Jesus gradually transferred more and more responsibility to them. In the process, he demonstrated a fundamental model of leadership and delegation: First, he showed them what he wanted done by doing it himself. He said, in effect, "I'll work; you watch." Next, he gradually involved the twelve in the work: "I'll work; you help." Then, he shifted still more responsibility to their shoulders: "You work; I'll help." Finally, he entrusted the work completely to his followers: "You work; I'll watch."

In Mark 6:7–13, we see the culmination of this process. Jesus called the twelve to himself, then sent them out with instructions and full authority to do the very same work that he had been doing: preaching, healing, and battling evil. The Master Delegator delegated everything to his followers. Jesus was one man; but through his followers, he multiplied himself twelve times over. He had reproduced himself through them—not by turning them into clones of himself, but by investing in their diversity and molding them into a unified force of unique individuals. They were a rainbow of personalities forming a single spectrum of light.

In delegating his work to them, Jesus made an amazing promise to his followers: "I tell you the truth," he said in John 14:12, "anyone who has faith in me will do what I have been doing. He will do even greater things than these." That is a transforming truth of leadership: Strong leaders dare to be weak, dare to entrust their work to others, dare to work through people rather than doing it all themselves—and in the process, their work is multiplied many times over through the people around them. The followers accomplish "even greater things" than the leaders can do alone.

Here, then, are seven keys to being an effective delegator and a great leader, as modeled by the Master Delegator, Jesus of Nazareth:

*Hire for attitude and recruit the best.*

The first key to delegating is choosing the right people to delegate to.

In their book *Nuts!: Southwest Airlines' Crazy Recipe for Business and Personal Success*, authors Kevin Freiberg and Jackie Freiberg outline the stunning success story of an airline that enjoys an industry-high customer satisfaction record and an industry-low employee turnover rate. Southwest Airlines has turned a profit every year since 1973 while offering the lowest fares in the industry—and the company has never furloughed a single employee. The company must be doing something right when it comes to hiring—and it is. Southwest practices a policy it calls "Hire for Attitude, Train for Skills."

"This is a huge area of focus for us," says Southwest CEO Herb Kelleher. "We're religious about hiring." Years ago a vice-president lamented to Kelleher about interviewing thirty-four people for a ramp agent position, without finding the right person. Kelleher replied, "If you have to interview a *hundred* and thirty-four people to get the right ramp agent, do it."

Attitude is largely a function of character, personality, and core values. You can't train a rude, dishonest, abrasive, amoral, insensitive, bigoted, or narcissistic person to be polite, virtuous, genial, principled, thoughtful, tolerant, or selfless. For some people, good character and simple human decency are just not in their nature and never will be. You want to find people who feel they have a stake in the success of the organization—not just people who want a paycheck. You want people who are self-starters and self-motivated, who are flexible and adaptable, who take responsibility and admit mistakes, who are able to get along with others and find solutions to problems with coworkers and customers. It's this kind of person you ultimately want to delegate to! The people you recruit and select today will determine the culture of your organization, the service your organization renders to the public, and the reputation your organization will enjoy (or endure) for years to come.

Kevin Freiberg knows how to hire for attitude. Freiberg, who was a Southwest employee for ten years, advises that you start by identifying the superstars in your company, then ask their coworkers, superiors, and customers what is it about those people that makes them so effective to work with. Compile a profile of common denominators—then hire people who fit that profile.

Begin by trying to attract applicants who fit the profile. Southwest

Airlines does this with creative advertisements designed to attract an applicant with a built-in "Southwest attitude." One successful ad showed a coloring-book picture of a Tyrannosaurus Rex that had been scribbled with crayons. A teacher's note read, "Brian, please try to color inside the lines!" The caption read, "Brian shows an early aptitude for working at Southwest Airlines. At Southwest Airlines you get check pluses for coloring outside the lines." In other words, Southwest wants to attract people who think outside of the box and challenge conventional thinking.

Freiberg suggests a number of ways to structure an interviewing process that is focused on hiring for attitude. For example, if you want to screen applicants for such attitudes as unselfishness or a willingness to take risks, then you must design questions that target those specific attitudes. Since the past is the best indicator of the future, questions should begin with, "Tell me about a time when you did such and such." Freiberg offers these examples:[1]

- "Tell me about the last time you broke the rules to serve a customer in need." (The answer will indicate the applicant's flexibility and judgment.)
- "Tell me how you recently used humor to defuse a tense situation." (The answer will show how creative the person is at resolving conflict, and will also show if this person has a sense of humor.)
- "Tell me about a time when you went beyond the call of duty to assist a coworker when you received no recognition or no credit." (The answer will say a lot about the applicant's unselfishness and sense of teamwork.)
- "Give me an example of how you've worked with an extremely difficult coworker. How did you handle it?" (The answer will show whether the applicant is adaptable and cooperative.)
- "Tell me about a time when you made a serious mistake with a customer or a coworker. How did you reconcile it?" (This will help determine whether the applicant is willing to admit and fix mistakes.)

When you frame your questions and interview applicants, keep the applicant focused on past performance—don't let him or her simply predict how he or she *would* perform for you, or slide into some rehearsed answer. Demand specific examples of past actions that demonstrate the attitudes you seek.

Too, as you recruit for your organization, remember that the best people generally have good jobs. Sure, there are also some qualified candidates who are out of work, but odds are, the people you want will have to be lured away from their present employers. That means you must offer that prospective employee something he or she wants, but does not now get (or doesn't get enough of). Don't automatically assume that money is the ultimate lure. The person might just want a bigger challenge, a more fun and friendly environment, more recognition, or more responsibility.

Carefully investigate applicants who are unemployed or unhappy. Sometimes applicants put their best foot forward and make a good impression in an interview—but once they are in the job, you find out what they are really like, toxic attitude and all!

Instead of hiring only to fill a slot when an employee leaves, consider being in a mode of continuous recruitment and hiring. In other words, be a full-time talent scout. Even if you don't have an open slot, consider custom-tailoring a position when you come across someone who would be an asset to the organization.

Don't be afraid to hire people who are brighter or more talented than you are. David Ogilvy, founder of the Ogilvy & Mather Agency, once said, "If you ever find a man who is better than you are, hire him. If necessary, pay him more than you pay yourself." Wise words.

In hiring, seek diversity. I'm not just talking about gender and racial diversity. Just as Jesus recruited for diversity, you need to assemble a team of individuals with unique gifts, personalities, strengths, backgrounds, and outlooks. You need both the outspoken and the reserved, both the extroverted and the introverted, both the cautious and the risk-takers, both the innovators and the implementers. If you can assemble such an organization, focused on one vision, you will have an unstoppable, transformational workforce.

The strong leader surrounds himself with the best people and then gets out of the way and turns them loose. Though he wants his followers to benefit from his teaching, mentoring, and daily example, he resists the temptation to force his followers into his mold. "Never tell people how to do things," said General George S. Patton. "Just tell them what to do, and they will surprise you with their ingenuity."

So hire the best. Harness their energy. Harness their diversity. And watch your organization soar.

## Delegate as much as you can.

The second key to becoming an effective delegator is to delegate as much as you can to as many as you can. The organization benefits when you, the leader, delegate responsibility to others. In the process, you develop leadership skills and abilities in your people and enhance their initiative, creativity, and competence. You build their confidence and self-esteem and let them flex their own leadership muscles. When people at every level feel they are trusted and empowered to act, the entire organization is able to move decisively and respond quickly to changing situations.

But it's not just the organization that benefits. You, the leader, benefit even more! Just think: You get more free time to think, plan, and lead. Operational decision-making is shifted to the appropriate levels, allowing you more time and energy for strategic, long-range planning. Your effectiveness is magnified and multiplied. Your image is enhanced; instead of being judged on your individual performance, you are judged by the magnified effectiveness of the team or organization you lead. Best of all, you get more time for your private life—for family, for relaxation, for hobbies, and for working on your backswing.

I didn't learn the lessons of delegating all at once. After Spartanburg I started managing such basketball teams as the Philadelphia 76ers, the Chicago Bulls, the Atlanta Hawks, and the Orlando Magic. I had graduated to the big leagues, yet when it came to delegating, my thinking was still bush league. The front office had a support staff filled with talented people—but I still banged out press releases and promotional materials on my own typewriter.

As the basketball business kept getting bigger and bigger, my workload got heavier and my hours got longer. Finally, it dawned on me: *I can't do it all by myself! And it's not enough to hire an assistant. I need to hand off chunks of my job description to other people—and not just the grunt work. I need to trust people to become decision makers and initiators.*

In the process of admitting my own weakness and recognizing the strengths of others, I made some amazing discoveries:

- Some of the people I had hired were better at doing the work and making the decisions than I was.
- Those people who worked around me were actually happier with more responsibility, because now they were making a meaningful contribution, and they felt that I trusted them.
- The more small stuff I delegated to others, the more important stuff came my way. No longer mired in minutiae, I was able to handle bigger issues and more important decisions.
- Delegating tasks to other people enabled me to get more work done—and their accomplishments made me look like a genius!

When a business or organization fails, it is usually because the leader failed to get things done through people. No matter how skilled, talented, hardworking, and energetic you are as a leader, you will never get very far unless you know how to get things done through people.

Looking back, I can see four reasons why it was so hard for me to delegate tasks and responsibilities to other people:

- *Insecurity.* I was afraid that if other people were as good at my job as I was, I might be replaced. Once I started delegating, I learned that there was no need to feel threatened when others succeeded. Their success became my success.
- *Perfectionism.* I wanted everything done just right—as good as I knew I could do it. I had to learn that it's okay if people don't do

it the same way, or even as well as, you do. If they get it done, and if they learn in the process, then they have been successful.

- *False pride.* I thought I had to prove myself. I was filled with an attitude of egotism that said, "I don't need anyone else. I can do it myself." But a truly strong leader has the clear-eyed humility to know his own limitations, so that he can draw upon the strengths, resources, and genius of others.
- *Lack of trust.* I had to learn that if I don't trust people enough to delegate tasks and responsibilities to them, then they haven't failed—I have. If I can't trust people to know what they are doing and where they are going, then I have failed to communicate the vision.

Once I overcame those four problems, I was more easily able to let go of the reins. In doing so I practiced the following four simple steps of effective delegation:

- *Set clear goals and expectations.* People need to know what they are striving for and whether or not they have met (or exceeded!) your expectations.
- *Give people the freedom to act.* Delegate the authority to make decisions. Resist the temptation to interfere. Overrule your people only when absolutely necessary.
- *Motivate and encourage.* Give your people plenty of credit, affirmation, and incentive.
- *Remember that the buck stops with you.* Even though you trust others to make decisions and get the job done, you are still in charge. You must stay on top of things, get regular reports, and hold people accountable.

Moses practiced effective delegation. He learned the art of delegating from his father-in-law, Jethro. Moses had been serving as the judge of the Israelites. They brought to him all their disputes, from puny squabbles to the weightiest Supreme Court cases. Jethro told Moses, in effect, "These people are going to wear you down to a nub with these petty disputes! You sit here from morning till night, settling one argument after another. Take my advice: Delegate. Assemble a group of trustworthy advisors, teach them God's laws and decrees, and let them handle the small stuff." Moses did take Jethro's advice, and was the better for it (Exodus 18:17–25). Even a strong leader like Moses dared to be weak—and learned to delegate.

*Focus on relationships, understanding, and love.*

The third key to becoming an effective delegator is to build relationships between leader and followers and to create an atmosphere of understanding and love.

You might be thinking, *Relationships? Understanding? Love? I'm running an organization! What's all this touchy-feely "love" stuff?* The truth is that relationships and love are not only essential components of the leadership model of Jesus, they are also essential components of the most successful leadership models operating in the world today. Jesus started the V.O.P. Club: the Value of People Club.

Jesus said that the two most important commandments are "Love the Lord your God with all your heart and with all your soul and with all your mind and with all your strength" and "Love your neighbor as yourself" (Mark 12:29–31). When you think about it, this is a very strange statement: We are *commanded* to love. Isn't love an emotion? How can you *command* someone to experience an emotion?

In our twenty-first century culture, love is thought of as a warm-fuzzy, sticky-gooey feeling toward someone. That's not the kind of love Jesus was talking about. The word that is translated *love* in our English Bible was a Greek word, *agape*, in the original Bible manuscripts. *Agape* does not refer to a feeling. It refers to a decision to seek the ultimate good for another person. So when Jesus said you are to love your neighbor as yourself, he meant that you should make a decision to seek the ultimate good for all the people around you. Love *is* a choice.

With that understanding it becomes easier to see why love is such an important component of leadership. Even so, you may not be convinced. Some people think a strong leader has to be a tough guy. A strong leader, they say, should not get too chummy or friendly with subordinates. There should be a wall of emotional distance between the leader and the followers. In fact, followers should be downright *scared* in the presence of the leader. I've known numerous leaders who looked at their leadership role this way.

And they are wrong.

Legendary Dallas Cowboys quarterback Roger Staubach remembers coach Tom Landry as a man of great caring and compassion. The compassionate side of Coach Landry might seem to be at odds with Landry's "tough guy" image—the famous square-jawed profile that stalked the sidelines of so many memorable games, from the infamous "Ice Bowl" to five Super Bowl appearances. But Staubach recalls another side of Tom Landry:

> There was always this about Tom Landry. If you needed him for something, he was always there for you. If you needed help, advice, anything, he was ready to do whatever needed to be done, all the time. He has a great compassion about him. He cares about everybody he meets. That's a part of him that only those who have spent a lot of time getting to know him have found out.

What are some practical ways of showing love for your people? It starts with letting your people know you care. Genuinely strong leaders don't have to prove their toughness. They feel secure enough to display a side of themselves that some might mistakenly call "weak"— a caring side, a compassionate side. John C. Maxwell says, "Loving people precedes leading them. People don't care how much you know until they know how much you care."

Amos Alonzo Stagg knew this. Some have called Amos the greatest coach in football history. Born shortly after the beginning of the Civil War, he began coaching American collegiate football at the University of Chicago just a few years after the rules of the game were officially established. He coached for some seventy years, retiring at age ninety-eight as a coach at Stockton Junior College in California. He died in 1965 at age 102. Looking back over all the young men he had coached over a seven-decade career, he said, "You must love your players to get the most out of them. I have worked with players I haven't admired, but I have loved them just the same. Love has dominated my coaching career."

Tommy Lasorda, former manager of the Los Angeles Dodgers, will tell you that another way leaders show their love is through demonstrating understanding when people make mistakes or fail.

> A guy asked me one time what are the number one qualities a manager or a leader should have. It was difficult to put it down in a certain category, but I went to church and I heard the priest give a sermon. He talked about Solomon, who was the paragon of truth, and he was pleasing to the Lord. The Lord said to Solomon, "I want to give you any gift you want," and Solomon said, "The greatest gift you can give me, Lord, is an understanding heart." I think that's what every manager or coach needs—an understanding heart. Because when a player doesn't do well, the manager or coach has to understand how that player feels.

Sadly, an understanding heart is often lacking in leadership. Motivational expert Bob Nelson notes that while most companies talk a good game about caring for their people, the reality is often pretty bleak. "It's funny," he says. "All bosses say, 'People are our most important resource,' but you never see that. Usually it comes down to, 'Don't screw up.'" The result of that kind of inattention and insensitivity to people is often a high rate of dissatisfied customers and costly turnovers. Hal Rosenbluth, CEO of Rosenbluth International, puts it this way: "I think that companies today have an obligation to create an environment where people are happy, because if people aren't happy and they don't like the company they are part of, if they don't like their leader, then they are really not going to be focusing on the customer. They are going to be focusing on their résumé."

Once, after speaking at a breakfast in Washington, Pennsylvania, I was driven back to the Pittsburgh airport for the flight home. Dwayne Durham rode with me. He had been a Pennsylvania State Trooper for twenty-five years before taking early retirement at age fifty-two. I asked him why he'd retired so young, and he replied, "Too much stress on the job—not from the public but from upstairs. I discovered that one 'You bonehead, you messed up' wiped out nine 'Attaboys.'"

Isn't that amazing? But it's absolutely true. The insults and condemnation of uncaring leaders can be much more discouraging and destructive than all the bad guys on the streets! Whatever the organization—a law enforcement agency, a corporation, or a religious group—morale always goes up and turnover goes down when superiors show empathy, caring, and love for the people who get the job done day after day. Author Henry Blackaby wrote, "When leaders stop loving their people, they stand tempted to use them, to neglect them, and to discard them."

John Wooden coached UCLA to ten national titles and is one of only two men (the other is Lenny Wilkens) to be inducted into the Hall of Fame as both player and coach. One of the ways Coach Wooden showed the love of a leader to his people was by making sure that every player—including the guys on the bench—got a measure of recognition and affirmation. "Players need to know that you really care for them," he once observed, "even though they might not be getting to play the amount of time they would like to play. You can do that in other ways—the pat on the back, the nod, the smile, the 'hello' for players who aren't going to play very much . . . I think it's necessary to make sure every player gets recognition, because we all want that."

My son Bobby, who coaches with the Cincinnati Reds organization, has become friends with Jim Hickman, a minor league hitting instructor with the Reds. Hickman is in his mid-sixties, having spent thirteen years as an outfielder in the big leagues. He played with the Mets, Dodgers, Cubs, and Cardinals, and he racked up some amazing statistics. Interestingly, all four of his big-league managers went into the Hall of Fame: Casey Stengel, Red Schoendienst, Leo Durocher, and Walter Alston.

Hickman told Bobby about one bad year he had in 1967 while playing for the Dodgers. He didn't play much, had ninety-eight at-bats, and hit .163—a rock-bottom season. Bobby asked Jim Hickman what he remembers about that year. Now, you'd think it would be a year he'd rather forget. Yet Hickman says he warmly recalls one thing about that season: "On two different occasions," Hickman said, "Walter Alston brought me into his office and thanked me for my good attitude. He said he appreciated the fact that I was working hard in practice, encouraging the other guys, and contributing any way I could. I can't tell you what that meant to me."

It doesn't take a lot of effort—just a little show of kindness—to make an impression that lasts for decades. If you want to be a leader who loves people, then show you are interested in the career growth and success of your people, not just your own success. Get to know your people. Talk to them and find out what really makes them tick. Take an interest in their interests. Show that you care about their families (especially their kids!). Colorado Rockies manager Clint Hurdle stated: "I want to know my players' wives' names and their kids' names. I want to know what they're doing away from the park. That way, when I come up to them, it's not always about hanging sliders or popups with the bases loaded."

Nothing builds a team or organization like the love of a strong leader. Love produces loyalty and builds morale. Love breaks down contention and strife between people in the organization. Love gives everyone a sense of trust, a sense of belonging to a family, not just working in a corporation. Love is the glue that binds an organization or team together into a unified force for transformation.

I often wonder where I'd be today if I hadn't received genuine love from some of the leaders and mentors in my life—people like Mr. R. E. Littlejohn, Bill Veeck, my college baseball coach Jack Stallings, and Rich DeVos. The encouragement these leaders have shown me over the years have truly shaped and transformed my life.

I vividly remember July 5, 1995, as the worst day of my life. It was the day after a glorious July Fourth holiday at the beach with my kids. I was still basking in the afterglow of that holiday when I entered my office at the Orlando Arena and saw the envelope on my desk. It had one of those ominous-looking "Return Receipt Requested" tags on the front, and the return address was that of an attorney. I won't go into the details, except to say that after twenty-two years of marriage, my wife was filing for divorce. I knew she had been unhappy for some time, but I had been trying to think, talk, and pray my way out of this eventuality. The letter on my desk was proof that divorce was inevitable.

My biggest struggle during that time was an overwhelming sense of shame and embarrassment. I didn't want anyone to know that my marriage had fallen apart—though I knew it would eventually become a very public matter. But over the next few weeks, several genuine leaders and dear friends demonstrated great love and caring toward me. In the process, they let me know that I was going to come through this calamity in one piece. Their support meant the world to me.

Great leaders don't hesitate to show caring and love for their people. That's the kind of leadership Jesus exemplified, and the kind of leadership that has transformed my life again and again.

## *Allow for human frailty, mistakes, and error.*

The fourth key to becoming an effective delegator, as exemplified by Jesus, is to give people room to make mistakes. Jesus was patient with the frailties and mistakes of his followers. In fact, after the disciple Simon Peter denied Jesus three times, Jesus accepted him and restored him, placing him in charge of his brand-new organization, the church.

Tom Watson, the founder of IBM, understood the importance of allowing for mistakes and failures. When one of his execs spent $12 million on a project that failed miserably, the young exec walked into Watson's office and offered his resignation.

"I don't want your resignation," Watson replied. "I just invested $12 million in your education! I can't afford to lose you now. Get back to work!"

When people land on their faces in the dust, great leaders pick them up, dust them off, and get them back into the game. Leaders allow for mistakes. The more room they give their people to fail, the more freedom and confidence those people have to risk, soar, and succeed.

## *Use authority sparingly.*

The fifth key to becoming an effective delegator is to use authority sparingly. In other words, be a leader, not a boss. In Matthew

20:26–27, Jesus told his disciples, "Whoever wants to become great among you must be your servant, and whoever wants to be first must be your slave." In other words, stop trying to be the Head Honcho, bossing other people around. Instead, show *real* leadership by setting an example of servanthood.

This advice is as relevant today as it was two thousand years ago. Conscientious workers don't mind hard work, they don't mind long hours, and they don't mind being challenged to achieve more. But they really hate being bossed around—or worse, bullied.

A leadership position is a position of power and authority. But the paradox of power is that authority is used most effectively when applied sparingly. Bossiness is a sign of insecurity, not genuine strength. The truly strong leader feels no need to assert his power, but is secure enough to keep his or her power under restraint. Authority doesn't make you a leader. It just gives you the opportunity to become a leader.

Take the example of the late H. Gordon Selfridge. Selfridge's in London is one of the world's great department stores. It owes a great deal of its success to its founder and namesake. Born in America, Selfridge went to London as a young man and founded his retail business on an unusual premise: Selfridge's would be operated by leaders, not bosses. He made a careful study of the differences between a leader and a boss. This is what he found:

- The boss drives his people. The leader coaches them.
- The boss depends on authority. The leader relies on goodwill.
- The boss inspires fear. The leader inspires enthusiasm.
- The boss says "I." The leader says "we."
- The boss fixes the blame for the breakdown. The leader fixes the breakdown.

Genuine leaders understand and embrace these principles. It's interesting, though, how many leaders do not. Why? I believe American pop culture and pop psychology have been heavily influenced by pop Darwinism, with the result that leaders are commonly compared to an "alpha male," the big ape in the jungle who gets his pick of the female apes and who pounds his chest to scare off the other male apes. Aspiring to be the "alpha male" in your organization is just fine—if all you want to be is an ape.

However, the authority of a leader has a specific function: It is designed to be used for the benefit of the organization—not the personal aggrandizement of the leader. So many people forget what power and authority are all about. Authority is about roles and responsibility—not about human worth or one's place on the food chain. All human beings are equals. A boss is not superior to the secretary or the kid in the mailroom. He may think he is, but he's not. A boss has more authority, more power, and more responsibility than others in the organization—but he is no more valuable than the least in the company. That's a paradox of power that few people in the world today understand.

And it's not just about the job, either! An eight-year study of two hundred employees at AT&T found that gentle leadership is actually good medicine. "A good boss offers genuine protection against illness," concluded one researcher, Dr. Fredrick Koenig, professor of social psychology at New Orleans' Tulane University. "Workers whose bosses are less than helpful are often more likely to become ill through stress. A bad boss can lead to problems including heart disease, insomnia, gastrointestinal distress, high blood cholesterol, and depression."

Koenig offered this prescription to business leaders who want to safeguard the health and effectiveness of their workforce.

1. Stand behind the decisions your employees make.
2. Sit down and talk things over with your employees.
3. Let your employees feel free to ask you to reconsider a decision you have made.
4. Respect your employees and ask for their opinions.
5. Listen to your employees' personal problems that could affect their work.
6. Compliment your people on their work.
7. Make it easy for employees to feel they're on top of what they're doing.

8. Allow your employees to offer constructive criticism without fear of reprisal.
9. Give your employees full credit for ideas they contribute at work so they will feel more a part of the organization.
10. Make suggestions that will help employees improve their work.

You can't scare people into doing their best. You can't browbeat people into doing their best. You can't make people winners by calling them losers. People give you peak performance only when they are inspired and motivated to do so.

## Acknowledge and affirm people.

The sixth key to becoming an effective delegator is to acknowledge people. One of the most powerful and transforming leadership abilities Jesus had was his ability to affirm people, to build them up, to enable them to see potential in themselves that they never imagined before. He had the gift of making people feel special and valued—particularly people who were sneered at and devalued by society. He called a despised, ostracized, hated tax collector named Zacchaeus, and he said, "I'm going to eat at your house today." He gave Zacchaeus the opportunity to serve, and Zacchaeus felt honored and affirmed in response (see Matthew 19). Jesus also affirmed Nathanael, saying, "Here is a true Israelite, in whom there is nothing false." And Nathanael became a follower of Jesus from that moment on (see John 1). Jesus reached out to people, and he raised them up and turned them into devoted, productive followers. He was a leader who transformed people. No one who encountered Jesus ever walked away unchanged.

On December 2, 1999, I interviewed Chuck Tanner on my Orlando sports-talk-radio show. Chuck managed major league baseball teams from 1970 to 1988: the Chicago White Sox, the Oakland A's, the Atlanta Braves, and the Pittsburgh Pirates. I asked Chuck his four keys to success as a leader in pro baseball. His answer was all about relating to people:

- You must be willing and able to communicate with people, individually and collectively.
- You must practice patience with people—lots of it.
- Remember, some people need a pat on the back and others need a kick in the rear. You must know the difference.
- If people know you care about them, they won't let you down.

If you go to Bangkok, Thailand, you will find many temples with statues of the Buddha. But there is one temple that stands out above all the others. It is not the size of the temple that is so impressive; the building itself is about the size of a modest two-car garage. Rather, the Temple of the Golden Buddha is famous for what is inside: a solid-gold statue of the Buddha that stands almost eleven feet high and weighs more than two and a half tons. At current market value, the gold in that statue is worth around $200 million.

The history of the statue is fascinating—and instructive. In 1957, a certain monastery had to be relocated to make way for a highway. One of the many art objects in the monastery that had to be moved was a massive clay statue of the Buddha. When a crane lifted the clay statue it developed serious cracks. Turns out underneath the clay was the golden Buddha. Historians theorize it had been concealed several hundred years prior to keep an invading army from carrying it away as loot.

The point is this: People are like that statue. There is gold inside every human being, even though that gold may be disguised by a layer of human clay. Our job as leaders is to penetrate that layer of clay, uncover the gold, and reveal the value and worth that is at the core of every human being. We do it by giving people an enlarged vision of who they are, how much they are worth, and what they can accomplish. When we make this effort, we can feel confident in delegating, because that person will feel up to the challenge.

Jack Stallings was my baseball coach at Wake Forest in the early 1960s. He retired in 1999 after thirty-eight years in coaching. At his retirement dinner, I heard him say, "When I was a graduate assistant at the University of North Carolina, head coach Walter Rabb said to me,

'Jack, you're not going to be coaching baseball. You're going to be coaching baseball *players*.'" Coach Stallings added, "I never forgot that. That became the guiding principle of my coaching career."

John 4 tells the story of Jesus' encounter with a Samaritan woman. They met at the well outside the town of Sychar. The woman was an outcast in her town, ignored as if invisible. Yet Jesus looked her in the eye, spoke to her, acknowledged her, asked her for water, took an interest in her story and her pain, and ultimately made her a part of his team, using her to take his kingdom message to her entire town. He pierced the clay disguise she wore, revealing the gold within her— revealing it even to herself.

Some people seem to have a natural gift for affirming others, for making people feel special and valued. Others have to work very consciously at acknowledging and affirming others. One leader who clearly has the natural gift of acknowledging people is former President Bill Clinton. (For the record: I didn't vote for him and I certainly don't approve of his irresponsible behavior in the White House—but was he ever great with people!)

*The New York Times*, on November 19, 1999, reported on President Bill Clinton's appearance at a state dinner in his honor, hosted in Ankara, Turkey, by the Turkish president, Suleyman Demirel. "Mr. Clinton startled several people in the receiving line," the *Times* reported, "by remembering them from years ago, and greeting them by name." One of those whom Clinton greeted by name was Henrik Liljegren, then the Swedish ambassador to Turkey, but previously the ambassador to the United States. Even before Liljegren reached Clinton in the receiving line, the American president stepped forward, took Liljegren's hand, and called him by name. Then he turned to the Turkish president and kidded, "You got my ambassador!"

Liljegren said Clinton "not only remembers faces, but you get the feeling that he really remembers people, thousands of them. Naturally, it's very flattering."

David Gergen, who has served in the White House under presidents Reagan, Bush, and Clinton, also remarked on Bill Clinton's ability to acknowledge people:

Long before he became president he would enter a group where he was virtually unknown. He would try to meet each and every person there, eliciting their stories, listening carefully, learning their names. Gradually, he would get a sense of who they were and how they thought . . . People gravitate toward him because he is so seductive. Only after he has had time with the group does he begin to put himself forward. By then, he seems their natural leader. That was the Bill Clinton who has become president or first among equals of every group of which he has been a part, from high school to college to Oxford to Yale Law to Arkansas to Renaissance to the National Governors' Conference to the Democratic Leadership Council to the White House.

The ability to acknowledge people, to make them feel valued and recognized, is an important leadership ability. Those who would lead by delegating to others must know how to make others believe in themselves. People who feel empowered and acknowledged by their leaders are capable of realizing any vision and achieving any goal.

## Be visible.

The seventh key to becoming an effective delegator is: Be visible. Jesus was probably the most visible and accessible leader in history. Though surrounded and pressed by crowds, he always took time for individuals in need. People came to him at all hours of the day, during his meals, his work, his travels, his sleep. He never resented these intrusions or turned anyone away. He understood the crucial need to be accessible—to build morale through his presence.

Julia Ward Howe, who wrote "The Battle Hymn of the Republic," once approached Massachusetts senator Charles Sumner and asked him if he could give some personal assistance to a needy family. Senator Sumner replied, "I'm sorry, Mrs. Howe, but I can't. I have become so busy that I can no longer devote any time to individuals." Mrs. Howe tartly responded, "That's amazing, Senator! Not even God is that busy!"

General George Patton was another who understood this important facet of leadership. In November 1942 General Patton was in charge of the American invasion of North Africa. His forces had landed on the beach at Fedhala, on the coast of Morocco. The region was controlled by the Vichy French, forces of Nazi-occupied France. The American landing was going badly. Troop transports would hit the beach, but before they could fully unload, French planes would strafe the beach and artillery would shell the area. Even though the planes and shells weren't hitting anything, they were causing the Americans to dive for cover, which delayed the unloading.

Patton knew that the first priority was to unload the ammunition from the beached transport boats so that the U.S. forces could return fire. So as the planes buzzed overhead and artillery shells exploded all around, Patton strode out onto the beach. He went straight to the transport, helped unload ammunition, then pushed the unloaded boat back into the water. Emboldened by his example, Patton's troops came out of their shelters and completed the job of securing the beach. The entire landing operation took eighteen hours, and Patton stayed on the beach the whole time, visibly leading his troops.

"People say that Army commanders should not indulge in such practices," Patton later reflected. "My theory is that an Army commander does what is necessary to accomplish his mission, and that nearly eighty percent of his mission is to arouse morale in his men."

One way a leader can become more visible is to spend mealtimes with his or her people. As author Bob Briner says:

> Food can be a great catalyst for building relationships and for teaching. Leaders do not neglect the power that food and mealtimes have to set the stage for building lasting productive relationships and imparting important lessons. . . . Nothing breaks down barriers like sharing a Coke and a hamburger or a quick breakfast together.

I once was talking to David McMakin, who played at Alabama for the great college football coach Bear Bryant. I asked him for his most vivid memory of the Bear. His answer surprised me, because it had nothing to do with Bryant's coaching:

> I remember the training table. The assistant coaches would grab their trays, jump line, and then all sit together—but Coach Bryant wasn't like that. He'd get his tray, wait in line, and then come sit with the players. He'd pick a different table, a different group of guys at every meal, but he would sit and talk with us. To tell you the truth, we were always praying he wouldn't pick our table! But looking back, I see that it was his way of keeping in personal touch with his players and making sure we all knew he was available and accessible.

When people can see their leader, look in their leader's eyes, and hear the strength in his or her voice, they can dare anything and accomplish any goal that is set for them.

## Make it fun.

Bill Veeck, the great baseball promoter and Hall of Famer, was also a great delegator. He impacted my life deeply from the very first day I met him. I was twenty-two years old, with stars in my eyes about this great American pastime called baseball. Bill preached to me the importance of having fun at the ballpark and in every aspect of a sports business—or even nonsports-related business. I bought into the importance of fun at an early point in my career and have believed it ever since.

At Bill Veeck's Baseball Hall of Fame induction, his widow, Mary Francis, said, "Bill was such fun to be around. He was a real pied piper." Bill's son Mike, who now operates a number of minor league baseball teams, has this same philosophy stamped on his tee shirts, hats, and letterhead: "Fun is Good."

You may think, "Well, what does fun have to do with delegating in the workplace?" My answer: Fun has everything to do with it! Fun keeps people loose, and staying loose is crucial to good performance.

Pressure and stress are found in every field of human endeavor: business, sports, government, religious ministry, and military. Stress degrades human performance. That's why we need fun! It keeps pressure from freezing the brain and prevents stress from wearing down the body.

Selling fun, as we do at the Orlando Magic, is serious business, involving serious money, serious deadlines, and serious pressure. But the leaders in our organization understand that as we *sell* fun to the public, we all need to *have* fun as well. How can we sell fun to the public with faces full of gloom?

I have found that fun is found in every successful enterprise, from great sports organizations to successful White House administrations to great retail companies to great high-tech companies and on and on. Fun makes working worthwhile. Fun makes us the kind of person people want to be around, do business with, and work alongside.

Truly great leaders are fun people to be around. Truly great politicians are fun people in private and in public. Truly great teachers and preachers find ways to make their lessons and sermons *fun*. When a leader knows his people are having *fun* at what they do, he can delegate with confidence, knowing that the work is going to be carried out with enthusiasm, eagerness, and a sense of excitement. Three of my favorite baseball personalities have strong feelings about the importance of having fun. Hall of Famer Willie Stargell said, "It's supposed to be fun! The man says 'Play ball!' not 'Work ball,' you know? You only have a few years to play the game, and you can't play if you're all tied up in knots." Hall of Famer Sparky Anderson stated, "If you don't have fun doing what you're doing, then you shouldn't be doing it in the first place. I might be old fashioned, but I always believed baseball was supposed to be fun." And Bobby Cox, current manager of the Atlanta Braves and future Hall of Famer, observed, "I've never lost that little-boy attitude of how much fun it is to come to the ballpark, put the glove on, and start doing something. It's still a lot of fun."

Former Jets quarterback Joe Namath once said, "When you have confidence, you can have a lot of fun. And when you have fun, you can do amazing things." And author and radio host Garrison Keillor touts fun as a lubricant for society and relationships. He once offered these words in a commencement address:

> We are meant to be a jazzy people who talk big talk and jump up on the table and dance. We aren't supposed to be dopey and glum and brood over old injuries. Laughter is what proves our humanity, and the ability to give a terrific party is a sign of true class . . .
>
> Put beans up your nose and tell limericks. Do what needs to be done . . . Get together in a comfortable place with people you like a lot. Dance, be romantic, be silly, and see if you can get each other laughing by making fun of your elders. Satire, kids, is your sacred duty as Americans.
>
> Be funny. Poke them cows and make them moo.

Fun energizes the body. The simple pleasures of playing and being silly get your circulation going, recharge your nervous systems, and clear the fog of stress and worry from the pathways of your brain. Laughter expands the lungs and charges your cells with oxygen. Fun is better than any medicine. As a leader, make sure you are having fun, spreading fun around, and making your organization a fun place in which to work.

# To Live, You Must Die

A few years ago, my wife, Ruth, and I were on our honeymoon in Scottsdale, Arizona. We stayed at the Phoenician hotel—an opulent resort on the edge of the Sonoran Desert. There happened to be a big convention going on with some high-powered guests: Bill Bennett, J. C. Watts, and Dick Vitale. I contacted Vitale, an old friend, to see if he could get us in. Since Ruth and I are both public speakers, we were excited about the chance to hear what these dignitaries had to say.

Although all three were impressive, I was particularly impressed by something J. C. Watts said on the subject of character. He asked these questions of the audience: "How many of you husbands think the character of your wife is important? And how many of you wives think the character of your husband important?" There were many affirmative answers, which Watts said he expected. "Now, don't tell me that the character of our leaders is not important," he said. "You can no more have leadership without character than you can have water without the wet."

It's true. We count on the character of the people closest to us. If they don't have good character, how can we trust them? In the same way, the people around us count on us, their leaders, to have character. If they can't trust us to be people of character, why should they follow us?

Peggy Noonan, speechwriter for Ronald Reagan and George H. W. Bush, knows a thing or two about character in a leader. She stated: "In a president, character is everything. You can't buy courage and decency, you can't rent a strong moral sense. A president must bring these things with him. He needs to have a vision of the future he wishes to create. But a vision is worth little if a president does not have the character—the courage and heart—to see it through."

The English word *character* comes from the Greek word *kharakter*, which is derived from *kharassein*, meaning "engraved" or "inscribed." The word literally means a "distinctive mark that is imprinted on the human soul." You cannot be a great leader without being a person of great character—that is, a fully integrated, morally consistent human being. Character is not something you have; it is something that shows itself in what you do.

Your character is the essence of who you truly are. It is greater than any monument that human hand could construct in your honor. Words inscribed on stone in a graveyard are at best a paltry monument to a human life. Even if your face were added to Mount Rushmore, it would mean little compared to the indelible marks of character that are forever inscribed on your immortal soul.

The fourth great paradox of power is this: *To live, you must die.* Jesus put it this way: "For whoever wants to save his life will lose it, but whoever loses his life for me will find it" (Matthew 16:25). The leader "dies to" all of his or her natural impulses: The impulse to gain power and wealth by cutting ethical corners. The impulse to protect oneself with lies, evasions, and shifting blame to others. The impulse to exalt the self in pride and arrogance. The impulse to gratify the self through laziness, stealing, or immorality. The impulse to safeguard the self through cowardice.

## THE CHARACTER OF JESUS

The greatest model of leadership in history was also the greatest model of character. Jesus was a man of incredible courage and toughness. He not only confronted the most relentless and dangerous political and religious leaders of his day, he also took on the forces of evil—Satan and his legions of demons. He willingly went to the most cruel and excruciating death imaginable—hands and feet nailed to a Roman cross.

Yet Jesus was also a man of gentleness, love, and compassion. As he hung on the cross, he offered forgiveness to the people who tortured and killed him. He reached out to the poor, the oppressed, the bereaved. He had influence on the great and small, the powerful and the powerless. Though he didn't hesitate to confront a king, a governor, and a corrupt high priest, he took time to give his blessing to children. All who encountered his powerful, magnetic personality were deeply impacted.

The character of Jesus is the standard by which you and I must measure ourselves as leaders. To build his character qualities into your life means nothing less than putting your selfish impulses to death. But the person who dies to self will gain his or her own soul—and will be a leader of character. Here, then, are some of the character qualities Jesus exhibited as a leader two thousand years ago.

## The Quality of Absolute Integrity

Mr. Hoess was a loving husband and father, and a devout Catholic. His five children respected and adored him. He was also a business leader. He had grown prosperous as a farmer, largely because of his administrative skills.

One of Mr. Hoess's acquaintances in the government took note of how he managed his farming business. He was offered a post in the government, where he proved himself very capable. This led to a series of promotions, and Mr. Hoess rose rapidly in a series of government offices.

Mr. Hoess had a regular routine every day: breakfast with his wife and children, then off to work—sometimes pausing to enjoy the fragrance of the flowers in his well-tended garden. Mr. Hoess worked diligently at his job, conducting staff meetings, making important decisions, reading reports, issuing orders. At the end of the day, he arrived home, where his children happily greeted him at the front door. They looked forward to his arrival, because he often brought them little gifts.

His loyalty and patriotism earned him the trust of the most important man in the national government. That man, whose name was Adolf Hitler, rewarded Rudolf Hoess by making him Kommandant of the Auschwitz extermination complex in southern Poland. Mr. Hoess's mission: to increase the killing efficiency of the camp to a level of ten thousand dead every twenty-four hours. Mr. Hoess was very good at his job, and he had no trouble meeting his quota.

From the bedroom window of his comfortable brick-walled house in the country, Mr. Hoess could see the chimneys of the camp. The smoke from those chimneys darkened the skies as thousands of human bodies were cremated, day after day, night after night, twenty-four/seven. He was proud of his work. Under his efficient management, Auschwitz exterminated 2.5 million people.

Rudolf Hoess was raised to work hard and live a productive life. He was a loving family man, a devoted Catholic, and possibly the greatest mass murderer in human history. Why didn't he see any contradiction in these various roles he played? Because Rudolf Hoess had compartmentalized his soul. He had constructed a wall of separation between his home life and his vocational life, between his Sunday morning faith and his job during the week as the Kommandant of Hell.

Rudolf Hoess lacked a character trait called *integrity*.

People of integrity do not compartmentalize their lives. They live consistently as fully integrated human beings. People of integrity are exactly the same in every situation, whether at home or in church or in the office. Total integrity is an absolute requirement for any leader in any organization or sphere of life. Vince Lombardi Jr., son of the legendary Packers coach, put it this way: "Any talk of being able to compartmentalize your life, so that what you do in private has no bearing on your public life, is a fiction. As a leader, you are no better than your principles."

Tom Peters once said, "There are no minor lapses of integrity." That's a powerful statement. We tend to think we can get away with *little* sins, *little* lies, *little* ethical lapses. But the reality is that if we are not faithful in the little things, we are far less likely to be faithful in the big things. Gerald R. Roche is the senior chairman of Heidrick and Struggles, a top executive-search company. He said: "The No. 1 criteria in every CEO search we do today is integrity. That used to be assumed. No one had to mention it. Not anymore."

Jesus was a leader of absolute integrity. When he was brought before the Roman governor, Pontius Pilate, to be judged, it was clear to Pilate that the charges against Jesus were trumped up. Pilate wanted to please the religious leaders who clamored for Jesus' innocent blood, so he questioned Jesus intensively, trying to find some legal pretext for crucifying him. But Luke 23:4 tells us that, after examining Jesus, Pilate announced to the crowd, "I find no basis for a charge against this man." How could there be a charge against him? Because Jesus was a person of complete integrity.

A leader of absolute integrity has put to death the natural human impulse to live only for the convenience of the moment. A well-integrated leader lives consistently, so that there is a seamless unity between the core inner being and the outer reputation, between the values of the home and the values of the workplace. A leader of integrity dies to self and selfishness—and, in the process of dying, becomes a living soul. As former president Gerald Ford said, "I do feel that absolute integrity is a cornerstone of a successful presidency."

## The Quality of Absolute Honesty

Colin Powell has collected many mementos from his long career in government and military service. One of his most prized possessions is a photo of Ronald Reagan and himself, inscribed in the following manner: "Colin, when you tell me something, I know it is so. Ronald Reagan." What a marvelous tribute! The same could certainly be said of Jesus: If he said it, you knew it was so. Upon the death of General J.E.B. Stuart on May 11, 1864, Robert E. Lee paid him the ultimate compliment for a cavalryman when in a shaken voice he affirmed that Stuart "never brought me a piece of false information."

Father Martin Tierney of Saint Audoen's Catholic Church in Dublin, Ireland, observed that the gospels present a picture of "the almost startling honesty of Jesus." Jesus did not attract followers by means of false promise or pretenses. He never promised them an easy way. With painful honesty, he told his disciples, "If anyone would come after me, he must deny himself and take up his cross and follow me." In other words, said Father Tierney, Jesus told each disciple that "he must be ready to be regarded as a criminal and to die. Jesus never sought to lure men to him by the offer of an easy way . . . He came not to make life easy but to make men great."[1]

You are either honest or you are not. There are no shades of honesty, no degrees of truthfulness. To be a person of honesty means to die to our natural impulses to cut ethical corners, to fabricate and scheme for personal gain, and to cheat our way to success. To be a leader, you must be trusted, and truth is the key to trust. Get caught in one dishonest act— one lie, one theft, one fraud—and you have destroyed trust forever. Once trust has been damaged, it is very hard to restore.

The great broadcaster Edward R. Murrow stated, "To be persuasive, we must be believable. To be believable, we must be credible. To be credible, we must be truthful." Dishonesty has been the downfall of scores of leaders. Political leaders from Richard Nixon to Bill Clinton have lost their legacies to lying. Religious leaders from Jimmy Swaggert to Jim Bakker have had their lives and ministries ruined by the Achilles' heel of dishonesty. Honesty must be absolute, pervading all levels of a leader's life. Complete and constant honesty is something these leaders could not seem to understand nor embrace—a fact that ultimately led to their downfall.

Coach Rick Pitino wisely put the issue this way: "Lying makes a problem part of the future. Truth makes a problem part of the past." The leaders who have succeeded are those who have dealt squarely and truthfully with their followers, even if the truth was harsh, painful, and embarrassing.

I know of no greater example of honesty than Dr. Billy Graham and his organization, the Billy Graham Evangelism Association. I first met Dr. Graham in 1962, when I was a student at Wake Forest University in Winston-Salem, North Carolina. He had come to speak at chapel, so I lined up an interview with him for my radio show (I did a sports interview show for the campus radio station). It was a great interview. Dr. Graham talked about all the sports he loved to play, especially baseball. He was an avid and knowledgeable sports enthusiast.

Later, as an NBA sports executive, I was invited to share my

Christian experience with the audience at two Billy Graham crusades, one in Syracuse, New York, and the other at McCormick Place in Chicago. Both times, I remember being profoundly impressed by Dr. Graham's appearance on the stage. As a leader, his presence dominated the arena. He had—and still has—a paradoxical mix of qualities: He carries himself with an air of authority and conviction, yet he speaks with genuine humility. There is one practical reason why Billy Graham regularly tops pollsters' lists of the most respected and admired people in the world: "The Modesto Manifesto."

It all goes back more than half a century, to the year 1948. Billy Graham was just becoming widely known in Christian circles in America. He and his team were traveling from city to city, holding large evangelistic meetings, during a time when the reputation of Christian evangelism had been tainted by a number of highly publicized scandals and claims of corruption and fraud.

Billy Graham called a meeting with his three closest associates: singer George Beverly Shea, music director and spokesman Cliff Barrows, and associate evangelist Grady Wilson. They met on the Barrows family farm outside of Modesto, California, to fast and pray for God's direction for the future.

Out of that meeting came a plan for holding each other accountable so that the entire evangelistic effort would remain above reproach. "The Modesto Manifesto" was not a formal document; rather it was a pact in which all members of the Graham team agreed to avoid the slightest hint of financial or moral impropriety and to be scrupulously honest in all publicity claims and reporting of results from the crusades. The organization's finances would be an open book, as would all aspects of the team's public lives.

To this day Reverend Graham and his organization have striven to live up to those standards. Nobody is perfect, but there is no doubt this supremely honest leader has done better than most—and this is because of a commitment he made many years ago and honored throughout his life.

A leader of absolute honesty has put to death the natural human impulse to seek momentary gratification, to "shade the truth" in order to advance himself, to lie in order to cover up past sins. A leader of absolute honesty dies to self and becomes a living soul.

## The Quality of Absolute Humility

If there is one character quality of Jesus that is universally recognized and admired, it is his absolute humility. Jesus himself said in Matthew 11:29, "Take my yoke upon you and learn from me, for I am gentle and humble in heart, and you will find rest for your souls." He exemplified the quality of humility in John 13:4–5 where, just hours before the crucifixion, he wrapped a towel around his waist, filled a basin with water, and began to wash the feet of his disciples. Jesus took the form of a servant, setting an example of humility for us all.

Humility means dying to our natural impulse to elevate ourselves and feed our own egos. In Philippians 2:3–7, the apostle Paul said that we should look to Jesus as the example of supreme humility:

> Do nothing out of selfish ambition or vain conceit, but in humility consider others better than yourselves . . . Your attitude should be the same as that of Christ Jesus: Who, being in very nature God, did not consider equality with God something to be grasped, but made himself nothing, taking the very nature of a servant.

The humble-servant quality of Jesus—though it cuts across the grain of our self-exalting culture—is the most compelling and attractive feature of his leadership ability. Arrogance is a fatal flaw in a leader. The most dangerous leaders of all are those who think the world revolves around them. They are dangerous to themselves, to their organizations, and to everyone in their sphere of influence. As John Stott, the great Anglican thinker, once observed, "Leaders have power, but power is safe only in the hands of those who humble themselves to serve."

A humble leader is quick to share credit with others. Ronald Reagan kept his favorite inspirational quotation displayed on his desk in the Oval Office: "There's no limit to what a man can do or where he can go if he doesn't mind who gets the credit." A humble leader focuses on making others feel important—not making himself or herself look important. Humble leaders underscore the achievements of others while downplaying their own.

A great illustrator of how strong a humble leader can be is General Omar N. Bradley, who commanded the largest American force ever assembled. He spent sixty-nine years on active duty—longer than any other soldier in American history. Dubbed "The G.I.'s General" during World War II because of his great rapport with the foot soldiers of the war, Bradley later became the first chairman of the Joint Chiefs of Staff. During his tenure as chairman, General Bradley happened to meet a man who had served under him during World War II. "General," said the man, "I served under you during the war. Because of you, sir, we won that war."

"No, sir," said Bradley, "it was because of *you* that we won the war."

Some leaders confuse humility with humiliation, mistakenly thinking that humility means degradation or disgrace. Others think humility and leadership are polar opposites, as if you can't be a leader unless you are a self-seeking egotist. Nothing could be further from the truth.

A humble leader treats everyone as an equal, never as an "inferior." In January 2002, I had dinner with Graham Lacey, a prominent businessman from England. When I learned that he had personally known Diana, Princess of Wales, I asked, "If she were with us at dinner tonight, what would it be like?" He replied:

> I know one thing. Lady Diana would have been fascinated with all of your children. In fact, she would have insisted on going to your house to meet them all. She'd have been down on the floor playing with them. Then, when she got back home, she would have sent each of them a handwritten note and then at Christmas mailed them a card.

That is the humility of greatness. Harry Truman's secretary of state, Dean Acheson, believed that the key to Truman's success was that "he was free of the greatest vice in a leader: his ego never came between him and the job."

Being humble also means being quick to admit fallibility. Even when we "know for certain" we are right, we can still be wrong. Motivational speaker Stephen R. Covey, author of *The Seven Habits of Highly Effective People*, has an audience participation exercise he sometimes does at speaking events. First, he asks everyone to stand up with eyes closed and point north. Then he says, "Now, open your eyes." Everyone looks around and sees fingers pointed every which way!

Then he says, "Now, only those who are *absolutely* certain you know your directions, close your eyes again and point north." On this second round, fewer people participate—only those who are dead certain. But when they open their eyes, they find that fingers are *still* pointed every which way! At that point, Covey takes out his compass and settles the matter.

The point is clear: Even people who are absolutely certain can be absolutely wrong—so a little humility is in order. As leaders, we must act on what we believe is right, but we should also be aware of our human fallibility. And when we are wrong, we should be the first to admit it. A good leader takes a little more than his share of the blame and a little less than his share of the credit.

A recent major five-year study on leadership reported some astonishing conclusions, according to the January 2001 issue of the *Harvard Business Review*. For instance, according to their data, one of the most important factors in transforming a good company into a great company is *a humble, determined leader*. The study, conducted by a Boulder, Colorado-based research group headed up by Jim Collins, set a very high standard in defining a "great company." Collins chose cumulative stock returns as his benchmark. Then he looked for companies that had (1) experienced returns at or below market par for fifteen years, and then (2) surged to three times greater than market par for the next fifteen years.

Collins weeded out companies that simply rode industry trends to higher profitability. He wanted to find *internal* factors that produced corporate transformation. He examined 1,435 companies listed in the Fortune 500 from 1965 to 1995, and found only eleven companies that met the high standards he had set. Then he examined the internal factors that produced such stunning performance over a sustained period, looking for common denominators. He found just one: Leadership.

He was astonished at the *kind* of leadership he found in those transformed companies. As executive coach Dr. Michael O'Brien stated on his company's web page, in response to the findings, the leadership style Collins documented was "not leadership based on ego. Or power . . . Each CEO of each of the eleven companies exhibited leadership characteristics that were paradoxical. The paradox was that the CEOs weren't cut from the cloth of charisma. They were cut from a different cloth, one that was made up of equal parts personal humility and professional will."[2]

It is widely assumed, of course, that major corporations need bigger-than-life leaders. But the Collins research didn't turn up any splashy headline-making celebrity CEOs like Lee Iacocca or Jack Welch. Instead, the typical CEO Collins found was like Darwin Smith of Kimberly Clark. Under Smith's quiet leadership, Kimberly Clark generated cumulative stock returns more than four times higher than the market average, outperforming such stock market megastars as 3M, Hewlett-Packard, and General Electric.

When a genuinely humble leader is willing to die to self, to crucify his own ego for the sake of a larger cause, the entire organization is transformed. As Samuel told King Saul in 1 Samuel 15:17, when a leader is humble and small in his own sight, then he and his organization become great. But when a leader becomes arrogant and great in his own sight, he and everything he touches becomes small. To truly live and become great, a leader must die to self.

## The Quality of Absolute Love

John 13:1 tells us that as Jesus was about to wash the feet of his disciples, just hours before the crucifixion, "Jesus knew that the time had come for him to leave this world and go to the Father. Having loved his own who were in the world, he now showed them the full extent of his love." The love of Jesus was demonstrated in acts of servanthood to others. And the ultimate act of service he rendered to the human race was in willingly submitting himself to the cross.

In 1 Corinthians 13, the apostle Paul describes love as patient and kind and humble. Love protects and trusts other people, hopes for the best in other people, and refuses to give up on other people. That is the love Jesus demonstrated to his disciples and to the whole world.

One of the great leaders of history was a man who led a lost cause. He was also a great model of love. His name: Robert E. Lee, commander of the Confederate Army in the Civil War.

The South was a genteel and cultured society with a great moral blind spot: The wealth and refinement of the South had been acquired at a huge and tragic human cost—the cost of human slavery and oppression. The baffling paradox of Robert E. Lee is that, though he commanded the army of a slave-holding society, he was morally opposed to slavery and he himself owned no slaves. As a man of deep Christian conviction, he opposed not only slavery but racism in all its forms.

Lee also opposed the secession of the South from the Union. He was originally appointed by Abraham Lincoln as a colonel in the U.S. Army's First Cavalry at a time when Lee's home state of Virginia was standing by the Union. But when Virginia seceded, Lee felt that the people of Virginia were his people, so he cast his lot with them.

One of the traits that most defined General Robert E. Lee was his love for his men. If there was one message he repeated often to his generals, it was "Look after your men." Lee never marched his troops longer or harder than he had to. He never exposed them to the enemy unless it was strategically necessary. After the men had won a battle, he increased their rations; hot food is a great morale-builder. He also made sure to take his men by streams where they could bathe and wash their uniforms—cleanliness, too, is good for morale.

Another way Lee showed his love for his men was by taking personal responsibility for losses. When Pickett's Charge failed at the Battle of Gettysburg (the single most decisive battle of the war), when almost three-quarters of Major General George E. Pickett's division was slaughtered, when the Confederate forces fell back in disarray, Lee met the returning remnants and said, "It's all my fault and no one else's. You men did your best, but I failed you." He took all the blame upon himself.

In response, Lee's men protested, "No, general! You didn't fail! It was us!" Lee's men loved him, because they knew he loved them—

because he showed it every day in every way he could. Even in defeat, his men would have fought on if Lee had given the word.

After Lee surrendered at Appomattox, he returned to his troops. They were weeping openly. "General, have we surrendered?" they asked. "Just say the word, sir, and we'll go after them again!"

Perhaps the most illuminating story of the character of Robert E. Lee is this one, which occurred in 1865, just weeks after the end of the war:

It was a Sunday morning. Robert E. Lee was sitting in his favorite pew at the Episcopal church in Richmond, Virginia. When Communion was served, a black man walked up the aisle and knelt to receive the wafer and a sip of wine from the Communion cup. There was an angry murmur from the white congregants when they saw this former slave at the front of their church.

But Robert E. Lee rose to his feet, walked to the altar, and knelt beside the black man. They shared the cup and received Holy Communion together. Then Lee turned and faced the congregation. "All men are brothers in Christ," he told them. "Have we not all one Father?"

Robert E. Lee was a leader of love. He taught his fellow Southerners to reunite with their Northern brothers as citizens of one nation. He once said, "Let the past be the past. We must move forward and bear no malice. Ought not we, who are governed by the principles of Christ, forgive our former enemies?"

On September 29, 1870, Lee stood at the dinner table of his home to say grace when he suddenly appeared stricken and sank into his chair—the victim of an apparent stroke. He died several days later. Throughout his life, and right to the very end, he was a man who died to self, who accepted blame that was not his, who rejected wealth and fame in favor of having an influence on lives, who sought national and racial reconciliation and rejected bitterness. He was a model of how a great leader must be a leader of love.

## The Quality of Influence

A leader must be continually aware of the influence he or she has on others. To be a person of influence means dying to our self-centered impulses and living to impact others for good. The minister or politician who gets caught in a sex scandal, the sports figure who spits in the ref's face, the rock star or actor who goes in and out of rehab, the corporate CEO who takes millions out of his company and leaves his employees and shareholders impoverished—these are all people of worthless character. They have scorned and wasted the opportunity they once had to influence people for good and instead lived for themselves.

Coach Bobby Bowden believes that "whether we want to admit it or not, we're all hero worshipers. We don't have cowboys anymore. We don't have war heroes to admire. So most of the heroes today are athletes." It's true. I have known former NBA star Charles Barkley for many years. I was general manager of the Philadelphia 76ers in 1984 when we drafted Barkley, the "round mound of rebound," from Auburn University. Though Barkley had a bad-boy reputation because of his confrontations with coach Sonny Smith at Auburn, I personally found him to be genial, coachable, hardworking, and a team player. He was also fiercely competitive and aggressive on the court.

Now retired from the game, Barkley still has a bad-boy reputation. That comes largely from the notorious scrapes he's gotten into *away* from the basketball court. Case in point: the 1997 incident where he tossed a man through a plate-glass window at an Orlando nightclub. (To be fair, the man who was forcibly launched by Sir Charles started the incident. Barkley was out with friends, minding his own business, when the man came over to him and dumped an icy drink on the 6'6" star forward, an act of about an 11 out of 10 on the stupid meter.)

Barkley has reflected, "I've done some good things, some bad things, some stupid things, some funny things, but so has everybody else. Mine have just been in the limelight."

Well, of course his actions get more media attention than your average barroom brawl. That's what the limelight is all about. People like Barkley who are in the limelight make the big money and get the big perks—but the limelight also confers a big responsibility.

Barkley doesn't see it that way. In a controversial TV ad he did for Nike in 1993, he said, "I am not a role model. I am not paid to be a role model. I am paid to wreak havoc on the basketball court."

Well, in a perfect world, young people today would look up to parents, teachers, and other responsible adults in their lives more than they look up to NBA stars. But that simply isn't the case. People who make their living in the limelight *are* role models, like it or not. The very fact that Barkley was being paid a lot of money to endorse Nike products is testimony to the fact that he is out there influencing people, for good or ill.

That's what a role model is—a person who is imitated by others. Leaders are role models. In 1 Timothy 3:1–7, the apostle Paul lays out the character requirements for a leader in the church, and most of those character qualities have to do with a leader's influence. A leader, says Paul, must be:

- *Above reproach*—living a life that gives no hint of scandal or wrongdoing
- *Temperate*—possessed of a reasonable and moderate demeanor
- *Self-controlled*—capable of controlling such impulses as anger, drinking, gambling, and sexual urges
- *Respectable*—engaged only in moral and decorous conduct, not conduct that is offensive to others
- *Able to teach*—capable of having a positive influence on others through instruction, training, and mentoring

As leaders, we are in the limelight, and we must be aware that people are watching us, taking cues from us, learning from us. So we must die to ourselves, to our selfishness, to our baser urges, to our temptations, to our lust and greed and pride. We must start living for the sake of others, for the sake of the influence and impact we have on the people around us.

Former Reagan aide Michael Deaver tells a story from Ronald Reagan's days as governor of California. Deaver's daughter, Amanda, was just a toddler, but she knew that her daddy worked for the man who was the leader of the whole state. It was around this same time, in 1974, that Richard Nixon resigned as president because of the Watergate scandal.

When Amanda saw her mother crying in front of the television, the little girl asked what was wrong. Carolyn Deaver explained it in simple terms. "The president had to quit being the president," she explained.

"Why?" asked Amanda.

"Because he lied, honey," said Mrs. Deaver.

A few days later, Mrs. Deaver stopped by her husband's Sacramento office with little Amanda in tow. They happened to run into Ronald Reagan. The governor reached down and scooped Amanda up in his arms. He was surprised when the child began to cry. She didn't just whimper—she bawled her eyes out. Mike and Carolyn Deaver were baffled. Amanda had never behaved this way before.

Reagan grinned. "I know what you need," he said, and he took Amanda into his private office and let her scoop a big handful of jellybeans out of the jar he kept on his desk. Even with all those jellybeans in her hands, it took a while for Amanda to settle down.

Mike and Carolyn Deaver waited in the outer office while Reagan and Amanda talked quietly in Reagan's private office. They strained their ears, but couldn't make out what the two were talking about. Finally, the governor and the child came out of the office. Amanda's eyes were dry and she was smiling.

"What was that all about?" asked Deaver.

Ronald Reagan shrugged. "Beats me," he said. "She just kept asking me, 'You'll never lie, will you?' I just told her, 'Don't worry, I won't lie.'"

Leaders must always be aware of the profound influence they have on the next generation. As John C. Maxwell observed:

> In a word, the goal of a leader is to leave a *legacy*. He wants to leave behind something important after he dies. He wants to have improved the lives of people in some corner of the world— or better yet, see them engaged in a cause that counts . . . Leadership is influence. It isn't about titles, positions, or flow charts. It's about one life influencing another.

A genuine leader dies to self and lives for the next generation.

## The Quality of Responsibility

True leaders die to the selfish impulse to cover up mistakes and failures. They die to the natural tendency to protect the self by shifting blame. Leaders are reliable, dependable, accountable, and trustworthy. Leaders take responsibility.

Bobby Bowden, head football coach at Florida State University, puts it this way:

> Everything that occurs within an organization reflects back upon its leader. If something bad happens on your watch, outsiders will wonder why you weren't watching. If an employee performs poorly, they will ask you why you hired that person in the first place. If poor decisions are made that damage your organization's reputation, people will cast a wary glance toward the ultimate decision-maker. Whether or not you should be blamed, you will be. The leader is ultimately responsible for all that occurs within the organization.

Rich DeVos, founder of Amway, once appeared as a guest on my sports-talk-radio show in Orlando. He told me a story about responsibility. Years ago he supported an older evangelist named Anthony Zeoli. Zeoli had become a Christian while in prison and had gone on to become widely respected. DeVos described how every Sunday morning at 9:00 A.M. Zeoli would call and tell him everything he had done that week:

> One week I finally said, "Anthony, you don't have to call me like this." He said, "Yes, I do. I'm accountable to you. You pay me, and I must account to you for what I do with the money. All of us are accountable to someone."

Former Pittsburgh Steelers quarterback Terry Bradshaw is a leader with a hard core of responsibility in his character. He was the first player taken in the 1970 NFL draft. Calling his own plays, Bradshaw led the Steelers to four Super Bowl titles. To him, being a leader meant taking responsibility for his actions:

I never made excuses. When I screwed up, I was vocal about it: "I don't know why I threw that ball into coverage. I don't know why I threw that ball over your head. I don't know why I messed up that hand-off, but I did it." During my career, I heard all kinds of excuses for making a physical error: "I lost it in the sun. The wind took it. That @#%& held me. The balls were bad. The field was torn up. It was too cold to get a good grip. The meteor shower made me nervous."

But I never heard excuses from the group of players who stayed together through our four championships. That was a stand-up group of people. If we screwed up, we admitted that we screwed up. When people took responsibility, when they apologized, we always forgave them.

The ability to take personal responsibility is a powerful ingredient for success. As long as a person says, "It wasn't my fault" or "It's her responsibility" or "I'm a victim of circumstances," that person is in a position of helplessness and hopelessness. He is saying, "I have no control, I have no confidence, I'm at the mercy of people and events."

But the moment a person says, "I'm responsible, I could have done this better," that person has taken a major step toward improvement, learning, growth, mastery, and control of the situation. A person of responsibility says, "I'm not anybody's victim. I just made a mistake, and I'm going to do better next time." That is a position of power! That is an attitude of confidence and self-empowerment.

Bill Russell is a leader in the game of basketball, and a man who lives life on his own terms. In 1955 he led the University of San Francisco to an NCAA title and led the U.S. Olympic basketball team to a gold medal. In 1957 he spurred the Boston Celtics to their first NBA title. The following year he collected his first of five MVP awards. From 1959 to 1966 he led the Celtics to eight straight NBA championships.

But Bill Russell was not just a leader on the court. He was a leader in American society. When he and other African-American players were barred from segregated hotel restaurants, he and other players boycotted a game in Lexington, Kentucky. He fought for justice and black American pride. One of the defining traits of Bill Russell, the American leader, is his sense of personal responsibility.

"Responsibility," Russell once said, "ultimately gravitates to the person who can shoulder it. We must all be strong enough. The more you stand behind what you do or what you decide, the more you will be able to feel that is a reflection of yourself. It is your integrity that is at stake when you genuinely take responsibility for what you do." The leader who dies to self takes responsibility, and in doing so he finds his own soul.

One of my never-ending jobs as a parent is trying to instill a sense of responsibility in my children. I'm always looking for teaching opportunities. Understand, I'm an old-fashioned father, and I'm totally opposed to the current rage of tattoos and body piercing. I can't stand seeing young ladies whose faces look like they've fallen into their father's tackle box. There are no tattoos permitted under my roof!

Well, there is one exception. In fact, I'd pay for this tattoo and I'd even offer a signing bonus. There are just two stipulations: (1) I determine the location on the body where the tattoo goes, and (2) I determine what the tattoo says. Location: The forehead. Wording: "I AM IN CHARGE OF ME!" No takers yet, but the offer still stands.

We are all responsible for the decisions we make. Those decisions determine the course of our lives and have a powerful effect on the people around us and on society as a whole. Immature people avoid responsibility, but great leaders understand it, live it, and teach it at every opportunity.

## The Quality of a Work Ethic

While campaigning for the Democratic presidential nomination in 1960, John F. Kennedy visited the coal mines of West Virginia. There he met one crusty old coal miner who eyed him with apparent distrust. They shook hands and the miner said, "Is it true that you were born to money, and everything you ever wanted was handed to you by your rich old man?"

"I suppose that's true," said Kennedy.

"And is it also true that you've never done a hard day's work in your entire life?"

Uncomfortably, Kennedy admitted, "I guess you could say that."

"Well," said the coal miner, "you haven't missed a thing."

Yes, it would be nice to live without having to work and with never a worry about where the next meal or the next car payment is coming from. But I wasn't born into the Kennedy clan, and in all likelihood, neither were you. So in order to succeed in this world, we're going to have to demonstrate a character quality called a *work ethic.*

To have a good work ethic means dying to our natural inertia and laziness, to our juvenile expectation that the world owes us a living. An industrious and hardworking leader inspires productivity in others by living a productive life. As the Bible tells us, "Do you see a man skilled in his work? He will serve before kings; he will not serve before obscure men" (Proverbs 22:29). Continental Airlines CEO Gordon Bethune said, "Success doesn't have an autopilot. You need to work every day."

I had the best education a kid could ever want—and I got it from hanging around a ballpark. One of my dad's best friends was Bob Carpenter, then owner of the Philadelphia Phillies baseball club. I was a star-struck, baseball-crazed kid who got to spend many glorious hours in and around Shibe Park. I not only got to go to more baseball games than I could count, but I also attended spring training sessions with the team. That's where I first learned what a strong work ethic is all about.

Most kids grow up thinking baseball is just a bunch of guys who go to the ballpark and have fun swatting the ball around. But I got to see the hours of conditioning, practicing, and training that goes on long before the first pitch on opening day. I learned from my earliest years that it takes a lot of work to be successful in baseball or in any other endeavor.

Walter Alston was one of the great managers in baseball history. He managed the only Brooklyn Dodgers team to win a World Series and managed the Dodgers in Brooklyn and L.A. for twenty-three seasons. Alston started out in the St. Louis Cardinals farm system under the legendary Branch Rickey (Rickey was the pioneering baseball exec who broke baseball's color barrier by signing Jackie Robinson to the Brooklyn Dodgers in 1945). When Rickey left the Cardinals organization and took over the Brooklyn Dodgers, he brought Alston with him. Alston became manager of the Dodgers in 1954 and continued in that role until his retirement in 1976. By that time, he had amassed a record of 2,063 wins (2,040 regular season and 23 postseason), seven National League pennants, and four World Series titles. He died in 1984.

The one character quality that defined Walter Alston more than any other was his work ethic. You can see Alston's unflagging industriousness in a story he recalled from his days as a manager in minor league baseball:

> I was managing in the Dodger system, and we'd be at Vero Beach, Florida, in the spring—twenty-four minor league managers and about fifty scouts. Every time the word went out that Mr. Rickey was coming to town, these guys would all bust their tails doing this, doing that. I'd think, "Well, heck, I can't do any more than I've been doing." I felt I'd been giving it everything I had and couldn't do any more just because Branch Rickey was coming. If I waited for him to show up before I put out, I had no business being there in the first place. I felt the same way when I took over the Dodgers.

Alston's long and successful career in baseball demonstrates an important truth about the character quality of a strong work ethic: Industriousness and hard work are not something you take out, polish up, and put on for show when the boss comes around. It's something that is a part of your makeup, 24/7. If you are not a hard worker all the time, even when no one is watching, then you are not a hard worker, period.

Hardworking leaders inspire workers to work harder. Boston Celtics forward Paul Pierce is one of the best players in the NBA. When Pierce heard that the legendary Michael Jordan was returning to the game for the 2001–2002 season with the Washington Wizards, Pierce decided to ratchet his work ethic up another notch. Pierce, who works hard at his game all year round, decided to increase his off-season workout schedule from two workouts a day to three workouts a day. Pierce called that third workout his "Michael Jordan session."

"The whole time I'm working out," the twenty-four-year-old Pierce explained, "I'm thinking 'Michael Jordan, Michael Jordan.' Michael sets the standard, even at his age. I'm not in there thinking, 'Vince Carter' or 'Kobe Bryant.'"

Michael Jordan himself is a leader with an inhumanly intense work ethic. Phil Jackson, Jordan's old coach with the Bulls, once talked about how Michael's enthusiasm and hard work elevated the work ethic and intensity of the entire team:

> After coaching him for eight seasons, I still marvel at how much Michael's enthusiasm energizes us, even at practice. I mean he never takes a day off. As a player, I had only modest skills, so I always had to operate at a maximum effort to compete. His work ethic is an important personal bond between us.

Today, we see many young people growing up with a disdain for hard work. It's an attitude I've seen again and again: "You won't ever catch me flipping burgers at McDonalds!" Many people in the working world today have been corrupted by the idea that there are shortcuts to success—that there's "easy money" out there and they are entitled to it. As leaders, we need to demonstrate in our lives and our words that hard work is a good thing, an enjoyable thing, not just a necessary evil to be grudgingly endured for the sake of a paycheck. Work is honorable, admirable, and it's the only way to succeed in life.

## The Quality of Relentless Perseverance

Perseverance is the breakfast of champions. The quality of perseverance is more crucial to success than brains, skill, talent, strength, and luck—combined! If you fall down a thousand times, and you get up a thousand and one times, then you have perseverance—and you *will* succeed. As my friend Richard DeVos, the cofounder of the Amway Corporation, often says, "Perseverance is stubbornness with a purpose."

Leaders are ordinary people who are extraordinarily determined, who never quit. Outstanding leaders don't give up. They don't say, "I failed." Instead, they say, "I haven't succeeded yet, but I will!" They stick with the problem until it is solved. They keep charging up that mountain until it is conquered. It's the quality Abraham Lincoln saw in General U. S. Grant when he said, "It's the dogged pertinacity of Grant that wins."

As I write these words, I have run twenty-three marathons. People ask why I do that. Why put myself through that kind of excruciating punishment four or five times a year? My answer: Running marathons is the best way I know to practice perseverance. When you run a marathon, your body and head are soon screaming at you, "Stop this foolishness! End this pain! Quit, quit, quit!" But what a feeling to cross that finish line after more than twenty-six miles of torture! When you can finish a marathon, my friend, you know you can persevere through any situation life throws at you!

In the thick of the 2001 football season, *USA Today* published a profile on Green Bay Packers quarterback Brett Favre. As you hear what Favre's teammates and other NFL stars say about him, you get the impression that the character trait that most defines Brett Favre is perseverance. To Favre, says *USA Today*, "leadership is a trust, a responsibility. That's one reason he has started an NFL quarterback-record 146 consecutive games, has been league MVP three times, and rarely misses a practice."[3]

Another Packers great from the 1960s, offensive lineman Jerry Kramer, shares Starr's appreciation for Favre. "The thing about him that all of us old-school Packers love," says Kramer, "is that competitive fire and that ability to withstand pain."[4]

Favre's brand of perseverance is not only good for motivating the entire team—it's great for recruitment, too. On November 15, 1992, the Packers played the Philadelphia Eagles at Milwaukee County Stadium. Thirteen minutes into the first quarter, an Eagles defensive lineman put a monster hit on the then-rookie QB. Favre was driven into the ground with a separated left shoulder. Packers coach Mike Holmgren told Favre he was finished for the day, but Favre took a massive shot of painkiller and returned to the game. Three plays later, he threw a touchdown pass for the lead, 6 to 3. During the first quarter, he completed 11 of 11.

The Eagles lineman who had flattened Favre was Reggie White. He had never heard of Brett Favre before. Now he was watching an amazing display of leadership, perseverance, and courage. White wondered, *Who is this guy?* By the end of the game, Favre and the Packers had beaten the first-ranked defense in the NFL, 27 to 24.

In 1993 Reggie White became a free agent, and he remembered the grit, perseverance, and leadership of Brett Favre. He stunned the sports world when he signed with Green Bay, turning down larger offers from the 49ers, Giants, and Redskins. Why Green Bay? Because Reggie White knew a winner when he saw one. And he was right. In January 1997 Brett Favre led the Packers to a championship in Super Bowl XXXI—a game in which Reggie White collected three sacks and a Super Bowl ring.

This nation was founded on grit and perseverance. Think of General George Washington. He lost two-thirds of the major campaigns of the Revolutionary war—but he persevered and he won the battles that settled the outcome of the war. The United States of America exists today in large part because of the perseverance of Washington.

Think of scientist Louis Pasteur. In the 1860s Pasteur discovered a revolutionary process for heat-treating certain foods to retard spoilage and prevent microbe-related food poisoning in humans. That process, called pasteurization, has safeguarded our food supply for generations. What few people realize, however, is that Pasteur's great discovery did not occur until after he had suffered a paralyzing stroke. "Let me tell you the secret that has led me to my goal," he later said. "My strength lies solely in my tenacity."

Think of Henry Ford, who failed and went broke five times before he finally succeeded. Though his successes were great, his failures were spectacular and embarrassing. The very first Ford car model had a glaring design flaw: Ford forgot to install a reverse gear! But he knew how to achieve his goals: *Just stick to it*. An ambitious young employee once asked Henry Ford the secret of his success. "When you start a thing," Ford replied, "*finish* it."

Finally, think of Tom Monahan. Monahan bought a little hole-in-the-wall pizza shop in 1960. The shop struggled along for eight years until a fire consumed his investment. The insurance company paid him ten cents on the dollar for his loss. He took that meager sum, invested in a new pizza shop, and persevered once more. Two years later, when he fell behind in his loan payments, the bank took over the business. In 1971, in hock to the tune of $1.5 million, facing lawsuits from angry creditors, Monahan asked himself, "What can I do to turn this around?" The answer: Start the nation's first pizza home delivery service. Today, Monahan's company—Domino's Pizza—has over sixty-six hundred corporate and franchise stores worldwide.

Whatever your organization, whatever your goal, whatever your vision, the key to success is to eliminate the word "quit" from your vocabulary. If you persevere, you *will* win.

## The Quality of Total Self-Control

As leaders, we must die to our baser selves, our selfish urges, our arrogant ambitions, our momentary impulses. We must place depth of soul over gratification of self. We must place the good of the organization over simply doing what feels good. We must keep ourselves, our lusts, our pride, our emotions, under control at all times so that we can achieve our goals and realize our vision. A leader who possesses the character trait of total self-control is able to:

- manage his or her temper when provoked
- stay calm in a crisis
- make quality decisions under pressure
- maintain strong convictions and pure conduct—even in times of great temptation

NBA star A. C. Green is a leader whose life has been characterized by self-control. He has played for the L.A. Lakers, the Phoenix Suns, the Dallas Mavericks, and the Miami Heat—and he's been a leader everywhere he's played. The durable power forward didn't miss a day of work for eleven straight years. He retired at the end of the 2000–2001 season with the longest iron-man streak in NBA history: 1,192 consecutive games played.

Green is intensely focused on being a leader and an example of self-control to today's youth. He established the A. C. Green Youth Foundation in 1989 as a means of helping young people build self-esteem and self-control into their lives.

Green credits his faith for his strong trait of self-control. As a role model, he doesn't smoke, drink, swear, or engage in sex outside of marriage. He says that his total self-control is intertwined with his total work ethic. That desire to keep his life pure, he says, is "inside me, like the will of not wanting to take time off."

Green unashamedly proclaims himself a virgin—an extreme rarity in our sex-obsessed, morally bankrupt society. His claim of total abstinence has drawn reactions ranging from polite skepticism to nasty ridicule. It has also provoked some amusing exchanges with opponents on the basketball court.

A. C. takes the needling about his sexual purity with a grin, but he's dead serious about the importance of total self-control. "Temptations come and go," he says, "but by the grace of God, I will hold myself sexually abstinent until I marry. I am single, and I have a wonderful girlfriend. For me, abstinence is more than a statement. It's a personal conviction." (Green has recently married.)

How does he do it? How does A. C. Green remain an iron man and a virgin well into his thirties? It is not just a matter of willpower, says Green. He attributes his total self-control to his faith in God. "I've stuck to it," he says, "but it's only been by God's grace. I keep looking to him to be my source and power. But at the same time, I keep looking to him because I love him, I want to please him, and I want to be committed to him."[5]

Of course, sex isn't the only area of our lives that demands total self-control. We all face temptations in different areas of our lives. We are tempted to give in to anger and rage when people let us down at the office. We are tempted to lose our cool under pressure, yielding to either panic or paralysis or discouragement. We are tempted to compromise our business ethics on the grounds that "everybody does it" or "nobody will ever know" or "you have to go along to get along."

Jesus, the supreme example of leadership, faced temptation just as we all do. He responded with total self-control. He regularly fed and strengthened his soul so that he could remain in total control of his conduct and emotions. He maintained a careful balance between an active public ministry and private times of solitude, prayer, and reflection. He made sure that his soul was in control of his self. His spiritual side was always the master of his natural human urges and impulses.

Jesus never lost sight of his vision of the kingdom. It drew him onward and motivated him to maintain self-control in spite of pressures, discouragements, obstacles, and temptations. As Hebrews 4:15 tells us, Jesus was "tempted in every way, just as we are—yet was without sin." Exceptional leaders display exceptional self-control. Exceptional leaders remain focused on their vision and goals, even when pressures and distractions attempt to pull them off course.

Total self-control is a defining characteristic of a great leader.

## The Quality of Unconquerable Courage

Courage means dying to our natural tendency to seek safety and avoid risk. Courage is not the *lack* of fear but the *management* and *subjugation* of fear. As leaders, we are all afraid of something, if only the fear of failure. The courageous leader acts in spite of those fears, and defeats them. The most courageous people of all are those who are afraid, yet do what must be done. NBA coach Paul Silas tells his players, "If you take the last shot and make it, you're the hero. If you don't, at least you had the guts to take it." We all need to learn to try for the shot.

Rudy Giuliani was known for his courage long before America was attacked by terrorists on September 11, 2001. As a prosecutor, he had courageously waged war against organized crime, and he put many vicious killers and corruptors of society behind bars. On September 11, when terrorists piloted two hijacked airliners into the towers of Manhattan's World Trade Center, Mayor Giuliani was called upon to step up to the next level of courage.

The moment Giuliani heard of the attack, he rushed to the scene. There he found that the emergency command post in Seven WTC had been evacuated, and a makeshift command post had been set up in the shadow of the twin towers. Looking up at the burning towers, the mayor was horrified to see people jumping from windows a hundred stories up.

From the makeshift command post, Giuliani and his aides went to set up an emergency communications center a short distance from the scene. They chose an office building at 75 Barclay Street and began working from the office phones on the ground floor. As Giuliani and his aides attempted to contact the White House, seeking air cover to prevent further attacks, there was a low rumble, like an earthquake. The phones went dead. The street outside turned dark, and someone yelled, "Hit the deck!" Then the windows shattered and chunks of debris blew into the building, along with thick black clouds of ash. To the mayor, it seemed as if a nuclear bomb had gone off.

Giuliani and his aides headed for the basement and tried the exits— all locked. They went back upstairs and looked out at the street beyond the shattered windows, but saw no signs of life, only a thick blanket of gray dust. Finally, they made their way through the building next door and onto Church Street.

Once outside, they encountered chalk-white people wandering through a gray haze, like ghosts in a fog—only some of these ghosts were bleeding. Over the next few hours, Giuliani worked intently, reestablishing lines of communication. He frequently faced the TV cameras, displaying a calm demeanor to the public. His reassuring presence was probably the most important factor in preventing panic. Swiftly and efficiently, he made hundreds of crucial decisions affecting the city's security and rescue operations.

At around 2:30 in the morning, Giuliani went to the apartment of some friends to spend the night. He watched the TV replays of the destruction for the very first time, then read from a newly published book, *Churchill: A Biography* by Roy Jenkins. He opened it to these words of Winston Churchill from the darkest days of World War II: "I have nothing to offer but blood, toil, tears, and sweat."

"I started thinking," he later recalled, "that we're going to have to rebuild the spirit of the city, and what better example than Churchill and the people of London during the Blitz in 1940?"

Though some of Giuliani's friends claim he was born without a "fear gene," Giuliani says he felt a lot of fear on September 11. When he and his aides were trying to find a way out of the building at 75 Barclay Street, he recalls, "I kept saying to myself, 'You've got to keep your head, and you've just got to keep thinking, *What's the most sensible thing to do next?*' Something I learned a long time ago, also from my father, is that the more emotional things get, the calmer you have to become to figure your way out."[6]

All of which underscores this truth: Courage is not the absence of fear, but the conquest of fear.

In August 1964, Winston Churchill lay in a London hospital. He was eighty-nine years old, and he had less than half a year of life remaining. Churchill's face came alight when an old friend from America walked into his room. It was Churchill's fellow warrior, Dwight David Eisenhower. During World War II, Eisenhower had been Supreme Commander of the Allied Forces when Churchill was prime minister of England. Later, when Eisenhower was president of the United States, the two men had worked together to oppose the spread of communism during the Cold War.

Eisenhower stood at Churchill's bedside. The old man had suffered a slight stroke a few weeks earlier and couldn't speak. But no words were needed. They clasped hands, and the memories of all that they had been through together seemed to pass in silence between them. After a while, Churchill released the hand of his friend and made his trademark V for victory sign.

Eisenhower nodded and smiled, then turned and left. Outside the room, he encountered one of Churchill's aides. "I just said good-bye to Winston," Eisenhower said, "but you can never say farewell to courage."

People like Winston Churchill and Rudy Giuliani are courageous not because they have no fear but because they have made a decision of the will to master that fear. What many people fail to understand is that courage is inseparable from fear. You cannot have true courage unless you are truly scared, because courage is a response to fear. Courage is saying to yourself, "I will not let my fears master me; I will master my fears." As John Wayne once said, "Courage is being scared to death—but saddling up anyway."

Gilbert Keith Chesterton pointed out the paradoxical nature of courage. "Courage," he said, "is almost a contradiction in terms. It means a strong desire to live taking the form of readiness to die." What a paradox! You cannot truly live unless you have the courage to die for the sake of what is ultimately important to you. Courage is the willingness to risk everything we possess, even life itself, for the sake of something larger than life. And until we are truly willing to die for that larger, greater thing, then we have not truly begun to live. Without courage, we simply take up space on the planet.

The character quality of courage is essential to authentic leadership. A great leader dies to fear in order to bring a vision to life.

## HOW TO SAFEGUARD YOUR CHARACTER

There is no real mystery to building and maintaining your character. It's just a matter of doing what you know you ought to do. It's a matter of living a principled life, of practicing the Golden Rule, of building quality habits, of making moral, ethical decisions and sticking by them.

But there's a paradox here. Notice, I said that there's nothing *mysterious* about building and maintaining good character; I never said it was *easy!* Safeguarding your character is hard work, and it requires serious intentions and hard choices. Here are some suggested steps for building and maintaining your character:

*Take regular time for reflection and restoration of your soul.*

Remember the example of Jesus, who regularly took time away from the crowds for prayer and meditation.

I have set up the porch in the back of our house as a weight and workout room. There's a beautiful view there, overlooking Lake Killarney.

That's where I am at the start of every day. That's where I exercise, meditate, think, pray, and commune with the Lord.

There's a bird-feeding station near the screened-in porch that attracts every kind of bird, from sparrows to pigeons to robins to ducks, with the occasional squirrel thrown in as well. I watch those animals come to feed on bird seed, peanuts, and bread, or to enjoy the birdbath, and I think of how God has provided for me and my family over the years. That porch is my refuge, where God restores my soul. I hope you, too, have a place for prayer, meditation, and restoration.

*When faced with an ethical choice or a temptation,
consider the example you set for others.*

Consider all the people who are watching your life and learning from you—and even patterning their lives after you. Imagine how hurt and disillusioned they would be if you were caught in a lapse of character.

In California, a banker sat down over coffee with one of his managers and said, "You're going to find out soon enough, so I want you to hear it from me. The bank examiners are closing in on me, so I've hired an attorney and I'm going to turn myself in. That's right, I embezzled half a million dollars."

The manager was stunned. "You?" he said. "Embezzlement? You're the last person I would have suspected."

"I'm looking at prison time and complete financial ruin," said the banker. "But that's the least of it. Now comes the hard part. I have to go home and tell my wife and two daughters what I've done."

I've seen it happen again and again—and so have you. A pastor caught in adultery. An attorney dipping into escrow accounts. A prominent Christian sports star nabbed for soliciting an undercover policewoman. Imagine the sense of horror and shame when your "secret" sin becomes a public disgrace. Imagine the look on the faces of those you love.

Whatever the temptation you face, you have to ask yourself: *Is it worth hurting and disillusioning the people who look up to me?* We are all one bad decision away from ruin.

*Make yourself accountable to a small group of trusted friends.*

Ask them to check in with you regularly about your character and conduct. Choose people you can be honest and open with, and share your struggles with them. Submit all areas of your life to a regular review.

Once a month I have dinner with Dr. Jay Strack. It's usually a three-hour session, wives included—the ultimate accountability session. Everything is aired out, no holds barred, no question out of bounds. We all need to have a few friends we can trust with our secrets and struggles—people we can open our lives to, people we can share our burdens with, people who will keep our confidences, pray for us, and hold us accountable for personal growth and integrity.

*Focus on integrity, not image.*

Focus on being real, through and through, not just an empty facade. Dr. Robert Terry, president of The Terry Group and author of *Reflective Leadership*, observes:

> Leadership is more about who you are as a human being than about what you do for a living. It's more about *being* than *doing*. If we don't have a deep soul and a deep sense of ourselves as we engage with the world, leadership becomes manipulative: "How can I get you to do what I want you to do and have you feel good about it?" To me, the profound challenge in ourselves is *authenticity*—being true and real in ourselves, in our relationships, in the world.

*Grow deep in your faith.*

Lakers head coach Phil Jackson put it this way:

> Ultimately, leadership takes a lot of what Saint Paul called faith: "The substance of things hoped for, the evidence of things not seen" (Hebrews 11:1). You have to trust your inner

knowing. If you have a clear mind and an open heart, you won't have to search for direction. Direction will come to you.

Every day, seek God's friendship and direction for your life—and he will guide your path.

*Deal firmly and uncompromisingly with*
*hidden sin and character flaws.*

I recently heard about something that took place in India. A cobra slithered under the front porch of a home. Understandably, the family panicked and called for the local snake specialist to come and rid their home of the cobra. They couldn't get under the porch, because there was no crawlspace. So they brought in powerful equipment to lift the porch up so the snake expert could gain access. As the porch was raised, a shocking discovery was made: There was not one, but four full-grown cobras under the porch—plus three thousand cobra babies! These cobras had been living and breeding under the house completely undetected and unsuspected. Worst of all, the cobra population under that house was about to explode!

Leadership guru John Maxwell says that hidden patterns of sin work the same way as hidden cobras under a porch. Those hidden patterns of sin, he says, generally take one of two forms in a leader's life: a time bomb or a cancer. Either way, the leader and the organization can end up destroyed. The time bomb of hidden sin quietly ticks away in the dark recesses of the leader's life. Then, when it is uncovered, it explodes, producing public humiliation and collapse. The cancer of hidden sin may work more slowly, but it is just as deadly. It eats away at character and confidence, producing a gradual corruption and decline of moral health. The leader, worried about the risk of being exposed, loses his boldness and begins operating out of fear and guilt rather than confidence and enthusiasm.

"Any time a leader neglects to repair flaws in his character," Maxwell concludes, "the flaws become worse and inevitably lead to a downward spiral, culminating in the destruction of the leader's moral foundation . . . Leaders cannot escape who they truly are and what they do in the dark comes out in the light." So don't give destructive habits and hidden sins a place in your life. Root them out and destroy them—before they destroy you.

*Make a commitment to pursue lifelong character growth.*

Think of character building as a marathon—and make a decision to finish strong. As you go through life, never stop listening, learning, and building good habits. As Stephen R. Covey has said, "Our character is basically a composite of our habits." Refuse to yield to temptation. Refuse to back away from your values and convictions. Refuse to compromise your principles or your integrity. Throughout your life, until your very last breath, be aware of the influence you have on others.

The result of taking all of these steps on a regular, persistent, continuous basis is something called *maturity*. Maturity is the sum total of all of these character qualities working together, enabling us to make right choices on a consistent basis. Mature people are people of character. Immature people possess character that is stunted, undeveloped, and ill formed.

We are not surprised when children behave in an immature way. We don't expect kids to demonstrate mature character. That's why kids have parents and teachers—to model and teach them about character, so that they can become mature. While they are learning, kids fib and cover up mistakes to avoid consequences. They are boastful and selfish, irresponsible and lazy. They are quitters, lacking in perseverance, deficient in self-control. They shrink from challenges and risks. That's normal behavior—for *children*.

Unfortunately, it is becoming increasingly commonplace to see *adults* who are as immature as children. Perhaps parents and teachers have failed these people along the way, so that they never learned character and never matured. Or perhaps parents and teachers tried, but failed. But at a certain point in life, every individual must take charge of his or her own personal growth. "When I was a child," said the apostle Paul, "I talked like a child, I thought like a child, I reasoned like a child. When I became a man, I put childish ways behind me" (1 Corinthians 13:11). Each of us is ultimately responsible for the choices we make that produce our mature or immature character.

## WHERE DOES CHARACTER COME FROM?

Building good character is nothing more or less than building ethical, moral, principled habits. "Good habits are habit-forming," says Bobby Bowden.

Sorry if that sounds redundant. But one of the wisest things a person can do is practice good habits until the habits become instinctive. Nowhere is this truer than in the arena of leadership, and no habit is more important than the habit of good character. Good character is a leader's greatest ally. . . . *Character* is an action word. We have good character only to the extent that we demonstrate good character. That's why it's so important for a leader to create good habits.

My daughter Karyn and I ran in the 2002 Boston Marathon. The night before the race, we attended a dinner honoring Bob Kraft, owner of the Super Bowl–champion New England Patriots. I went up afterwards, introduced myself, and congratulated him on his team's success. Kraft greeted me warmly, and just before we parted he said, "You have a nice reputation." I thought to myself, *Sixty years of living went into those five little words!* And to have my daughter hear it just thrilled me beyond words. How can you put a price tag on that experience?

That experience reminded me of the words of Pete Rozelle, the former commissioner of the National Football League. He said, "Character is what you are and reputation is what people think you are. But if your reputation is bad you might as well have bad character."

There is a catch-22 involved in becoming a person of sound character: It takes good character to make good decisions—and it takes good decisions to build good character. Character is the result of the accumulation of choices we make over a lifetime. The better the choices we make, the stronger our character. And the stronger our character, the better the choices we make.

"We are not born with character," observes General Charles C. Krulak, retired commandant of the United States Marine Corps. "It is developed by the experiences and decisions that guide our lives. Each individual creates, develops, and nurtures his or her own character. . . . It requires tough decisions, many of which put you at odds with the more commonly accepted social mores of the times."

My collaborator on this book, Jim Denney, puts it this way:

> I often hear people say, "I have a decision to make, and I'm confused about what I should do." That is rarely true. Usually, there is no confusion whatsoever about what a person *should* do. The confusion is between what he *wants* to do and what he knows is the *right* thing to do. For people of character, these decisions are fairly simple—they do the difficult but right thing, and they suffer few regrets. . . .
>
> Some would say, "But that's tough!" Of course, it's tough. Everything worth doing is tough. Interviewing for a job is tough. Running a marathon is tough. Getting a degree is tough. Losing weight is tough. Quitting cigarettes is tough. Getting off drugs or booze is tough. Maintaining a healthy relationship is tough. Resisting temptation is tough. Raising kids is tough. Writing a book is tough. Life is tough—really, really tough . . . And that's why character matters.[7]

Only a leader of character can make the tough decisions that can turn a vision into a reality. To live, a leader must die—to selfishness, pride, anger, sin, fear, self-indulgence, and everything else that is corrosive and destructive to good character. This is one of the great paradoxes of power, one of the great truths of leadership:

The leader who sacrifices the *self* preserves the *soul*. Only the leader who dies, lives.

# The Successful Leader Encourages Failures

It's something I do at many speaking appearances: I look out across a sea of faces and ask, "How many here are fathers?"

Hundreds, sometimes thousands, of hands go up.

"How many of you dads were in the birthing room when your child was born?"

Nearly the same number of hands.

Then I ask another question: "How many of you remember the doctor handing you your newly minted son or daughter and saying, 'Sir, it looks like we've got a natural-born leader here!'? Any hands?"

It doesn't matter what kind of crowd I'm speaking to—business, sports, religious, or wannabe leaders—the answer is always the same. I scan the audience. Not one hand goes up.

You know what that tells me? It tells me that leaders are not born. Leaders are *made*. To a great degree, they are *self* made. Leaders are people who want to lead so badly that they invest time in learning the skills and acquiring the competencies that leaders must have in order to lead. If leaders can't be developed, if competencies can't be increased, then you're wasting your time reading this book.

But I assure you—you're not wasting your time.

# FAILURE, THE DOORWAY TO SUCCESS

A young magazine reporter once interviewed a billionaire business leader. "Sir," asked the reporter, "what is the secret of your success?"

"Two words," replied the billionaire. "Right decisions."

The reporter wrote those two words in his notebook, then looked up with a puzzled expression. "But sir," he asked, "how did you learn to make right decisions?"

"One word," said the billionaire. "Experience."

"Ah," the reporter said, nodding. He wrote in his notebook—then he looked puzzled once more. "But, sir," he asked, "how did you gain the experience you needed to make those right decisions?"

"Two words," said the billionaire. "Wrong decisions."

Failure is the doorway to success. Failure is the act of making wrong decisions and suffering the consequences. Failure teaches through experience; experience informs our decision making; informed decision making produces competence; and competence produces success. The successful leader is one who has learned through failure and who allows others to learn the wonderful lessons of failure as well.

Harvey Mackay, that great Minnesota entrepreneur and phrase-maker, put it this way: "It doesn't matter how much milk you spill as long as you don't lose the cow." In other words, don't worry about a few mistakes and minor failures along the way—that's just a little "spilt milk." What we are trying to avoid is "losing the cow." In other words, we learn from our mistakes to avoid a truly *catastrophic* failure.

The successful leader knows that the worst failure of all is the failure to learn from failure. So the successful leader encourages failures, and uses the lessons of failure to generate and propagate success.

Jesus knew this paradoxical principle. He practiced it daily with his twelve closest followers. In so doing, he transformed the world.

There is a baffling statement about Jesus in the Bible: "Although he was a son, he learned obedience from what he suffered" (Hebrews 5:8). I have to wonder exactly what that means—Jesus, the Son of God, had to learn obedience? As you read the account of his life in the Gospels, there is no suggestion that Jesus had to learn *how* to obey

God the Father. There's not the slightest hint that he ever went through a rebellious or sinful phase in his life.

So what does it mean that Jesus "learned obedience from what he suffered"? It can only mean one thing: By going though trials, pain, temptation, setbacks, and sufferings, Jesus experienced what obedience was all about. He experienced what obedience feels like. He experienced how hard it is to live a life of absolute obedience. The result of that obedience: unjust accusations, humiliation, shame, torture, and death on a cross. In short, abject failure.

But out of that failure came a transformed world.

Though I believe that Jesus, as the Son of God, was fully God, I am convinced that he had the keenest perception of human nature and the human condition of anyone who has ever lived. He understood the human condition from the inside out. He had a personal experience with human suffering, human limitation, and human temptation. He was the Great Empathizer.

So when Jesus approached his leadership role with the twelve, he understood them better than they understood themselves. He knew what these men could learn through failure—and he made sure they learned those lessons well. Why? Because his job was to transform them from failures into successes, from a bunch of bumbling incompetents to the most competent force for change the world has ever known.

Jesus took them to school, and eleven of the twelve—all but Judas, who betrayed him—graduated with Ph.D.s, *magna cum laude*, from the School of Hard Knocks.

Peter failed repeatedly. His most spectacular failure of all was his claim in Matthew 26:33, "Even if all [the other disciples] fall away on account of you, I never will." This arrogant boast was soon followed, of course, by his three denials of Christ. These denials were a far more humiliating failure than the mere "falling away" of the other disciples. They just fled. But Peter renounced and disowned Jesus with a vile curse.

Later, Jesus made sure that Peter had learned the valuable lesson of his failure. In John 21 Jesus brought the disciples together around a meal of fish beside a lake. He turned to Peter and said, "Simon son of

John, do you truly love me more than these?" Notice the irony! Jesus is saying, in effect, "Peter, you once told me you loved me more than all the rest of the disciples. You claimed that, even if they all fell away, you never would. But you denied me three times. Do you still say you love me more than all of these other disciples?"

What could Peter say? "Lord," he answered, "you know that I love you." He professed his love for Jesus—but the old arrogance was shattered. Peter could no longer compare himself to the others. He no longer claimed his love for Jesus was greater than that of the rest. He had been humbled and chastened by failure.

During the course of that meal, Jesus asked Peter the same question three times, in three slightly different ways, one question for each act of denial: "Peter, do you love me?" And each time, Peter answered yes—but it was a shamed and painful yes. Then, after those three questions had been asked and answered, Jesus was satisfied that Peter had learned the lesson of failure. He reinstated Peter with the words, "Feed my sheep. . . . Follow me!" (John 21:16, 19).

There were other ways that Jesus used failure to teach his disciples. For example, he sent the twelve out to extend his ministry in outlying villages—a ministry of preaching the kingdom, healing the sick, and confronting evil spirits. The disciples went out as he commanded and had amazing results. They returned exuberant and excited over the fact that even the evil spirits obeyed them because of the authority they exercised in the name of Jesus.

But then, in Mark 9, we come to a moment where the disciples attempted to accomplish the same result—and failed miserably. A man brought his son to Jesus and said, "Lord, have mercy on my son. He has seizures and is suffering greatly . . . I brought him to your disciples, but they could not heal him." Jesus commanded the evil spirit out of the boy, and the disciples asked him, "Why couldn't we drive it out?"

Jesus answered that their faith was misplaced. The disciples had started thinking that it was they themselves who were driving out evil spirits. They needed to experience a failure to remind them that it was only by the authority and power of God that evil could be defeated (Mark 9:17–29).

Jesus wanted his followers to have the faith to launch out, to risk, to sometimes fail, and to profit from their failures. He didn't want to make fools of his followers, but to show them their foolish mistakes in order to make them wise.

The successful leader encourages failures—and transforms those failures into even greater successes. That is one of the great paradoxes of power, one of the most transforming of all lessons of leadership. As John C. Maxwell said, "Great leaders fail forward." It's true. Failure produces competence, and competence produces success—if we learn the lessons of failure. That is a paradox of power that Jesus taught and lived and used to transform the world. It is a paradox that you and I need to master in our own pursuit of leadership excellence and organizational success.

## FAILURE IS NOTHING TO FEAR

Radio commentator Paul Harvey once called Lewis Timberlake "America's Apostle of Optimism." Timberlake, a renowned public speaker who has devoted his life to leadership training and enhancing the vision of organizations, once said leaders "never expect to fail, but leaders aren't *afraid* to fail."

This is absolutely true: Great leaders do not fear mistakes or failures—not their own, not the mistakes or failures of others. Leaders are quick to admit their own mistakes and quick to forgive the mistakes of others. That is the key to setting a tone and creating a culture in which innovation, imagination, and risk taking are encouraged and celebrated.

As a leader, as a coach, as an executive, I want to see mistakes happening in my organization on a regular basis. I want to see people taking chances—not stupid, foolish gambles, of course, but prudent, calculated risks. When I look at the résumé of a job candidate, I want to see a track record of success. But if there are a few flops in the mix, I will consider that a plus! It means that here is a candidate who has made some mistakes and has learned a thing or two along the way.

In 1981, while I was general manager of the Philadelphia 76ers, the team was bought by Harold Katz, a very colorful and unusual personality who ran the team with a lot of emotion. From the moment he took the reins, he was always looking for ways to improve attendance. I approached him with an idea for a God and Country Night promotion, involving cooperation with all the Philadelphia churches and holding a Christian rally after a game. Though Harold is Jewish, he was very open to the idea of an event aimed at Christians and he endorsed the plan.

So we held the event in November 1981. Our speakers at the postgame rally included Christian 76ers stars Julius Erving and Bobby Jones, plus Phillies third baseman Mike Schmidt and Christian football stars from the Eagles. The event was mobbed—completely sold out. The idea was so successful that we did God and Country Night twice a year for the next five years.

The night after that first event, we attended a roast for head coach Billy Cunningham. I sat at the table next to Harold Katz. At one point, he leaned over to me and said, "Brilliant promotion last night! I'm as proud of you as if you were my own son." Well, that was high praise! I was walking two feet off the ground for the next week.

A couple of months later, I came up with another promotion, but this one flopped big time. The next day, Harold Katz called me into his office, and he was furious. "I'm taking this out of your paycheck!" he roared. (Well, he didn't—but only because he would have had to give me a raise in order to cover the losses.)

I learned my lesson that day. After that, I still tried to come up with creative promotion ideas. But every time I brainstormed, I could hear Mr. Katz's voice in the back of my mind: "I'm taking this out of your paycheck!" After that, I was never quite the risk taker I once was. And I therefore avoided major mistakes.

I've tried to carry that lesson with me into my own leadership role. If the people in my organization see me as a leader who rewards prudent risk taking, I'm going to see an occasional failure—but on balance, I'm going to reap huge returns. But if they see me as someone who punishes failure, they'll quickly learn to keep their mouths shut, keep their heads down, keep their best ideas to themselves, and play it safe. When that mind-set takes hold, the organization loses—and so does the leader. Nothing demoralizes and immobilizes people like knowing that any misstep could be their last.

How's this for an example: Henry Ford was not an immediate success as a carmaker. Fact is he went bankrupt *five times* before becoming the head of the largest automobile manufacturing company in the world. He once said, "I strongly believe that there is often more to be learned from failure than there is from success—if we but take the time to do so." Smart man!

Leadership is the art of taking negatives and transforming them into positives, of taking problems and turning them into opportunities, of taking failures and transforming them into successes. Leadership is the art of facing up to mistakes, learning from them, and making sure those mistakes are never repeated.

## THE CONFIDENCE OF COMPETENCE

In the spring of 1996 I was stunned along with the rest of the world by the news of the tragic loss of eight mountain climbers on the cruel slopes of Mount Everest. It was the worst disaster in the history of Everest climbs, and the story was later recounted in Jon Krakauer's book *Into Thin Air.*[1] The moment I heard that story, I became obsessed with the idea of mountain climbing. I love physical challenges, which is why I run marathons. Climbing a mountain was something I had never done before. So I kept thinking, *I wonder if I could climb a mountain.*

Understand, I'm so scared of heights that when I was a kid, my tree house was built on a stump. But I also figure that if a challenge doesn't scare you, then it isn't a challenge. So I checked around and found an organization that conducts climbs up Mount Rainier, a semidormant volcano in the Cascade Range of west-central Washington State. Mount Rainier is the tallest glacier peak in the forty-eight contiguous states, topping out at 14,410 feet. It is often used as a practice slope by climbers who are preparing an assault on Everest. Though it's only half the elevation, its terrain and climbing conditions are comparable to those on Everest.

I arrived in September 1996 and joined a group of amateur climbers. Most were novices like myself, though one couple was moderately experienced. They came from Michigan, Wisconsin, and Ohio. And me? I was just a guy from Orlando who didn't know a crevasse from a hole in the ground. Our leader was a man named George Dunn—one of the world's elite climbers, 6'3" and ruggedly constructed, with a marked resemblance to Bill Walton. George had lived in the mountains his whole life and had been to Everest four times.

I have been a leader in many areas of my life. But there, on the slopes of Mount Rainier, I was perfectly content to be a follower. I had placed my life under the truly competent leadership of George Dunn, and I followed him around as if I were a puppy. I was riveted by his knowledge, his skill, and the confidence he exuded.

A competent leader is one who has experienced success—but the most competent leaders have also experienced failures. When I met him, Dunn had been to the top of the world—the summit of Everest—one time out of four attempts. In other words, he had failed three times.

George Dunn had also been to the summit of Mount Rainier some 365 times. But on the day I went with him, we didn't make it to the summit. After being slowed down by an unseasonal blizzard, high winds, and deep snowdrifts, it became clear we would fail to reach our objective. About three thousand feet from the summit, most of us turned back and went back down the mountain with George's associates. (George took the more experienced husband-wife team from Wisconsin on up to the summit.)

I didn't reach my goal that day—but I learned a lot. I intend to tackle that mountain again someday.

My point, though, is this: Every experience is a learning experience. Every time we try something—win or lose—we learn, we grow, we attain more confidence and competence for the next time. A leader like George Dunn isn't born. He's self-made. From the time he crawled as a baby to the time he took his first step as a toddler on up to the moment he made those final steps to the highest point of the Himalayan range, he was stepping out, daring new experiences, acquiring new skills, attaining new levels of competency.

So it is with you and me, in every area of our leadership lives. We risk. We fail. We learn. We risk again. We succeed. We achieve confidence and competence. We become leaders.

# THE FIFTEEN CORE COMPETENCIES OF LEADERSHIP

There is no common cloth out of which all great leaders are cut. There is no single "leadership personality." When Jesus chose the twelve, he chose an array of diverse personality types and experience ranges. Of the twelve Jesus chose, all except Judas became leaders. Each was unique. Each led in his own way, according to his own individuality.

But having said that, it is important to note that there are some core competencies all leaders should strive to attain. A competency is a *skill*, not merely an innate gift or talent. True, some people seem to have a natural aptitude for certain skills—but the skill itself must still be honed. One of the ways we hone these skills, of course, is through experience, including the experience of failure. As IBM founder Thomas Watson Sr. observed, "If you want to increase your success rate, double your failure rate."

The more experience we gain, the more we learn and grow. The more we learn and grow, the more completely we master the core competencies of leadership. The more we master each of these core competencies, the more effective and successful we are as leaders.

After spending years researching, observing, and practicing the role of a leader, I have come up with a list of fifteen competencies that leaders can and should acquire:

## The Competency of Organization

The competency of organizational ability breaks down into a number of specific skills. A person with good organizational ability establishes clear priorities, manages time well, thinks logically and clearly. He or she sets and meets objectives and deadlines, demonstrates multitasking ability, maintains an orderly and uncluttered work environment, and keeps tabs on all areas of the organization (that is, he or she has a keen awareness of the functioning of the organization, how the various parts relate to the whole, how well the organization delivers on its commitments, and so forth).

A leader with good organizational ability also expects organization and efficiency from others. He or she does not accept lengthy reports loaded with jargon and detail, but asks for concise executive summaries. Well-ordered, well-organized leaders perform tasks quickly so there is no wasted energy. They know the difference between essentials and nonessentials, and they coordinate their efforts around the essentials. Nonessential tasks are delegated to others without hesitation. Those who become burdened and exhausted by trivialities are called "micromanagers." They cheat themselves out of greatness as leaders.

One of the brightest, best-intentioned, most idealistic presidents we ever had was Jimmy Carter. He is also widely regarded as one of the weakest leaders ever to sit in the Oval Office. His presidency was marked by mile-long gas lines, a 14-percent inflation rate, a debilitating Iranian hostage crisis, and a disastrous rescue attempt called Desert One. Trained as a nuclear engineer, Carter had an engineer's grasp of every fine detail of his presidency. He personally managed everything from the White House tennis court schedules to the operational details of the Desert One operation in Iran. Micromanagement was the template of his leadership style—and it ultimately sank his presidency.

The man who succeeded Jimmy Carter was Ronald Reagan—Carter's exact opposite as a leader. Carter was focused on details, Reagan on the big picture. Carter managed every little part; Reagan managed the whole, and delegated the parts to subordinates. Carter was a micromanager; Reagan was a macromanager. Carter demanded in-depth briefings and worked long hours; Reagan read executive summaries, selected his decision from a menu of options, then took a nap. Carter was intellectually gifted; Reagan was intellectually average, and readily said so. Carter is seen as a failed president; Reagan is considered (even, grudgingly, by his opponents) a great success as a leader.

Organizational ability is an essential competency of a great leader. I have never met a great disorganized leader. I don't believe any exist.

## The Competency of Preparation

Some 2,400 years ago, Sun Tzu stated that every battle is won or lost before it is fought. In his treatise *The Art of War*, he wrote, "Now the general who wins a battle makes many calculations in his temple ere the battle is fought." In other words, preparation is the key to success.

Great leaders prepare for success by anticipating failure. They are realistic optimists—they expect the best, but plan for the worst. Those who have invested time and resources in preparing for success are never caught off guard when circumstances change. If you plan out your worst-case scenario in advance, then when worse comes to worst, you'll know exactly what to do—and you'll be able to transform a worst-case scenario into a champagne-uncorking success.

Kenny Smith played basketball for coach Dean Smith at North Carolina before being drafted by the Sacramento Kings in 1987. He recalls one game North Carolina played at Clemson. The Clemson arena was rocking, the fans were screaming and yelling, and number one-ranked North Carolina was down by twenty points at the half. Coach Smith gave his team a pep talk during halftime, and the team went out on the floor and slowly, agonizingly managed to cut the deficit to fifteen points.

With eight minutes remaining, Coach Smith called a time out and gave his team another talk. "We're right where we want to be," he told them. Kenny Smith was astounded. *With eight minutes remaining, we want to be down by fifteen?* he thought to himself.

But then Kenny Smith remembered Coach Smith had repeatedly drilled the team on exactly these kinds of situations—eight minutes to go, down by fifteen; thirty seconds to go, down by three. He had put the team through those kinds of drills on a daily basis. Suddenly, Kenny and his teammates understood. Coach Smith had been preparing the team for this very moment. And they all knew exactly what to do.

Coach Smith did not diagram any plays. He didn't give them a single word of explanation. He just said, "We're right where we want to be," and he sent them back onto the floor. The team then proceeded to do everything they had done in practice. They ran their plays, they ran their defenses, and Dean Smith didn't need to call another time out. By the end of regulation play, North Carolina had stunned Clemson with an incredible run down the stretch, winning by a comfortable nine-point margin, 108 to 99.

Kenny Smith learned a valuable lesson in that game. "If I prepare myself," he said later, "I can be down fifteen points and still come out on top. I use that lesson in every area of my life. Whatever happens, I'm prepared."

NBA coach Pat Riley has formulated a set of rules for success. Here is his Law of Preparation: "Few people realize that, beneath the surface glitter, the players bring a fanatical depth of preparation to every game. Their apparently spontaneous creativity and effortless innovation are actually the product of hundreds and hundreds of hours of hard practice sessions." Preparation is one of the crucial competencies of a great leader.

## The Competency of Salesmanship

A great leader is a salesman. My friend Chuck Daly has coached basketball in the NBA with the Philadelphia 76ers, the Cleveland Cavaliers, the Detroit Pistons, the New Jersey Nets, and the Orlando Magic. He also coached the U.S. "Dream Team" in the 1992 Olympics. He once told me, "I'm two things as a coach. Number one, I'm a salesman; and number two, I'm a teacher. That's all I do all day long—I sell and I teach. I have to sell my players on the game plan and the strategy, I have to sell the front office, I have to sell the media, and I have to sell the fans."

What is salesmanship? I would define it as *the ability to communicate with persuasion*. What do leaders do? They move people to action. And the only way to move people to action is to persuade them. Persuasion is selling. Whether you are leading a business, a government, a team, or a church, you must be able to communicate persuasively so people will join your cause, buy into your vision, and take action to make your vision a reality.

Ronald Reagan has been called The Great Communicator. In many ways, he was also The Great Salesman. He sold an optimistic vision of the future to Congress, to the American people, and to the world. He told Mr. Gorbachev, "Tear down this wall!"—and the Berlin Wall is now just a memory. Ronald Reagan wasn't a born salesman. During the years of acting workshops, commercials and speeches for General Electric, and such films as *Knute Rockne, All American,* and *Bedtime for Bonzo* he never realized he was honing his leadership skills and preparing for the presidency.

Good salesmanship requires clarity and brevity. A leader must have focused ideas that can be stated briefly and simply. A great leader, says Vernon C. Lyons, "talks little but says much." The skill includes establishing good rapport with customers and organization members, greeting and acknowledging people by name, listening to and understanding people's wants and needs, displaying enthusiasm and energy along with nonverbal cues (eye communication, body language, tone and inflection, gestures) as part of one's communication style, "closing the sale," and moving the audience or listener toward positive action. Salesmanship is a key competency of leadership.

## The Competency of Teaching Ability

Chuck Daly said he was a salesman—and also a teacher. It's true. If you can't teach, you can't lead. Whereas a salesman persuades people to a certain course of action, a teacher persuades people to become a certain kind of person. Great teachers inspire and motivate people to become learners with a hunger and thirst for knowledge. Great teachers inspire people to seek wisdom, to grow in character, to find solutions, to pursue knowledge, and to stretch their understanding. They are mentors, coaches, guides, counselors, and empowerers. They attract and influence minds. They set a good example. They exemplify values. They embody the organization's vision through their words and deeds. Historian Peter Henriques wrote, "George Washington knew that he was the first, and everything he would do would set a precedent for the country."

When necessary, teachers confront negative behavior. They seek to change people's negative attitudes and actions in order to produce growth and transformation. Teachers demonstrate empathy and concern for individuals. They encourage and coach people toward positive change. They share knowledge and personal experiences. Danny Wuerfell, former University of Florida quarterback, was once asked about the greatest strength of his college coach, Steve Spurrier. Wuerfell answered, "What makes him special is that he can transfer knowledge to you. He teaches you what he knows. A lot of coaches can't do that."

Great teachers are the kind of people others want to emulate. As Jesus himself said, "A student is not above his teacher, but everyone who is fully trained will be like his teacher" (Luke 6:40). The greatest teachers teach by example and modeling. The deepest learning takes place not in a classroom, but in the laboratory of life. A teacher cannot impart what she does not possess, and learners cannot emulate what the teacher does not exemplify. So a teacher must be a good role model.

Someone once observed that some of the best teachers in universities are coaches. Why? Because coaches have a strong incentive to teach. Coaches must get results or they are out of a job. Your average classroom teacher gets tenured and is no longer accountable for results. But coaches are told, "Win games or seek employment elsewhere." A coach's players go out on the field or the track or the court, and they show exactly what they have learned. Their performance is easily measured with a scoreboard or a stopwatch. If the players fail to learn, all eyes turn in the coach's direction—and they *glare*. And that is as it should be.

UCLA basketball coach John Wooden often said, "I'm not a coach, I'm a teacher. I'm teaching basketball and life to my players." And before Vince Lombardi became a coach in the NFL, he spent seven years as a high school teacher. He said this about his coaching philosophy: "They call it coaching, but it is *teaching*. You don't just tell them it is so, but you show them the reasons why it is so. And you repeat and repeat and repeat, until they are convinced, until they *know*." The ability to teach is an essential competency of a great leader.

## The Competency of Ability to Learn

You can't be a great teacher unless you are a lifelong learner. Why? The answer is obvious: change. The world is changing at "Internet speed" (which is about a thousand times faster than a "New York minute"). You can't learn everything you need to know as a leader on a once-and-for-all-time basis. You can't get your university degree and say, "I don't need to learn anymore." The world changes so quickly that if you are not constantly learning, you'll soon be left behind. The great peace activist Gandhi was once challenged on an inconsistency in his life. The critic said, "How could you say one thing last week and now something different this week?" Gandhi replied, "Ah, because I have learned something in the last week."

Historians agree that the modern era began around A.D. 1500, soon after Europeans discovered the Americas. During the three centuries from 1500 to 1830—the period of the Enlightenment—all known knowledge doubled. The year 1830 marked the birth of the era of modern science and technology.

In that one year, the first commercial railroad opened between Liverpool and Manchester, the word *scientist* was coined by William Whewell, Michael Faraday conducted his pioneering experiments in plasma physics, and Patrick Matthew advanced his theory of natural selection (the basis of Darwinism). Thomas Graham, Justus von Liebig, and Friedrich Wöhler made giant strides in the science of chemistry and Sir Charles Lyall formulated a new scientific discipline called *geology*.

From 1830 to 1930, human knowledge doubled once more. Today, human knowledge doubles in roughly *fifteen to seventeen months*.

To lead, you must keep abreast of rapid change in the world around you. The old saying that "readers are leaders" happens to be true. "Successful leaders recognize that developing leadership skills is a lifetime pursuit," observes John C. Maxwell. "In their study of ninety top leaders in all fields, Bennis and Nanus found, 'It is the capacity to develop and improve their skills that distinguishes leaders from their followers.' The researchers also came to the conclusion that 'leaders are perpetual learners.'" As John Wooden advised, "Learn as if you are going to live forever, because if you stop learning, you're through."

A person with good learning habits is in a continual mode of self-improvement and personal development. My wife, Ruth, and I both have master's degrees, and we hope someday to take the time to get our Ph.D.s. We're committed to being lifelong learners. Why? Because we know that the mind is a muscle, like any other. It needs to be vigorously exercised on a regular basis. Without exercise, the mind becomes a pitiful mass of flab, fit only for absorbing *The Jerry Springer Show*.

Brian Tracy, that great guru of success and accelerated learning, says that if you read an hour a day, you can read a book a week. Break it up any way you like—one sixty-minute session, two thirty-minute sessions, or thirty two-minute sessions. Read an hour a day, and you'll be reading a book a week, fifty-two books in a year, and 520 books in ten years. Comic books don't count, and neither do trade journals, *Sports Illustrated*, or your local daily birdcage liner. We're talking *books* now, and you can pick any book you like on any subject that interests you.

If you read five books on any one subject, you can consider yourself a world-leading authority on that subject. So if you take Brian Tracy's advice, you can become an expert on a hundred subjects in just ten years! All that knowledge is bound to change your life, make you more successful, and make you a more fascinating conversationalist. It will certainly make you a better leader.

I always have ten or twelve books open at any one time—books on sports, history, biography, leadership, and inspiration. I have several on my desk, a couple on my bedside table, a few more in my car and at the office. I finish four to six books a week. When I take a trip, my most important decision is not what clothes to wear or which airline to fly, but what books I am taking on this trip. When my contract with the Magic was last negotiated, I turned down a raise and accepted instead a monthly stipend to cover the purchase of books. As many books as I read per month, I feel I'm about two hundred books behind where I want to be.

The competency of lifelong learning doesn't just happen. It is the result of a conscious commitment to a vigorous schedule of systematic learning and personal development. There is no room for stagnation or complacency in your leadership role. You must be able to adjust to changing conditions in the world. Continuously learning leaders build continuously learning organizations that adapt, evolve, and grow. Leaders and organizations that do not meet the challenge of a changing world are doomed to wither and die. Peter Henriques wrote that "George Washington went to school all the time. The lack of formal education didn't stop him from learning."

So keep learning and growing—and above all, keep learning from your experience and your failures! A capacity for continual, lifelong learning is an absolute necessity for all great leaders.

## The Competency of Flexibility

"In matters of style, swim with the currents," Thomas Jefferson once said, "and in matters of principles, stand like a rock." In other words, learn to be flexible and adaptable when the situation demands. Flexibility is a key competency of leadership.

In 1860, with only 39.8 percent of the popular vote, Abraham Lincoln became president. When asked what his policy as president would be, Lincoln replied, "My policy is to have no policy." In other words, he knew that as a minority president, he needed to be flexible and open to change in order to be the president of all the people.

Lincoln once told Maine congressman James Blaine, "You must lead a country as you would steer a riverboat. You don't just set your compass and head south, or you will quickly run aground. Instead, you steer from point to point according to how the river is running and the obstacles that appear in your path."

Lincoln opposed slavery, but he knew that a frontal attack on slavery would have destroyed the Union—and nothing was more important to Lincoln than preserving the Union. So Lincoln advanced his cause by slow and incremental steps. Some have said Lincoln wasn't truly interested in ending slavery. They misunderstand that Lincoln was demonstrating a crucial competency of great leaders: flexibility. By being flexible in his actions and words on the subject of slavery, he was able to move quietly toward his ultimate objective: liberty and justice for all.

The competency of flexibility opens a leader up to innovative solutions and alternative ideas. Flexible people brainstorm with an open mind. They listen to all viewpoints and opinions. They sift information with dispassionate objectivity. This doesn't mean a leader should have no opinions, but great leaders are able to hold their opinions in abeyance while giving a fair hearing to the opinions and ideas of others. Flexibility is an essential competency of a great leader.

## *The Competency of Problem-Solving Ability*

Great leaders know that problems are normal and natural. They don't feel ill used by fate when problems come their way. They accept the fact that problem solving is one of the primary functions of leadership. As pastor David Jeremiah puts it, "A leader is built for problems. If there were no problems, there would be no need for leaders."

Another word for problem is *challenge*. Great leaders love a challenge. They stand tall in adversity, plow through misfortune, overcome obstacles, and rebound from setbacks. Great leaders display complete confidence and optimism even when things go wrong. Enthusiasm is contagious, and times of adversity are great laboratories for teaching the people around you about perseverance, mental toughness, and problem solving.

My whole career has been spent throwing myself into hopeless situations and trying to resuscitate them. At age twenty-four, the Phillies sent me to Spartanburg, South Carolina, to run their minor league baseball team. Community interest had died, the ballpark had fallen into disrepair, and my job was to come in and energize the whole situation. From there, I went into pro basketball. Everywhere I went in the NBA, from Chicago to Atlanta to Philadelphia to Orlando, had a problem crying to be solved. In each case, the problem seemed insurmountable. But to me, a hopeless situation is a magnet. Tough problems fascinate and challenge me. I look at one of those situations and figure, "Hey, there's no place to go but up!"

Competent leaders find stimulation in the opportunity to apply their knowledge and personal resources to the task of solving problems. They don't complain about problems—they go looking for them! Great leaders want to catch problems early, solve them quickly, then move on to the next problem in line.

Another thing all good leaders, teachers, coaches, and parents have in common is that they are *proactive* problem solvers. You have to deal with seemingly little issues immediately and consistently to keep them from growing into big issues. In coaching these might include showing up on time, maintaining good practice habits and respect for teammates and coaches, and dozens of other factors. They might even be something as seemingly trivial as footwear. When John Wooden was coaching at UCLA, the first thing he taught all his players was how to put their socks and shoes on properly to keep blisters from developing. A little thing? You bet—but a team with blisters can't play very good basketball.

In parenting these seemingly little issues might include making sure kids keep up their chores and their studies, maintain a good attitude, show respect to parents and others, and so forth. In business, they might have to do with promptness, courtesy, professionalism, diligence, follow-up, excellence, and workmanship.

"As weather shapes mountains," says Warren Bennis, "so problems make leaders." When we as leaders face adversity with grit, determination, and a positive attitude, we grow. Problems serve to shape a leader's character. "Problems," said M. Scott Peck, "call forth our courage and our wisdom. Indeed, they create our courage and our wisdom. It is only because of problems that we grow, mentally and spiritually."

As leaders, we should welcome problems and thrive on them. Problem-solving ability is one of the most essential core competencies of a great leader.

## The Competency of Ability to Withstand Criticism

Leaders need the capacity to absorb criticism without taking it personally. Criticism is part of the job. Leaders are visible, and the person most visible is inevitably a target. If you don't want to be criticized, don't be a leader. "To avoid criticism," wrote Elbert Hubbard, "do nothing, say nothing, and be nothing."

David J. Vaughn, author of *The Pillars of Leadership*, observes:

> Criticism is one of the most painful, yet inevitable, tests of leadership. Leadership is not, as some would like to think, a

popularity contest. It is not about pleasing people, striving to be liked, or attempting to gain admiration. Rather, leadership is about making the hard decisions, despite competing claims and wishes of others. It means acting conscientiously, even though it will engender hostility.

Complaints and criticisms are annoying. They can also be time consuming. Some criticisms are unfounded and unfair; some are constructive. Leaders must learn to sift the constructive criticisms (designed to help) from malicious criticisms (designed to hurt). It can be hard to tell the difference; a constructive suggestion can often sting every bit as much as a hateful barb. But the intention of the two is 180 degrees apart. The inability to distinguish between the two kinds of criticisms can be a major blind spot in a leader.

The great preacher John Wesley was approached by an elderly lady one Sunday after the morning worship service. "Pardon me, Mr. Wesley," she said, "but I must give you a little constructive criticism."

"Oh," said Mr. Wesley, "and what would that be?"

"Your tie is too long," she said. "It distracted me all through your sermon this morning. It is offensive."

"Have you a pair of shears?"

As it happened, she had her sewing bag with her. She took a pair of scissors from the bag.

"You may cut my tie to whatever length pleases you," said John Wesley. "Clip it so that you will never be offended by it again."

The lady was pleased to do so. After she had reduced the length of John Wesley's tie, the preacher said, "Is it the right length now?"

"Oh, yes," the lady said. "That is much better."

"May I borrow the shears for a moment?"

"Certainly."

John Wesley took the shears and said, "Now, would you mind a little constructive criticism? You see, your tongue is a great offense to me because it is a little too long. Please stick it out so that I may clip some of it off."

Mr. Wesley's critic didn't get her tongue bobbed—but she did get the point.

Former NFL coach Bill Parcells says:

> Can you take the scrutiny? Can you take everybody booing
> you? Can you take people second-guessing everything you do?
> If you can't deal with that, you're not going to be a head coach
> in this league for very long, because you're going to get that . . .
> If you let that stuff get to you, you're not going to last.

Well, you and I can take it. We're going to last. We're leaders. And
we know that the ability to accept criticism is one of the core competencies every leader needs.

## The Competency of Ability to Empower Others

We talked about delegating authority in Paradox 3. Let's look at it
from another angle: Delegating authority is really nothing more or less
than empowering other people to decide and take action. When we
delegate, we bestow a measure of our own power and authority on
others. A crucial aspect of empowering others is making sure that we
do not waste time second guessing the decisions others make.

A woman hired a man to paint the upstairs rooms in her house. She
let him in, showed him the rooms, and watched him lay out his tarps,
paint cans, rollers, and brushes. Then she went downstairs to do
chores. After a while, she went to the foot of the stairs and listened.
Hearing nothing, she called up to the man, "Are you working hard?"

"Yes, ma'am," the painter called back.

"Well, I can't hear you working," the woman shouted.

"Lady," the painter replied, "I ain't putting it on with a hammer!"

The leader who empowers people does not hire a painter and
demand to hear hammering. He or she focuses on final results, not on
making sure the process is noisy enough.

When Conrad Hilton was twenty-one, his father delegated responsibility for the business to him. Unfortunately, the elder Hilton was
not a good delegator. He kept breathing down Conrad's neck, second
guessing every decision, and generally keeping his son on a very short

leash. Years later, Conrad Hilton recalled, "I learned at twenty-one how a man feels when he's been given a job, but complete confidence has been withheld. Perhaps that is why, in later years, when I had carefully selected a man for a job, I left him completely alone, knowing I had either made the right selection or I had been wrong."[2]

Great leaders do not micromanage their people. You can't empower people and micromanage them at the same time. You empower people by giving them the knowledge and resources to solve problems, by giving them the authority to create their own solutions, by encouraging initiative and risk taking, by providing feedback and encouragement, and by managing the results rather than the processes used to achieve those results. If your people achieve quality results on time, then why would you care what process was used to achieve those results?

The ability to delegate and empower others is an indispensable competency of the leadership role.

## The Competency of Intrinsic Motivation

Great leaders operate on intrinsic rather than extrinsic motivation. In other words, they are motivated from within, not from without. A great leader doesn't need praise and acclaim, a pat on the back, or promises of a bonus or a raise in order to feel energized and inspired to lead. A great leader is motivated from within by the challenge of achieving something important, of accomplishing a goal with excellence, even if nobody celebrates the achievement or rewards the accomplishment.

Pat Riley put it this way: "If you feel you have to be validated by your coach or your boss, then you are not a leader. If you just do your job with efficiency and energy, leadership automatically comes to you." Riley has formulated what he calls "Riley's Law of Motivation," which says:

> You motivate yourself by trying to develop another reason above and beyond the natural motivation of just wanting to be successful. Everyone wants to win a championship. The ones

who can really separate themselves from the pack are those who understand what it takes to sustain excellence. They understand that you have to get away from a "to have" mentality and prioritize "to be" ahead of "to have." And when you're thinking about being the very best, you're thinking about making sure that you're being a person, a performer, of whom you can be proud.

Some people simply will not perform unless they get something in return. But genuine leaders have an inner spring of competitiveness, an artesian well of excellence that bubbles up from some mysterious source in the soul.

Oscar Hammerstein II once remarked on an aerial photo he saw of the Statue of Liberty. The picture revealed the amazing detail that was designed into the top of the statue's head by the sculptor, Frédéric-Auguste Bartholdi. The statue was designed in the 1870s, decades before the invention of the airplane, and Bartholdi had no reason to suspect that those details would ever be seen by anyone other than some high-flying seagulls. But Bartholdi was motivated from within to pursue absolute excellence. He refused to cut corners on his masterpiece. Maybe no one else would know—but he would know. That was motivation enough.

"When you are creating a work of art or any other kind of work," Hammerstein concluded, "finish the job off perfectly. You never know when someone will fly over your work and find you out."

All great leaders possess the competency of intrinsic motivation.

## The Competency of Initiative

You might call this the willingness to take the bull by the horns. Some people just seem to know when a given situation needs their leadership, so they step in, fill the void, and start calling the shots. Even though this ability seems innate in some people, it is a skill that can be practiced and acquired by everyone. Many shy, retiring people have learned to identify leadership needs, put themselves forward, and fill a leadership vacuum. People can *learn* to take charge and initiate action.

Those who are able to take charge have a desire to be empowered, to be responsible, to exercise independence and authority. They have confidence in their own decision-making ability. They do not need other people directing their actions. They are capable of initiating action and directing the actions of others, and doing so for the benefit of the organization—not the glorification or aggrandizement of the self (taking charge for selfish reasons is mere bossiness—not leadership).

General George Patton devised an ingenious method for identifying the take-charge leaders among his men. He would line up the soldiers and give them a task. "Men," he'd say, "I want a trench dug behind that warehouse. I want you to dig that trench eight feet long, three feet wide, and six inches deep." That was all the instruction he would give.

While the soldiers got their tools, Patton would go inside the warehouse and watch through a knothole. He would see the men stand around for a few minutes and wonder why that crazy old man wants them to dig such a shallow trench. He'd listen to the men argue with each other: "Are you sure he said six inches deep? That's crazy! He must have meant six feet!" "Look, we all heard him. He said six inches, and he meant six inches!" He'd listen to them gripe about the cold or about having to do menial labor that made no sense.

Finally, one of the men in the group would say, "Look! What difference does it make why the old so-and-so wants this trench? He gave us a job to do, so let's do it and get out of here! You, measure and mark the site of the trench! You, pass out those shovels. The rest of you, line up—three men on this side, three men on that side . . ." And Patton would have his leader.

The leader is the guy who gets the job done—and he's the guy who gets the promotion. The ability to take charge is one of the most fundamental and essential of all leadership competencies.

## The Competency of Decisiveness

A good leader must be a good decision maker. He or she must be able to make high-quality decisions in real time within the limits of available information—and that requires a level of judgment and intuition that only comes with experience and learning. Decision making is thought translated into action. The decision maker gathers all available information, considers and weighs that information, looks for an overall pattern (the big picture) in that information, analyzes the pros and cons, listens to opinions, and then renders a verdict.

Once the decision is made, good decision makers do not obsess about whether or not it was the right decision. They know that a decision has to be made; they know they have made the best decision possible with the information available, and having made the decision, they are at peace with themselves.

Good decision makers are good listeners. They seek clarity and ask incisive questions. They apply logic and analysis to the issue at hand, as well as the lessons and insight they have gained from past experiences. Good decision makers have confidence in their reasoning ability and their judgment. They are able to take a stand—and, if need be, take the heat for that stand.

The ability to make good decisions is not a gift. It is a honed skill, a learned ability—and it is a key competency for all leaders.

## The Competency of Originality

Some people say, "I'm not imaginative. I never have any original ideas." But imagination and creativity are *thinking skills*, and they can be learned and mastered, like any other skill. It's not so much a matter of talent as it is a style of thought.

The in-vogue phrase is *thinking outside the box*. It simply means the ability to be creative and unorthodox. It means to be open to new ideas, to be willing to brainstorm and let your mind roam through previously unexplored possibilities.

Imagination is one of the biggest differences between managers and leaders. People sometimes confuse management with leadership. There is certainly a need for both in every organization. But the difference between the two is that managers tend to accept the organizational context, existing processes, and accepted structure. Leaders are constantly reexamining the status quo, looking for ways to revise and improve the processes and structures, and constantly keeping pace with evolving realities.

Let's put it this way: A manager's job is to feed and pamper sacred cows. A leader thinks sacred cows make good hamburger. Managers help preserve rules and traditions. Leaders question rules and challenge traditions.

Great leaders are never satisfied with the status quo, but constantly look at all sides of every issue, seeking new and ever more flexible solutions to problems, finding nontraditional approaches. Leaders constantly ask, *How can we do this better?*

## The Competency of Professionalism

Professionalism is the ability to project an image of excellence, confidence, and proficiency. An aura of professionalism enables customers and members of the organization to feel assured of their leader's competence. A leader of professionalism is seen as showing taste and refinement in the way she presents herself, objectivity in the way she conducts herself, and poise in word and action.

The leader reflects and embodies the organization, so a leader of professionalism conveys to the world that this is an organization of professionalism. People in the organization see that, from the leader on down, business is always to be conducted in a courteous, dignified, cultivated manner, without emotionalism, coarseness, or any hint of unseemliness.

A friend recently told me, "Our family dentist retired and sold his practice, but we stopped going to the new dentist."

"Why is that?" I asked.

"It's simply a matter of professionalism," said my friend. "He looks in my mouth and starts criticizing the dental work I've had in the past. I think it's very unprofessional for professionals to bad-mouth other professionals."

"Anything else?"

"Well," said my friend, "sometimes he's working on my teeth and something goes wrong—so he starts swearing a blue streak. There's nothing that makes me more nervous then to have a guy start cussing while he's drilling on my teeth!"

No question, that's unprofessional! Leaders *must* project a cool, collected, professional demeanor to others in the organization and to the public.

## The Competency of Poise

Poise is the ability to remain cool, calm, and focused under pressure. It's the ability to keep your head while everyone around you is losing theirs. It's the ability to remain steady amid the storm and therefore have a steadying influence on others. Leaders with poise are not necessarily fearless. Instead, they have learned to control their fears; they resist the temptation to panic and continue to get the job done amid pressures, distractions, and perils. Former Braves star Dale Murphy praised manager Joe Torre by saying, "His steady influence and long-term approach to the season let players ride out the down times. He never pushes the panic button."

Napoleon described the competency of poise this way: "The true genius in war is the one who can do the average thing when those around him grow hysterical with emotion or fright." When a leader panics, the organization becomes paralyzed. When a leader stays calm and poised, the organization continues to function. Former Cleveland Indians manager Mike Hargrove said, "The best compliment [former GM] John Hart ever gave me is that I could walk into a room where there was complete chaos and forty-five minutes later I'd leave and things were peaceful. That's a manager's job. Not to get in the players' faces but to create an environment where it's easy to work and perform to the best of their abilities."

Poise is a learned skill, and it has a lot to do with learning how to talk to yourself in times of crisis. If you tell yourself, *Ohmygosh, this is a disaster. I'm toast,* then you probably *are* toast. But if you tell yourself, *I can think my way out of this; let's just get the facts, figure this thing out, and get the job done,* then you'll probably be okay. If you can check your emotions and maintain your ability to think logically and analytically, you'll be able to shut down panic (your own and everyone else's) and find a solution to the problem.

Great leaders accept the fact that there's never a good time for a crisis. Things always go wrong at the worst possible moment. As Henry

Kissinger once quipped, "Next week, there can't be any crisis. My schedule is already full." A poised leader does not whine about the timing of crises. After all, if the crisis came at a convenient time, it wouldn't be a crisis. A poised leader simply accepts what is and seeks to transform it into a positive outcome.

The leader who seeks to personify these fifteen competencies is the leader who is bound to succeed. No one is born with all of them, but all of us can master each of these competencies. As we acquire and polish these skills in our lives, we become the kind of leaders we were meant to be.

## THE DANGER OF LEADERSHIP FAILURE

One of the most spectacular leadership debacles in American history was the dramatic meltdown of the Enron energy corporation. When Enron collapsed in late 2001, it became clear that people in the highest echelons of Enron leadership had enriched themselves by creating partnerships designed to disguise over a billion dollars in company losses. Sitting in the highest corner office of this financial house of cards was CEO Kenneth Lay, who had transformed a modest company of gas pipelines and power plants into the world's largest energy trading company. An internal investigation concluded that Lay had done nothing wrong—he was guilty only of a "*laissez-faire* management style."

CFO Andrew Fastow has been portrayed as the real villain of the Enron fiasco, since he created the borderline-legal partnerships called "special purpose entities" that were used to hide the company's losses. Fastow made over thirty million dollars from the scheme, and millions more went into the pockets of people in Fastow's office.

Also at fault was the accounting firm Arthur Andersen, which designed the creative ledgers that helped Fastow keep his partnerships afloat for so long. Top executives at Arthur Andersen's home office in Chicago dumped blame on the Houston office, where Enron's audits were carried out. Not surprisingly, Andersen's internal investigation cleared the company's top brass of responsibility.

I don't claim to understand all the labyrinthine ins and outs of the Enron implosion. I'm not saying that anyone at Enron or Andersen did anything that was criminal; as of this writing, the story is still unfolding.

But one thing is clear: Top management at Enron and Arthur Andersen cannot duck responsibility for this massive corporate failure—a failure that cost many small investors and Enron employees their life savings. Andersen's top brass in Chicago tried to pass the buck to the Houston office—but the Houston office is just as much Arthur Andersen as the Chicago office. That buck just won't pass.

Kenneth Lay, who resigned as Enron CEO in February 2002, tried to make the case that he was a victim of subordinates, that he didn't have a clue what was going on in his own company. Well, perhaps it is better from Lay's perspective to have the whole world think him a fool than a villain.

Those are the only choices we have—the scope and scale of the Enron implosion allows no third alternative. The Enron debacle took place on Lay's watch, and in the final analysis, it makes little difference whether Ken Lay wasn't watching on his watch, or whether someone should have been watching Ken Lay. He was the leader, he was the captain of the *Titanic*, and when his ship went down, he was called upon to answer for it.

When an organization fails, it is because the organization's leadership has failed. If the leader doesn't know about an impending disaster, it's because he failed to find out. If he did know and let the ball drop, it begs the question: "Why didn't he do anything about it?" Either way, the buck stops with the person in charge. That is how it is, and that is how it should be—no excuses, no shifting of blame.

Organizations fail for many reasons, but those reasons always come down to a leadership failure:

- The leader failed to set a clear vision for the organization.
- The leader failed to make the right business decisions.
- The leader took stupid risks.
- The leader was too timid and took no risks whatsoever.
- The leader failed to delegate and empower subordinates.
- The leader failed to hold subordinates accountable.

- The leader lacked knowledge about the competition.
- The leader lacked originality, imagination, and innovation.
- The leader allowed the organization to incur excessive overhead.
- The leader allowed the organization to acquire excessive debt.
- The leader did not maintain effective financial control.
- The leader failed to encourage continuous improvement.
- The leader did not encourage effective communication.
- The leader was not responsive to changing conditions.

In every case, whenever an organization fails, the blame can be traced squarely to one person: the leader. Either the leader was incompetent or the leader was a villain—the organization is just as bankrupt in either case, as are the investors.

In the case of Arthur Andersen and Enron, there was still another failure, and it is the most unforgivable failure of all: *the failure to learn from failure*. Enron was just the latest and biggest in a string of costly Arthur Andersen auditing blunders. In recent years, Andersen settled a fraud lawsuit with Sunbeam Corporation for $110 million, ran afoul of the Securities and Exchange Commission over its audit of Waste Management Corporation, and was implicated in the collapse of Global Crossings, another company with Enron-style inflated earnings. Arthur Andersen was also asleep at the switch during the collapse of Banca Nazionale del Lavoro (BNL) some years ago in Atlanta.

Failure is forgivable if you learn from it. Failure is fatal if you don't. As I write these words, it's too early to say what the outcome will be for Arthur Andersen—but the prognosis looks mighty terminal from where I'm sitting.

The lesson is clear: Be a good leader, a great leader, a competent leader. Above all, be the kind of successful leader who embraces failures and learns from them. The great leader understands that failure can be the key to ultimate success when it produces learning, growth, and increased competence. That is one of the great paradoxes of power, one of the enduring truths of leadership.

# Your Toughest Crises
# Are Your Best Opportunities

The 1995–96 season was the best season in the history of the Orlando Magic—and the worst. That season, we posted a record of sixty wins and twenty-two losses. We went to the playoffs—and were swept in the Eastern Conference finals by Michael Jordan and the Bulls. But that wasn't the worst of it. Immediately after that season, we found ourselves on the losing end of one of the boldest moves in the history of professional sports. It's a story that has never been fully told in the media, so sit back and enjoy.

Though the Orlando Magic and I were in the middle of this tale, it's not a story about the Magic. It's about the Los Angeles Lakers and the man who personified the Lakers for some forty years: Jerry West. At that time, Jerry was executive vice president of basketball operations, overseeing a Lakers team that was good but not great. The Lakers finished the 1995–96 season with a 53–29 record, eleven games behind Seattle in the Pacific Division. The team made the playoffs, but got knocked out in the first round by Houston, eliminated in four games. So for Jerry and the Lakers, the season ended on a low note.

As a player, Jerry West was legendary for his boldness and his ability to achieve the impossible under pressure with apparent ease and non-chalance—hence his nickname, "Mr. Clutch." Case in point: In game three of the 1970 NBA finals, Jerry and the Lakers were tied with the Knicks at 100. Thirteen seconds remained. Then the Knicks' Dave DeBusschere hit a jumper. Now the Lakers were down by two with just three seconds remaining and no timeouts. So what did the Lakers do? Something unbelievably bold.

Wilt Chamberlain inbounded to Jerry West from the far end of the court. And West fired from deep in the backcourt and nailed the shot from sixty feet! In those days, there were no three-point shots, so Jerry's sixty-footer only tied the game and sent it into overtime. Under today's rules, that shot would have won the game, but the Lakers lost in overtime, 111–108.

Jerry has shown that same kind of daring and boldness throughout his career with the Lakers, whether on the court or in the front office. Looking at the shambles of the 1995–96 season, Jerry hatched a plan that was sheer madness. Here's what he did.

First, he cut a deal to trade the Lakers' 7'1" center Vlade Divac to the Charlotte Hornets. Divac was not an All-Star but he was certainly one of the better centers in the league. Big men who can play center in the NBA are tough to come by, and many people (including some in his own organization) thought Jerry was nuts to unload Divac—especially when they saw what Jerry got in return: the thirteenth pick in the first round of the NBA draft.

What did Jerry plan to do with his draft pick? Amazingly, he did *not* have his sights set on a top college prospect. Instead, he wanted a seventeen-year-old 6'7" guard from Lower Merion High School in Philly—a player by the name of Kobe Bryant. Jerry had worked Bryant out privately before the draft and absolutely fallen in love with him. What's more, Jerry had worked things out with Kobe's agent, Arn Tellem, to make sure Kobe would still be available by the time that lucky thirteenth pick rolled around. When the perennially rebuilding New Jersey Nets talked about taking Bryant with their number-eight pick, Tellem waved them off, saying that Kobe would rather play in Italy than New Jersey. The Nets left Kobe alone.

When the NBA draft rolled around and the Lakers picked Bryant, the sports world was stunned. Jerry West had, in effect, traded his starting center for a high school player. Even worse, by the end of the draft, the Lakers *still* had no center.

Then, on July 1, immediately after the draft, free agency kicked in. Shaquille O'Neal, star center of the Orlando Magic, turned free agent. We, of course, were trying to re-sign Shaq, and we weren't overly concerned that we might lose him. Obviously, we thought, the Lakers would have liked to sign him, but they couldn't; they didn't have enough room under the salary cap.

We underestimated Jerry West's boldness as a strategic thinker.

One morning in July, we woke up to learn that Jerry had traded two players, both starters or near starters, to Vancouver. Those two players, George Lynch and Anthony Peeler, had been making big money in L.A., and Jerry had just moved them off the payroll. A whole lot of cap room had suddenly opened up. The instant we heard that Lynch and Peeler were leaving L.A., we knew we were in big trouble. The Lakers could now afford Shaquille O'Neal.

Within hours, the Lakers made their move. We got a call in the dark of night from Shaq's agent, Leonard Armato, telling us that Shaq was going to sign with the Lakers. We said, "Don't let him sign; we'll top the Lakers' offer." And we did—but it didn't matter. Shaq had made up his mind to go to L.A. and the Lakers' offer was close enough.

Now Jerry West had the greatest center in the NBA and he had an eighteen-year-old kid. Time would tell: Kobe and Shaq were about to become the nucleus of a Lakers superteam.

The Kobe-Shaq combination didn't click right away. The Lakers took three years to rebuild and in the meantime got knocked out of the playoffs in 1997, '98, and '99. But in 1999 the Lakers acquired Phil Jackson as head coach, and the Lakers' picture was complete. In 2000 the Lakers broke through and won the NBA championship. They repeated that feat in 2001, and in June 2002 won their third straight crown by whipping the New Jersey Nets in four games.

It had all been a huge gamble on Jerry's part—a complex chess game in which he had traded away three starters on the chance (which was far from guaranteed) that he would be able to acquire Kobe and Shaq. The stakes were high, the odds were long, and the entire scheme could have easily ended in disaster. If Kobe had been taken twelfth in the draft, the Lakers would have traded away their center for nothing. If they hadn't been able to deal Lynch and Peeler away, they couldn't have cleared the cap room and signed Shaq.

But Jerry West took his bold gamble and he won big time. It was the boldest sports move I have seen in my entire career. Even though my team was on the losing end of that deal, I had to admire the sheer chutzpah of Jerry West.

## THE BOLDNESS OF JESUS

The sixth great paradox of leadership: *Your toughest crises are your best opportunities*. The issue: boldness.

A wise leader knows that crises are opportunities for growth, learning, change, leverage, and expansion. A wise leader knows how to boldly seize opportunities when others would shrink in fear. If you want to succeed—and succeed *big!*—you must be willing to take a chance and leave your security blanket behind.

The great model of bold leadership, of course, was Jesus of Nazareth. One of the boldest things about him was his powerful personality. In John 18 is the famous scene where Jesus was in the garden with his disciples—all but Judas. Judas entered, bringing with him a detachment of Roman soldiers and Jesus' religious opponents, the chief priests and the Pharisees. When Jesus saw his enemies and Judas the betrayer approaching, he stepped forward and asked them, "Who do you want?"

"Jesus of Nazareth," they replied.

"I am," Jesus said simply—using precisely the same words that God spoke to Moses from the burning bush (Exodus 3:14).

When Jesus spoke those words, John 18:6 records, the soldiers and religious extremists "drew back and fell to the ground." Now that's boldness! That's a powerful personality! With just two monosyllabic words, "I am," Jesus knocked his enemies flat on their posteriors.

Jesus stood up to kings and rulers. He preached to crowds. He confronted every kind of evil, from human hypocrisy to demonic assault. He afflicted the comfortable, and comforted the afflicted. He healed the lame, blind, crippled, and mute. Matthew 15:31 tells us that "the people were amazed when they saw" all the things Jesus had done. Bold action always produces astonishment, and generates credibility in a leader. Jesus took bold action, and his boldness attracted many to his cause.

Jesus also spoke powerful words. Again and again, we read that people were amazed at what he said, because he taught boldly, as a person who had full authority (see Matthew 7:28–29; Luke 4:32). His message was attractive to many people and swelled the ranks of his followers—but it also alienated some. Bold words can make you a target as a leader. Mark 11:18 tells us that when the religious leaders heard of Jesus' teaching, they "began looking for a way to kill him, for they feared him, because the whole crowd was amazed at his teaching."

Bold actions as a leader can make you a target. Great leaders do not go out of their way to alienate people, but if you are not making some enemies, then you are not leading as boldly as you should. Boldness is divisive; it attracts some people and repels others—and that's as it should be.

Finally, Jesus transformed the world. His message of love, compassion, and human brotherhood has influenced every great humanitarian movement in history.

For example, the modern hospital movement is rooted in the stories of Jesus going from town to town, healing the sick. That movement continued through the earliest days of the Christian church. When plague swept Rome under emperor Flavius Claudius Julianus, Christians risked death to feed and care for the sick, making Julianus complain that the "Galileans" (as he called Christians) cared for "not only their poor, but ours as well." The eighteenth-century English preacher John Wesley opened England's first free hospital. Christian missionaries founded more than 1,200 hospitals and dispensaries, plus over eighty leprosariums throughout India.

The abolition movement that fought slavery had its roots in the bold teachings of Jesus of Nazareth. The Christians abolitionists who followed in Jesus' footsteps ranged from the Quaker activist Lucretia Mott to black itinerant preacher Sojourner Truth to evangelical activists Charles G. Finney of America and William Wilberforce of England.

The civil rights movement is something else that stems from Jesus' teaching. The great Christian preacher and civil rights leader Martin Luther King Jr. encouraged his followers to adopt "that spirit born of the teachings of the Nazarene, who promised mercy to the merciful, who lifted the lowly, strengthened the weak, ate with publicans, and made the captives free."

The boldness of Jesus transformed the world in so many ways and he created a legacy that impacts us still today. He was persecuted for his boldness because of it. That is why his leadership model is the greatest leadership style the world has ever seen.

# PATTON'S OUTLINE FOR BOLD LEADERSHIP

General George S. Patton was a bold leader—a man who thrived on crisis. The United States Military Academy at West Point maintains a library of books that were owned and annotated by General Patton. Reading his margin notations in those books, you get a glimpse into the mind of one of the greatest military leaders of all time. One of the books in that collection is a textbook called *Elements of Strategy*, which Patton studied when he was a West Point cadet. Opening the flyleaf of that book, you find an interesting note in Patton's own hand. It reads:

*Qualities of a Great General*

1. Tactically aggressive (loves a fight)
2. Strength of character
3. Steadiness of purpose
4. Acceptance of responsibility

5. Energy
6. Good health

That fascinating entry is dated 29 April 1909, meaning he wrote that observation near the end of his final term at West Point and shortly before he received his commission as a second lieutenant in the U.S. Army. Even at that early point in his career, Patton was committed to studying the lives of great leaders, understanding the qualities of great leadership, and building those qualities into his own life. When you boil down the six qualities of a great leader that he espoused, you find one common thread running throughout: *boldness*. His approach to any crisis in life was to tackle it boldly.

"Daring is wisdom," Patton once said. "It is the highest part of war." On another occasion, he observed, "Decisive action is the key to success. Indecision is, in fact, a decision to do nothing. Failure to act appropriately and decisively when an opportunity presents itself is to concede the initiative to the enemy." And in a field notebook he once wrote, "Success in war depends upon the golden rule of war: speed, simplicity, boldness . . . The fog of war works both ways. The enemy is as much in the dark as you are. BE BOLD!"

The rest of this chapter will take a closer look at what Patton's six qualities mean, and how they can help you turn your crises into opportunities. We will see that all great leaders possess these six bold qualities.

*Tactically aggressive: Be boldly decisive.*

Bold decision making is the key to radical transformation. There is risk to any decisive move—but the risk of failure is usually far outweighed by the unlimited upside. Some people avoid risk and avoid decision making until all the information is in. What they are really doing is deciding *not* to decide.

Look at it this way: If you know everything there is to know about a situation, there's no decision to be made—just an obvious conclusion to be drawn. Leaders make decisions precisely because the best course of action is *not* obvious. You don't need leaders to point out the obvious; you need leaders to point the way through confusion.

A time of crisis does not give us time to calmly, patiently collect all the facts. Decision making means choosing a course of action before all the facts are in. It involves taking the incomplete information you have, analyzing it as logically as possible, computing the odds as closely as possible, combining those results with intuition, experience, and gut instinct—then taking a deep breath and going for it.

On the morning of May 1, 1863, the Army of Northern Virginia was camped on the south side of the Rappahannock River, near Chancellorsville, Virginia. General Robert E. Lee and General T. J. "Stonewall" Jackson had spent a year battling the more numerous and better equipped Union forces, winning battle after battle. But the Union forces had rallied and were closing in on Lee's army. It was a time of crisis—and opportunity. Everything was riding on the decision Lee and Jackson would make on that cold morning on the first of May. It would be one of the shortest councils of war ever held—and one of the most crucial.

"Well," said Lee, "how do you intend to get at those people, General?"

Jackson showed Lee a hand-drawn map. "I plan to go around there," he said, indicating a route through the woods that passed perilously close to the Union pickets.

"What do you propose to make that movement with?" asked Lee.

"With my whole corps," Jackson replied. "Twenty-eight thousand men."

Lee saw at a glance that what Jackson proposed was the most daring gambit that had ever been attempted—not only in the Civil War but perhaps in any war in history. It was risky for Jackson's forces because it would involve moving thousands of men stealthily across the Union front—a dangerous twelve-mile journey on narrow backwoods trails. The chances of detection were high, and if Jackson's troops were attacked while strung out along the trail in the woods, the results would be disastrous.

It was also risky for Lee in that he would be left with nothing but two divisions—a mere fourteen thousand men—to face General Hooker's forces of seventy-five thousand Union soldiers. The idea of splitting up his already outnumbered forces flew in the face of every tenet of conventional military wisdom. But Lee was convinced that General Hooker had lost his nerve. Though Hooker could have attacked and defeated Lee at any time, Hooker waited—and that hesitation on the part of the enemy emboldened Lee to accept Stonewall Jackson's risky plan.

"Well," Lee said after only a few seconds' consideration, "go on." Those three words constituted a military decision of unimaginable boldness. Jackson took his men on a march through the woods. The corps made its way undetected and arrived on schedule at the vulnerable right flank of Hooker's Union forces. On May 2 General Lee spread his vastly outnumbered forces thinly across the main battlefront and launched an assault. Hooker's forces thought the entire Army of Northern Virginia was attacking from that direction. The Union forces fought back—only to be thrown into a panic when Stonewall Jackson's men appeared from the woods and shredded their right flank. By May 3 Lee's and Jackson's forces had joined up. The Battle of Chancellorsville was a great victory, and it was won by sheer, outrageous, audacious boldness. It stands as a masterpiece of military leadership.

I've almost always found that delaying a decision is far more dangerous then deciding before all the facts are in. When a decision is called for, decide quickly, decide boldly. If you don't have all the facts, settle for 75 percent. Settle for 50 percent. If the situation demands, settle for 25 percent. Get your best sense of the situation, take counsel of your boldness rather than your fears, then *go*.

"Leaders take risks," observes John C. Maxwell. "That's not to say they are reckless, because good leaders aren't. But they don't always take the safest route. Rarely can a person break ground and play it safe at the same time. Often, leaders must take others into the unknown and march them off the map."

Sometimes people take risks and the decisions turn out to be bad. But you can't beat yourselves up about it. One of my big struggles over the years has been to learn not to second guess myself to pieces.

In 1970 I was general manager of the Chicago Bulls. I was going into my first NBA draft. Our coach, Dick Motta, wanted us to take a kid named Nate Archibald from the University of Texas at El Paso as our first pick. But our college scout, Jerry Krause, really wanted Jimmy Collins out of New Mexico State. We decided to take Collins first, then Archibald on our second round, if he was still available. Dick Motta wasn't happy with that decision, but he was outvoted. Dick was even less happy when Archibald was taken by Cincinnati just a few picks ahead of us.

If you were following pro basketball in those days, you know how it turned out. Nate Archibald had a brilliant career, and went into the Basketball Hall of Fame. Jimmy Collins just never panned out. Two years after we took him as our first pick, he was out of the game.

It's been years since Nate Archibald retired, yet the memory of my decision still gives me heart pangs. Fortunately, I've made more good decisions than bad, and I've lasted thirty-five years in the NBA. As Hall of Fame baseball manager Connie Mack observed, "You can't grind grain with water that's already gone down the creek." When a decision has been made and the die cast, then murder the alternatives.

Sometimes boldness seems like foolhardiness. At a moment of crisis, when you make your bold decision, the path before you may seem impossible. You don't have the people or the resources to pull it off. But boldness inspires boldness. Bold leaders inspire and attract bold followers.

The 1967 NFL Championship game in Green Bay, Wisconsin, is probably the most famous game in football history. It is better known as the Ice Bowl. The reason it is so famous is that it was a hard-fought contest under adverse conditions, and it came down to a single bold decision on the very last play. The Green Bay Packers were hosting the Dallas Cowboys in sub-zero weather. The two coaches are men of legend—the Packers' Vince Lombardi and the Cowboys' Tom Landry. The two quarterbacks in that game are equally legendary: the Packers' Bart Starr and the Cowboys' Don Meredith.

It was so cold, the football was like a rock. Receivers had to catch with near-frostbitten hands. Deep passing was impossible on the ice-slick field, so most plays were short-yardage passes and runs. At halftime the Packers narrowly led, 14–10. No one scored in the third quarter. Dallas halfback Dan Reeves (now the Atlanta Falcons' head coach), recalls, "I remember getting my lip busted, and no blood came out. My throat burned from breathing in that cold air."

A Dallas touchdown in the fourth quarter put the Cowboys up, 17–14. With 4:50 to play, Green Bay got the ball on its own 32. Bart Starr knew he didn't have much time to score. Carefully managing the clock, Starr and the Packers steadily gained yardage with short slants and handoffs. Finally, with sixteen seconds remaining in regulation play, it was third and goal, and the Packers had the ball inside the Cowboys one-yard line. Starr burned his last timeout and went to the sidelines to confer with Lombardi.

The Packers had two choices. Option 1: An easy field goal to send the game into overtime. That would have been the prudent choice. Downside: Nobody wanted to spend one more second on that frozen field than necessary. Option 2: Go for it. Run or pass it, but just go for the win. Downside: If the attempt failed, there were no timeouts remaining and no time to bring on the kicking team or run another play—and the Packers would lose the championship.

At the sideline, Starr gave Coach Lombardi the best information he had about the situation. He told the coach that linemen Jerry Kramer and Ken Bowman had assured him they could wedge Cowboys' defensive tackle Jethro Pugh off the line. That would open a hole for Starr. "If they move Pugh," said Bart Starr, "I can keep the ball and sneak it in."

Lombardi pondered for all of about two seconds. "Run it," he said, "and let's get outta here."

So Starr went back on the field and called perhaps the most famous play in NFL history. The ball was snapped, guard Jerry Kramer leaped forward and stood Pugh up, center Ken Bowman knocked Pugh back from the line, and Bart Starr lunged across the goal line.

In that instant, the Packers had the touchdown, the win, and the league championship.

Lombardi's decision was the right decision. It was proof of the paradox that your toughest crisis is your best opportunity—if you are a tactically aggressive, boldly assertive leader. When a crisis presents itself, act boldly and decisively, and if you are prepared, if you make your decision on the basis of the best possible information, odds are you will win.

*Strength of character: Be boldly right.*

Leadership is not just about winning. It's about being right—morally, ethically, spiritually. And that means, of course, that we must be leaders with bold, strong principles. That way, when we win, we will be winning on behalf of a just and righteous cause.

Christian X was king of the Danes during World War II. The people of Denmark remember him as a man of character, courage, and principle—a leader who was bold and boldly right in what he did. Every morning, he rode without bodyguards in an open carriage through the streets of Copenhagen. He trusted his people and wanted them to feel free to come up to him, greet him, and shake his hand.

In 1940 Nazi Germany invaded Denmark. Like so many other European nations that fell before the Nazi juggernaut, this small Scandinavian country was quickly conquered. But the spirit of the Danish people and their king proved unquenchable. Even after the Nazis had taken control of the nation, King Christian X continued his morning carriage rides. He boldly led his people in a quiet but courageous resistance movement.

On one occasion, the king noticed a Nazi flag flying over a public building in Copenhagen. He went to the German kommandant and asked that the flag be removed. "The flag flies," the kommandant replied, "because I ordered it flown. Request denied."

"I *demand* that it come down," said the king. "If you do not have it removed, a Danish soldier will go and remove it."

"Then he will be shot," said the kommandant.

"I don't think so," said King Christian, "for I shall be that soldier."

The flag was removed.

Later, the Nazis decided that all eight thousand Jews in Denmark would be rounded up and sent to concentration camps in central Europe. Georg Ferdinand Duckwitz, a German diplomat with a troubled conscience, secretly informed King Christian of the Nazi plans. So the king organized a resistance effort that smuggled 7,500 Jews to Sweden within a single two-week period. The remaining five hundred Jews were rounded up by the Nazis and sent to Theresienstadt, an internment ghetto in Czechoslovakia. King Christian interceded on their behalf and all but fifty-one survived their treatment at the hands of the Nazis.

King Christian paid a price for his bold courage. The Nazis imprisoned him from 1943 until the fall of the Third Reich in 1945. An old man in his seventies, imprisonment was hard on his health. He died two years after his release.

We all want leaders who will boldly do the right thing, no matter what the cost or the consequences. We want heroes of character and courage. You and I must be leaders who will boldly do the right thing.

How do we know what is the right thing to do?

One rule of thumb: *Do what is unpopular; the majority is usually wrong.* That is not as undemocratic a statement as it sounds.

Pure democracy is mob rule. And mobs are not very good at making decisions. But that is the genius of our American representative democracy. We don't have a pure democracy, in which voters decide on every government policy. Instead voters choose representatives who make the tough decisions the mob is incapable of making.

Leaders must often buck the tide and lead their people where the people themselves would never go. Great leaders take the heat, bear the criticism and scorn, and see their bold, unpopular decisions through to a successful conclusion. After the dust settles, the people look back and say, "We were with you all along."

Wal-Mart founder Sam Walton affirms this advice. "Swim upstream," he once said. "Go the other way. Ignore the conventional wisdom. If everybody else is doing it one way, there's a good chance you can find your niche by going in exactly the opposite direction—but be prepared for a lot of folks to wave you down and tell you you're headed the wrong way."

The first task on any leader's job description should read, "Willingly become unpopular." Leaders must fight popular opinion and do what is unpopular whenever it is necessary. And great leaders know that it is often necessary—because it's more important to do what's right than to do what's popular.

Another rule of thumb: *Do what is risky; the safest choice is probably wrong.* "Safety first" is not a leadership motto. It is not an ethical principle. It is usually just an excuse for cowardice.

Dietrich Bonhoeffer was a leader who took risks to do the right thing—and he willingly paid the ultimate price. Bonhoeffer, a German theologian, studied at the University of Berlin and Union Theological Seminary in New York. Bonhoeffer was appalled by Adolf Hitler and his anti-Semitism. He and other courageous Christian leaders founded the "Confessing Church" to oppose anti-Semitism and Nazism in Germany. Although the organization, and the seminary at which he taught, came under increasing persecution, Bonhoeffer continued to teach and preach, traveling secretly from village to village throughout Germany, confronting the doctrines of Nazi hate. It was around this time he wrote *The Cost of Discipleship*, a book about what it means and what it costs to be a radically committed Christian.

During the early 1940s, as Hitler's war machine roared across Europe, Bonhoeffer devoted himself to "Operation Seven," helping Jews escape from Germany into Switzerland. He also became involved in another project, a strange one for a man who had once been a devout pacifist: He became a conspirator in a plot to assassinate Adolf Hitler.

The Gestapo arrested Bonhoeffer in April 1943 for his "Operation Seven" activities. On July 20, 1944, while he was in prison, members of the resistance carried out the attempt on Hitler's life. Colonel Claus von Stauffenberg, one of several conspiring German officers with access to Hitler, left a suitcase bomb in Hitler's fortified offices at Wolf's Lair in East Prussia. The bomb exploded but Hitler escaped—shaken, but unharmed. Von Stauffenberg was executed, and Bonhoeffer's role in the plot was discovered.

The Gestapo transferred Bonhoeffer from a prison in Berlin to the famous hellhole called Buchenwald, and later to the Flossenburg concentration camp. There he was hanged on April 9, 1945. He was thirty-nine. Less than three weeks later, Hitler committed suicide, the Flossenburg camp was liberated, and the war in Europe was over.

A German doctor who watched Bonhoeffer's execution later said he went to his death "brave and composed . . . I have hardly ever seen a man die so entirely submissive to the will of God."

Some might say Dietrich Bonhoeffer took a bold gamble and lost, and that he gave his life for nothing. I say he was a bold leader who took a bold stand. He was boldly right. Great leaders do not operate out of fear or timidity. In a crisis, leaders must be people of strong character, choosing to do what is a morally and ethically right, regardless of the personal price to be paid.

## *Steadiness of purpose: Be boldly committed.*

In 1997 I had the privilege of hearing former prime minister Margaret Thatcher, England's renowned "Iron Lady," when she spoke at a luncheon in Orlando. Though she had been away from the corridors of power for years, she had an unmistakable presence, an aura of strength and power about her.

During the Q&A session after her talk, she was asked about the ingredients of a successful leader. There are four ingredients to being a great leader, she replied:

> First, know what matters to you. Have a set of principles and follow them. Your principles serve as the foundation of your leadership. Second, speak up! Be bold and fearless about asserting your principles. Third, anticipate problems. Use information, instinct, and intuition to foresee problems and crises before anyone else does. Fourth, make bold decisions. Base your decisions on your principles and on the information and insight you have. Meet problems and opportunities head-on, then take bold action. Those are the four ingredients of a great leader.

Lady Thatcher was talking about steadiness of purpose. It means being committed to your vision ("Know what matters to you"), boldly committed to asserting your vision ("Speak up!"), committed to solving problems and removing obstacles to that vision ("Anticipate problems"), and committed to making sound, firm decisions to advance that vision ("Make bold decisions").

Lady Thatcher gave basically the same advice to President George H. W. Bush after the 1990 Iraqi invasion of Kuwait. When President Bush appeared to be wavering in his resolve to turn back the invasion, she told him, "George, this is no time to go wobbly." And she was right. Steadiness of purpose and bold commitment won that war and liberated the people of Kuwait.

Unfortunately, many leaders today have compromised their commitment and steadiness of purpose. Instead of leading, they seek consensus. Instead of deciding, they take polls.

Understand, there's nothing wrong with involving people in the process of solving problems and setting goals. It's important that leaders listen to people. It's healthy for leaders to invite criticism and debate. Want to have a knock-down, drag-out discussion in which all sides of the issue are presented? I'm all for it—as long as you don't abdicate your role as a leader and a decision maker, as long as you don't compromise your commitment to your goals and purpose.

Many so-called leaders today are really just facilitators of groups or committees. They don't lead, and they don't decide. They just moderate discussions. They let the group decide. But there is a fundamental and fatal design flaw in any group decision-making process: Groupthink is never bold-think. Margaret Thatcher framed it succinctly in this rhetorical question: "What great cause would have been fought and won under the banner, 'I stand for consensus'?"

Consensus is almost always the pooling of the fears, timidities, and cautious inclinations of the group. Boldness comes from solitary, committed leadership—not from a committee. Boldness comes from the power of a single, committed personality remaining true to his or her purpose. The great leaders of history have shown this to be true.

"Most important decisions in corporate life," says Lee Iacocca, "are made by individuals, not by committees. My policy has always been to be democratic, all the way to the point of the decision. Then I become the ruthless commander: 'Okay, I've heard everybody. Now here's what we're going to do.'" That's exactly what former secretary of state Dean Acheson meant when he said, "The capacity for decision is God's rarest gift of mind to men."

But you may ask, *What about self-doubt? How can I maintain steadiness of purpose when I'm riddled with self-doubt?* The truth is that most (and perhaps all) great leaders have been afflicted with self-doubt. It's part of the human condition. George Washington told the Continental Congress: "I do not think myself equal to the command."

Question: Who was the most forceful, confident, courageous leader of the twentieth century? Most historians would name Winston Churchill. But few people realize that Churchill, in his private moments, was tortured by doubts. Throughout his adult life, the great British statesman suffered chronic bouts of depression, gloom, and self-deprecation that he called "the Black Dog." During World War II he often questioned whether he had the ability to lead the English people through the most terrifying era in human history.

Even after the Allies defeated Hitler, Churchill expressed misgivings. On V-E Day—the day the Allies won victory in Europe—Churchill publicly announced the victory of "the cause of freedom in every land," but wondered aloud to his private secretary, "What have we accomplished? What will lie between the white snows of Russia and the white cliffs of Dover?"

Nevertheless, Churchill's public pronouncements were always tough statements of fierce commitment and determination. In his first speech as prime minister, Churchill vowed "to wage war until victory is won." One month later, as the Nazis were advancing and the Allied front in Europe was collapsing, he told the British people:

> We shall not flag or fail. We shall go on to the end, we shall fight in France, we shall fight on the seas and the oceans, we shall fight with growing confidence and growing strength in the air, we shall defend our Island, whatever the cost may be. We shall fight on the beaches, we shall fight on the landing grounds, we shall fight in the fields and in the streets, we shall fight in the hills. We shall never surrender!

Bold words of uncompromising commitment—especially given the fact that the Nazis were advancing, and the Allied front in Europe was collapsing at the time!

Churchill conducted himself with complete steadiness of purpose. In so doing, he boldly imposed his will upon history. His iron will made up for what he couldn't summon from his heart.

Sometimes boldness is a bluff. But all poker players know that a bluff can become reality. A bold poker player with a pair of threes can steal the pot. It's boldness that wins, not the cards you are dealt.

So set aside your doubts. Remember that great leaders are not people without doubts and fears. They are people who have *mastered* their doubts and fears.

Act boldly, stay committed, and doubt will ultimately be replaced by confidence—the confidence that comes with achievement. Act boldly, remain committed to your vision, and your vision will ultimately win. President Theodore Roosevelt said, "In any moment of decision, the best thing you can do is the right thing; the next thing is the wrong thing; and the worst thing you can do is nothing." Which do you want to do?

## *Acceptance of responsibility: Be boldly accountable.*

In February 2001 the nuclear attack submarine USS *Greenville* rapidly surfaced and collided with a Japanese fishing trawler, the *Ehime Maru*, off the coast of Hawaii. The trawler, which was being used to train students for the Japanese fishing industry, sank quickly. Nine people died, including several Japanese students. The incident set off a diplomatic crisis between the U.S. and Japan.

The captain of the *Greenville* later stood before a military court of inquiry, suspected of dereliction of duty and negligent homicide. The result is a case study in what it means (and what it does not mean) to accept responsibility. "I accept full responsibility and accountability for the actions of the crew," the captain testified. "For the rest of my life I will live with the horrible consequences of my decisions and actions that resulted in the loss of the *Ehime Maru*."

Fine so far—but then the captain went on to blame the officer of the deck for taking inadequate precautions during the surfacing maneuver. When it was pointed out to the captain that he had ordered the officer of the deck to conduct a ten-minute maneuver in five minutes, the captain claimed he had only given his subordinate a "rough time target," and it was up to the officer of the deck to perform the maneuver safely.

He went on to say, "I did not micromanage my crew. I empowered them to do their jobs." Well, that's what a leader is supposed to do—delegate and empower, not micromanage. But *delegate* does not mean *abdicate*. Although a leader empowers others to get the job done, the leader is still fully responsible and accountable for the results.

The captain of the *Greenville* accepted "responsibility and accountability" for the accident—then passed it off on a subordinate. But a leader can't have it both ways. A leader can't say, "I'm responsible, I'm accountable—but don't blame me, it's not my fault!" That makes no sense at all.

When you accept a leadership position, you place yourself at risk. Your success depends on the success of your subordinates. If they fail, you fail. You cannot say, "Well, they failed, but I'm not responsible." Responsibility for the success or failure of your people is precisely the risk you accept when you become a leader. If you want to have it both ways, you are not fit to lead.

One leader who truly understood the meaning of responsibility and accountability was John F. Kennedy. Kennedy was once on the receiving end of a collision at sea. Before dawn on August 2, 1943, a young Lieutenant Kennedy was commanding an eighty-foot boat, *PT 109*, in the waters around the Solomon Islands. Kennedy and his crew were hunting a Japanese warship, the destroyer *Amagiri*. In the predawn darkness they suddenly found themselves in the path of the destroyer. It struck the PT boat amidships, slicing it in half.

Two crewmen went down with the boat. Other crewmen suffered burns and lacerations. Kennedy suffered a back injury, but was able to swim over three miles while towing an injured crewman with a strap of the man's life-vest in his teeth. There were eleven survivors in all, and it took them four hours to reach the nearest island. They were stranded for six days, with nothing to eat but coconuts until they were rescued. JFK took responsibility for the safety of his men, helping to keep their spirits up through a harrowing ordeal.

Years later, as a newly inaugurated president, Kennedy showed he could take a different kind of responsibility—the kind that accompanies failure.

In April 1961, just three months into his presidency, he gave the go-ahead to the infamous Bay of Pigs invasion of Cuba. The three-day battle was an ill-conceived disaster from start to finish. The mission involved 1,500 U.S.-trained Cuban exiles who were expected to invade Cuba and trigger an uprising that would unseat Castro. The strategy was flawed, the forces were too few, the weapons inadequate, and the intelligence virtually nil. The tiny force of exile invaders was quickly overpowered by twenty thousand of Castro's well-armed, well-trained troops. The U.S. was humiliated, and Castro's stature soared.

JFK refused to duck the blame. He went on television and accepted full responsibility and accountability for the fiasco—and didn't proceed to parcel off pieces of blame to subordinates. The buck stopped with Kennedy.

Great leaders are big enough and strong enough to accept full responsibility for their own decisions—and the actions of subordinates. And the result? Almost always, the leader experiences a surge of respect. After Kennedy's unconditional acceptance of responsibility for the Bay of Pigs failure, the Gallup poll registered a 61-percent approval rating for the president. Obviously the public didn't approve of Kennedy's military failure—but they did approve of the character he displayed in accepting the blame. Great leaders are boldly accountable. They accept full responsibility for themselves and their people.

### Energy: Be boldly vigorous.

It is not enough to be mentally, morally, and spiritually committed to your bold course of action. You must also commit every ounce of energy to ensuring that your course of action succeeds. Great leaders are energized and energetic and they radiate energy to the people around them.

Energy is contagious. If you live boldly, people around you will be emboldened. If you have confidence in yourself, people around you will be confident. If you display energy and enthusiasm, you will inspire energy and enthusiasm in others.

As leadership guru Tom Peters says, "I trust a leader who shows up, makes the tough call, takes the heat, sleeps well amidst the furor, and aggressively chomps into the next task in the morning with visible vitality."

Postmodern writer-philosopher Jean Baudrillard, author of *The Murder of the Real*, likens the energy of a business leader to the energy of an athlete. "Executives are like joggers," he observes. "If you stop a jogger, he goes on running on the spot. If you drag an executive away from his business, he goes on talking business. He never stops hurtling onwards, making decisions and executing them."

That is how great leaders are: Always in motion, always vigorous, always in action. Great leaders pause, but they rarely stop. They are energized by their vision, and their energy will not allow them to slow down for long.

### Good health: Be boldly physical.

"Baseball," said Yogi Berra, "is 90 percent mental, and the other half is physical." Well, Yogi's math is flawed, but other than that, he's right on. The same can be said of leadership—90 percent mental, 50 percent physical. Great leaders are healthy people. They are people who are boldly physical.

Being boldly physical has to do with a certain mind-set, an aggressiveness, a willingness to get into the game with your elbows, forearms, and knees, and mix it up. Being boldly physical is about having a love for competition and contact.

One year when I was general manager of the Philadelphia 76ers our owner, Harold Katz, told the team he wanted his players to adopt a new approach to the game: a physical one. "This is a team of nice guys," he said. "We lead the NBA in helping guys to their feet. That's gotta stop. I want this team to lead the NBA in knocking guys on their can." So the 76ers adopted a more physical approach to the game. Incidentally, that was the year we won an NBA championship.

Being boldly physical also has to do with physical preparation—with being better conditioned and having more physical stamina than your competitors. Bob Griese, quarterback of the 1972 Miami Dolphins—the only NFL team ever to have a completely undefeated season—recalls the grueling workouts that coach Don Shula used to put his team through. The team would work out in pads under the hot Florida sun from 7:00 A.M. until dark, with breaks for meals and team meetings. Shula would pit offense against defense in intensive Oklahoma drills, seven-on-sevens, and scrimmages, and he'd have them do endless sideline-to-sideline sprints to build up their endurance.

"It was punishing, it was a murderous schedule," Griese recalls, "but there were few complaints, because [Shula] had pared the team down to a hard-core bunch of guys who wanted to win. We knew that to win, we needed to be tougher and more dedicated than the guys on the other side of the ball." Griese said they knew pro football was not the kind of job where you put in eight hours and pick up a paycheck. "If you're not ready to do whatever it takes to win, you shouldn't be there."

The payoff came in a game against the reigning Super Bowl champions, the Kansas City Chiefs, on Christmas Day 1971. At the end of regulation play, the game was tied at 24. So they went into sudden death overtime. The first overtime period expired without a score.

Going into a second overtime period, Griese recalls thinking, *Geez! They can't beat us! They're tiring out, and we've still got plenty of steam left!* That's when the Dolphins understood why Coach Shula had subjected his team to so many grueling workouts. The game had come down to a test of endurance—and the Chiefs were tiring out! The Dolphins were the better-conditioned team and they knew it—and they won the game by a field goal.

You can't be at your best as a leader if your mind and body are not at their best. The stress of leadership can cause physical, emotional, and behavioral disorders. If your body is not getting the rest and nutrition it needs, you not only risk your health and vitality, but also your personal relationships and effectiveness and productivity as a leader.

So a key dimension of being boldly physical involves taking good care of your health. Take exercise regularly—a great stress reliever. Follow a healthy diet. Avoid alcohol and caffeine, both of which can disrupt your sleep patterns. Get plenty of rest (many of the world's most effective leaders take afternoon naps!). And make sure that you balance your work with a healthy dose of play.

Another key dimension of being boldly physical involves mental toughness. Physical toughness is impossible without mental toughness. You must *want* to be boldly physical, you must crave the process (no matter how painful) in order to acquire the prowess. Former NHL hockey player Bobby Clarke put it this way: "I'm convinced the head goes before the body. You end up not wanting to pay the price. It happens to every athlete eventually. In a physical contact sport, it shows up quicker. A guy gets tired of hitting or being hit. You can't hide that once it happens."

Great leaders are mentally tough and physically bold. They know that good health supports great leadership. Great leaders know that ninety percent of the leadership role is mental, and the other half is physical—boldly, aggressively physical.

These, then, are General Patton's six keys to bold, effective leadership:

1. "Tactically aggressive"—Be Boldly Decisive!
2. "Strength of character"—Be Boldly Right
3. "Steadiness of purpose"—Be Boldly Committed
4. "Acceptance of responsibility"—Be Boldly Accountable
5. "Energy"—Be Boldly Vigorous
6. "Good Health"—Be Boldly Physical

I never knew a great leader who didn't have all six of these crucial qualities of boldness. So if you want to be a great leader—*be bold!*

## BOLD MEEKNESS

For great leaders, the toughest crisis truly is the greatest opportunity. This is a paradox, and that is why this truth is so hard for us to learn and practice. We consider a crisis something to dread, something to avoid. But almost every crisis that ever bedeviled a leader was really an opportunity in disguise. Met head on, with an attitude of boldness and daring, a crisis can be transformed into an opportunity beyond our wildest dreams.

Over half a century ago, Brooklyn Dodgers general manager Branch Rickey recognized a crisis. It was a crisis in baseball and a crisis in American society. The crisis was called *racism*. But Branch Rickey saw in that crisis an opportunity for transformation. He believed that the time had come to transform the game of baseball and to transform society. But, of course, the key issue for Branch Rickey was that he wanted to win baseball games. He believed that African-American players were a great untapped source of talent—and he was right. The Dodgers would later become very successful with such black stars as Jackie Robinson, Roy Campanella, and Don Newcombe.

Rickey called Robinson to his office for a meeting, so they could size each other up. Robinson came, but he thought it was a gesture on Rickey's part, not a serious attempt to bring him onto the team. Rickey had never been more serious in his life.

The meeting lasted three hours. Rickey did most of the talking, and what he told Jackie Robinson wasn't pretty. He told the black player to expect the worst indignities imaginable: racial slurs, threats, even assault; hostile teammates and even more hostile opponents; abusive fans; hotel and restaurant managers who would refuse him service. Rickey even role-played some of the vile behavior he expected Robinson to have to face. Robinson found himself angry by the end of that meeting.

"Mr. Rickey," he said at last, "do you want a player who's afraid to fight back?"

"Absolutely not!" snorted Branch Rickey. "I want a player with the raw guts to *not* fight back!"

What Rickey was asking of Robinson went completely against the man's grain. Jackie Robinson was a proud man, a fighter, and fiercely competitive. In the Army, he had risked court-martial when he refused to move to the back of a military bus.

"I see," Robinson said after a few moments' reflection. "You want me to turn the other cheek."

"You're getting it," said Rickey. He pulled out a book—Giovanni Papini's *The Life of Christ*—and he opened it to a passage dealing with the peaceful nonresistance of Jesus of Nazareth. Robinson read it . . . and understood. From that day forward he took his glove and his bat and he followed in the footsteps of Jesus. He was booed and spat upon and called names and abused and heckled. And he never fought back. It wasn't that he was afraid to fight. He had the courage *not* to fight. In the process, Jackie Robinson changed the game of baseball and the attitudes of millions of people.

There is a word that is used in the Greek New Testament to describe the kind of attitude shown by Jesus and by Jackie Robinson: *praus*. There is no good equivalent to that word in the English language, but it is usually translated as *meek*. It is the word used in Matthew 5:5, where Jesus said, "Blessed are the *meek*, for they will inherit the earth." Unfortunately, when people hear the word *meek*, they think it means weak and timid.

The Greek word *praus* actually means a gentleness of spirit, a willingness to rely on God rather than ourselves as a defense against injustice. It is not rooted in weakness, but in a trusting faith in God's strength. And here, again, we find another great paradox of power.

What both Jesus and Jackie Robinson demonstrated through their lives was not weakness, but strength under control. They were not intimidated into a posture of weakness and meekness. Rather, they projected a bold and courageous meekness to the world.

Bold meekness! What a paradox!

And what a transforming truth.

Jackie Robinson boldly faced his toughest crisis and turned it into a golden opportunity. That is one of the greatest of all lessons of leadership: The toughest crisis you face is just the flip side of your greatest opportunity.

# The Greatest Leader Is a Servant

The final paradox of power is the most profound of the seven: *The greatest leader is a servant of all.*

I was fortunate that the man who first mentored me in the principles and practice of leadership was a true servant leader. I've talked about him before: Mr. R. E. Littlejohn.

The poet Longfellow once wrote:

> Lives of great men all remind us
> We can make our lives sublime,
> And departing, leave behind us,
> Footprints on the sands of time.

Mr. R. E. Littlejohn left footprints on the sands of my life. I watched his life, I had long talks with him, and I learned from him. He was the first and greatest influence on my professional life.

Throughout my four years in Spartanburg, South Carolina, managing the Spartanburg Phillies, and long after I left in 1968, I called and talked to my mentor every other week or so. Whenever I faced a big decision, I would be sure to get his counsel and observations. Throughout my career, I never made a major move without running it past Mr. Littlejohn.

Why? Because I knew a great leader when I saw one. And what was it that made Mr. R. E. Littlejohn great? His humility. He was a servant. I knew that he was the kind of person I wanted to become, and I made up my mind to learn everything I could from him.

I wasn't the only person who was drawn to the servant leadership of this man. Every Christmas Day, Bob Carpenter, the owner of the Philadelphia Phillies, would call Mr. R. E. to pay his respects. Mr. Carpenter also often went to Mr. R. E. whenever he had a big decision or a problem to solve. Though he was a major league baseball owner and Mr. R. E. was an owner in the low minors, Mr. Carpenter knew big-league wisdom and character when he saw it.

Once, in 1965, Mr. R. E. and I drove together from Spartanburg to Florence, South Carolina, to talk to a prospective player. We got back to Spartanburg a little past midnight, and there was a message waiting for Mr. R. E.: "Please call John Quinn! Urgent!" Quinn was the general manager of the Philadelphia Phillies.

It turned out that he had a major personnel decision to make at the front office level, and he didn't want to make a move until he had input from Mr. R. E. I was astounded. It reaffirmed my belief: If Bob Carpenter, a big-league owner, and John Quinn, a big-league general manager, thought that much of Mr. R. E., I knew he was a leader I needed to listen to. And it spoke volumes to me about the greatness of this humble and self-effacing servant leader.

One of the lessons Mr. R. E. underscored for me again and again was the importance of humility in the leadership role. He told me that a leader should never be above doing any chore the people on the lowest rung were expected to do. A leader shouldn't hesitate to get dirt under his fingernails. "Pat," he once said, "never give the other fella the impression that you know more than he does or that you have a superior rank or attitude. When you give the impression that you are up and the other guy is down, you can no longer have any influence with him. You want to keep the lines of communication open with others? Then keep a humble spirit."

I wanted Mr. R. E. to know how much esteem I had for him, so one day I told him, "I really believe that Jesus must have been a lot like you."

I meant it as a compliment. But he was clearly embarrassed that I would say such a thing—it offended the genuine core of humility in his soul. Yet I don't think it was a sacrilegious thing to say. Certainly, Jesus is unique and his example can never be fully attained or imitated. But that should be our ambition. Jesus told his disciples that they were to make it the goal of their lives to become like him. "Follow me" (Luke 9:23), he urged them. That is, become like me, follow in my footsteps, imitate me. "I have set you an example that you should do as I have done for you" (John 13:15). And Peter wrote that Jesus left us an example, and that we should "follow in his steps" (1 Peter 2:21).

The net-net: We are to be imitators of Jesus. We are to copy his example. We are to become replicas of him—this man who exemplified leadership. Only if we work toward becoming more and more what he was can we become what he intended us to be.

## LEADING ON HIS KNEES

Jesus sure knew how to get a point across.

It was the night before he was to be taken out and crucified. Jesus knew what lay ahead of him. He had been predicting it for months. But the disciples didn't have a clue. On that particular night, they were all gathered in an upper room to celebrate the Passover. But while the disciples were all together with Jesus on that special and holy occasion, an argument broke out—an argument over *leadership*.

You can read the story in Luke 22 and John 13, but here's what happened: The disciples began to argue over which of the twelve was the greatest. After spending three years with this model of servanthood and humility, they were actually sitting around bragging and comparing egos!

There was a custom in that culture that when guests came into your home for dinner, you had a servant go around to each guest and wash their feet. In those days, travel was by foot along dusty roads, so a traveler's feet usually got tired and dirty, and a foot-washing was a refreshing experience. Obviously, foot washing was menial labor, done only by the lowliest of servants. So, as Jesus' disciples sat around trash-talking each other and acting full of themselves, a lowly servant wrapped a towel around himself, took a basin of water, and began washing the feet of the disciples.

That lowly servant's name was Jesus.

Perhaps these self-important disciples didn't notice what was happening at first. Imagine the scene: All twelve are talking and boasting. Gradually, one by one, their voices fall silent. Perhaps while Peter is blustering about some great accomplishment, he feels an elbow in his ribs. He turns, and there's John, whispering to him, "Hey! Look at that! What is Jesus doing?" There is Jesus, down on his knees, washing and drying the feet of Thomas. Then Andrew. And on down the line. Jesus even washes the feet of Judas Iscariot, the one who will betray him.

Jesus did something no leader, no master would ever do. He rendered the most menial and demeaning form of service there was in that culture. He washed and dried twenty-four grungy feet. At that moment, the discussion about who would be the greatest was ended. It was replaced by a vivid and humbling object lesson in true greatness, true leadership. Jesus, the greatest leader of all time, got down on his knees to lead.

Seeing what Jesus was doing, knowing that Jesus would soon get to his feet, Peter stood up and pridefully objected, "No! You shall never wash my feet!"

"Unless I wash you," Jesus said, "you have no part with me."

"Then, Lord," Peter answered, "don't just wash my feet, but my hands and my head as well!"

And Jesus answered, "A person who has had a bath needs only to wash his feet, and his whole person will be clean." So Peter submitted to the servanthood and leadership of Jesus (John 13:10).

I have read that story many times, and it never ceases to amaze me. Two thousand years later, it is still a disturbing image: Jesus, the Master, washing dirty feet.

If I had been Jesus, I would have handled that whole situation much differently. I would have done some big, flashy miracle to shut the disciples up. I would have said, "You dummies! You're going to sit there and argue about who's the greatest while I'm here? You want to know who is really the greatest? I'll give you three guesses, and the first two don't count!"

But Jesus had other plans. He wasn't out to impress his followers. He simply wanted to set a quiet example for them—an example of true leadership, an example of a servant. When he had finished modeling servant leadership to them, he said to them:

> You call me "Teacher" and "Lord," and rightly so, for that is what I am. Now that I, your Lord and Teacher, have washed your feet, you also should wash one another's feet. I have set you an example that you should do as I have done for you. (John 13:13–15)

Perhaps the most powerful and instructive lesson in servant leadership is that which was penned by the apostle Paul:

> Do nothing out of selfish ambition or vain conceit, but in humility consider others better than yourselves. Each of you should look not only to your own interests, but also to the interests of others. Your attitude should be the same as that of Christ Jesus: Who, being in very nature God, did not consider equality with God something to be grasped, but made himself nothing, taking the very nature of a servant, being made in human likeness. And being found in appearance as a man, he humbled himself and became obedient to death—even death on a cross! (Philippians 2:3–8)

No one in human history had more power, more authority, more right to be called great than Jesus. But the greatest leader of all emptied himself of all power and discarded all of his rights. He willingly became a servant as an example to his disciples.

And to you and me.

## THE JOURNEY OF A SERVANT LEADER

The term *servant leader* was coined by a retired AT&T executive, Robert K. Greenleaf, in an essay entitled "The Servant as Leader."

Greenleaf's essay was inspired by Herman Hesse's 1932 novel *Journey to the East*. In that novel, the narrator tells of a journey he takes with a mystical group of artists and poets, The League. Traveling with them is Leo, a servant who carries luggage and performs other menial tasks. At one point Leo disappears. A search is conducted but Leo can't be found. The League is thrown into disarray. The once-unified group is torn by strife and arguments. The narrator and others in the group lose their enthusiasm for the journey. Depressed, angry, filled with distrust, the narrator deserts The League and goes off alone.

Why was humble, self-effacing Leo the glue that held The League together? Why did his disappearance cause the group to implode? Could it be that the group could not exist without the quiet, invisible leadership of a servant?

Ten years pass, and the narrator encounters a man he is convinced is Leo, the long-lost servant. He follows the man through the streets, and up to a building—a hall where members of The League are holding a meeting. The man loses Leo in the crowd. The meeting begins, and a voice announces the arrival of the leader of The League. The leader makes his way to the platform, dressed in a regal robe trimmed in gold.

It is Leo. The long-lost servant is the leader of The League.

In his article Greenleaf says all truly great leaders are like Leo. We meet them first as servants, as people who are deeply driven by a desire to help others, love others, and serve others. Their leadership role emerges out of their servanthood. Greenleaf concludes:

> The servant leader is servant first. It begins with the natural feeling that one wants to serve. Then conscious choice brings one to aspire to lead. The best test is: Do those served grow as persons: do they, while being served, become healthier, wiser, freer, more autonomous, more likely themselves to become servants?

In recent years, Greenleaf's concept of servant leadership has been adopted and expanded by other experts in the leadership field. Numerous books have been written on the subject. They include books by James Autry, Warren Bennis, Peter Block, John Carver,

Stephen Covey, Max De Pree, Joseph Jaworski, Larraine Matusak, M. Scott Peck, Peter Senge, Peter Vaill, Margaret Wheatley, and Danah Zohar. The essence of what all of these experts tell us is that servant leadership is the way leaders *must* lead in the twenty-first century. The old leadership model of the top-down hierarchy is a dinosaur, a relic of another organizational age.

Amazingly, what's old is new again. The servant leadership model is as old as Jesus of Nazareth—yet it is paradoxically the leadership model of the future (surprise, surprise!). After thousands of years of bosses bossing people around, we have finally rediscovered the truth that Jesus demonstrated so clearly the night before he was crucified: Only leaders who serve should serve as leaders. If you don't grasp servanthood, you don't grasp leadership.

And yet, many don't. Even after all that has been written on the subject of servant leadership, most people—even, I daresay, most leaders—still don't get it. Even in the Christian church, the two-thousand-year-old organization that bears Jesus' name, we don't get it. If we did, we would never hear such terms as "church hierarchy" (a contradiction in terms!). We would not hear pastors described as the "CEO" of a church. We would not see church leadership structures depicted as pyramids, with the pastor sitting in the boss's chair.

Servant leadership is like the third rail of the New York City subway: That's where the electricity is, my friend! Grab it with both hands, embrace it, and let its power surge through you!

Ah, but we're afraid of that power, aren't we? We don't understand it. It makes no logical sense. *Servant leadership* to our rational, commonsense thinking is just another oxymoron, right in there with *government organization*, *death benefits*, *airline food*, and *act naturally*. But no. Servant leadership isn't an oxymoron—it's a paradox, a profound truth contained in a seemingly contradictory statement.

## BOSSES VERSUS SERVANTS

In this world, there are two kinds of leaders: bosses and servants. Bosses wield power, issue edicts and commands, and expect to be obeyed and served. Bosses use their power to elevate the self. But servant leaders empower others, delegate authority to others, and exemplify obedience and servanthood. Servant leaders elevate others.

Do servant leaders ever take charge? Hold people accountable? Exercise authority? You bet they do! But they do so for different reasons, and with different motives, than bosses do. A boss exercises the authority of reward, punishment, and compulsion. The servant leader exercises moral authority and wields the power of love.

There are times when the actions of a boss and the actions of a servant leader will be indistinguishable from the outside. Both a boss and a servant leader sometimes give orders, confront problems firmly, talk tough, discipline people, and even fire people. But even when those actions look the same on the outside, people can usually tell the difference between the spirit of a boss and the spirit of a servant leader.

Jesus used a metaphor to describe his own leadership style, a metaphor that makes the boss-servant distinction totally clear: Again and again, he referred to himself as a shepherd—the Good Shepherd. The meaning of that metaphor is unmistakable. It is an image that was familiar and understandable to every person who heard him; the people had all seen shepherds caring for flocks of sheep.

The Good Shepherd didn't boss his sheep; he served them. The sheep did not exist for the shepherd; the shepherd existed to serve the sheep. That is what a servant leader is all about, and the best leaders in every arena—church, business, government, military—have figured it out.

Herb Kelleher, CEO of Southwest Airlines, puts it this way:

> I'd describe leadership as servanthood. The best leaders, I think, have to be good followers as well. You have to be quite willing to accept other people's ideas even when they are in conflict with your own. You have to be willing to subjugate your ego to the needs of your business. You have to be willing to take risks for your people. If you won't fight for your people, you can count on your people not fighting for you.

The greatest leader who ever lived took his towel and his basin, and he stooped to wash the feet of eleven followers and one traitor—and a world was transformed. If you can't or won't wash feet, if you reject the leadership model of the towel and basin, then what are you left with? The same old leadership model that has ruled this world since club-wielding man first shambled out of the cave. Force, dominance, superiority, egotism, elitism—the same old, tired leadership model followed by Alexander, Julius Caesar, Napoleon, the Czars, Hitler, and Saddam Hussein.

Do you buy that?

Or do you resist it?

I've heard all the reasons why servant leadership "sounds great in theory but won't work in our organization." Some people say they would have to completely overhaul the structure of the organization. I say, "So? What are you waiting for?" Some say it's just another leadership fad. I say, "A two-thousand-year-old fad? Not many fads have that kind of staying power." Some say it'll never work; a leader has to have power and servant leadership means giving up power. I say, "Open your mind to the paradox of power!"

If you have to ask, "How can I lead without power?" you still don't understand. Servanthood *is* power. It's a power you can tap into. But you can't control the power of servant leadership. It's a power that controls *you*.

It's true: Leaders cannot lead without power. But there are many kinds of power, and not all power is created equal. Different kinds of power come from different sources and produce different results. Here are some examples:

- *Deadly Force.* This is the favorite of totalitarians, despots, and terrorists. Their power comes from the muzzle of a gun. Like Hitler, they're always trying to conquer the world—killing and terrorizing the masses.
- *Economics.* This is the type of power wielded by business hotshots and tycoons. They write a check and make things happen. Money talks and they know the world listens.
- *Personality.* This is the weapon of the charmers—people who manipulate through charisma, persuasive words, and a smooth voice. Some charmers have personalities that intimidate; they

manipulate people and events with threatening glares or destructive words.

- *Politics.* Some of the previous also wield political power. They manipulate decision-making processes behind the scenes, dispense favors and largesse, build coalitions, and cut backroom deals.

The paradoxical power of servant leadership is unlike any of these other forms of power. Leaders do not wield the power of servant leadership. The power of servant leadership wields *them.* Servant leaders do not always wind up in the corner office or at the head of the parade or on the platform in front of cheering crowds. Servant leaders sometimes find themselves nailed to a cross. But even though crucified, servant leaders win, and the world is transformed.

## POWER TO TRANSFORM THE WORLD

When Jimmy Carter was voted out of the White House in 1980 he was reviled by fellow Democrats and considered to be one of the poorest presidents in the history of the United States. Today, however, he is one of our most admired presidents because of his actions since he left office. Jimmy Carter has become a servant leader.

In the May 21, 2002, issue of *Christianity Today* Philip Yancy wrote:

> Due mainly to his emphasis on human rights, many developing nations looked to [Carter] as a great leader, and Carter responded with visionary projects. A democracy project began monitoring elections all over the world. His support of Habitat for Humanity brought publicity and funding to that fledgling organization. His foundation targeted a handful of major diseases that plague poor nations and mobilized dollars and expert knowledge to address the problems.

In addition, President Carter frequently teaches a Sunday school class at Maranatha Baptist Church in Plains, Georgia. He made the offering plates in his home carpentry shop. He takes turns cutting the church lawn and his wife, Roslyn, helps clean the bathrooms.

Jimmy Carter, who held the most powerful position in the world, and his wife have dedicated their entire lives to serving others all over the world. It brings to mind what Jesus said in Mark 8:35: "For whoever wants to save his life will lose it, but whoever loses his life for me and for the gospel will save it."

Dr. Martin Luther King Jr. was another servant leader. He lived in a modest neighborhood among the people he served, drove a second-hand Nash Rambler, put in long hours, and took no salary from the Southern Christian Leadership Conference. He often quoted the words of Jesus: "If anyone wants to be first, he must be the very last, and the servant of all." And he didn't just quote those words. He exemplified them.

Dr. King was stalked by death, and he was conscious of his mortality. Asked how he would like to be remembered at his funeral, he said:

> I'd like somebody to mention that Martin Luther King Jr. gave his life serving others, that he tried to love people, that he tried to feed the hungry, that he tried to clothe those who were naked, that he tried to visit those who were in prison, that he tried to love and serve humanity.

One January night in 1956, Dr. King went to a meeting at the Dexter Avenue Baptist Church, not far from his home in Montgomery, Alabama. It was less than two months after Rosa Parks made headlines by refusing to obey Montgomery's rules mandating segregation on city buses. Dr. King had also made headlines, leading a boycott of the city bus lines and demanding an end to segregation. During the church meeting, someone burst in and told Dr. King the terrible news: "Someone has fire-bombed your house!" It was a moment of horror, for Dr. King's wife and baby were in that house.

When he arrived home, smoke was rising from his house and a huge crowd of followers was gathered in the front yard. The bomb had exploded on the porch, and had blown glass shards into the living room. King pushed his way into the house and found his wife and baby safe.

Going back out on the shattered porch, he saw scores of people filled with legitimate rage. They wanted justice. There were people there with guns and broken bottles in their fists—and they were engaged in a loud, tense confrontation with the police. King saw that the situation was teetering on the brink of chaos.

He called out to the crowd, and the people went silent. "My wife and baby are all right," he said. "I want you to put down your weapons and go home. We have the weapon of nonviolence, the breastplate of righteousness, the armor of truth. We will not solve our problems with violence, because that would only harm our cause. Remember what the Bible tells us: 'Do not be overcome by evil, but overcome evil with good.'"

For a moment, no one knew what would happen next. Then someone in the crowd said, "God bless you, Dr. King!" And someone else said, "Amen!" And the crowd began to disperse.

There were news photographers there, and they captured that moment. Photos of Dr. King standing on his bombed-out porch, delivering a message of nonviolence and peace, appeared in newspapers across the nation. Support for Dr. King and the civil rights movement soared. The transformation of America had begun.

Servant leadership is the only form of power that can truly transform the world. Servant leadership does not compel or coerce people; it draws and attracts people. It is the most attractive form of power in the world.

In Matthew 26 we see Jesus about to be taken prisoner in the Garden of Gethsemane. Judas had betrayed his master. The soldiers had come. Peter stepped forward, drew his sword, and hacked at the servant of the high priest. Jesus rebuked Peter for wielding the power of the sword, and added, "Do you think I cannot call on my Father, and he will at once put at my disposal more than twelve legions of angels?" A legion, in Roman terms, was about five thousand soldiers. Jesus was saying that he had roughly sixty thousand angels at his beck and call—more than enough force to handle the situation. Jesus had all the power in the world.

But he chose to be a servant. He chose to submit to the iron nails and the wooden cross. A servant leader has the power to transform the world; all he has to do is die.

# WILL THE REAL LEADER PLEASE STAND UP?

"When I try to tell people what Ronald Reagan was like," says Peggy Noonan, former White House speechwriter, "I tell them the bathroom story."

The what? The bathroom story:

> A few days after President Reagan had been shot, when he was well enough to get out of bed, he wasn't feeling well, so he went into the bathroom that connected to his room. He slapped some water on his face and some of the water slopped out of the sink. He got some paper towels and got down on the floor to clean it up. An aide went in to check on him, and found the president of the United States on his hands and knees on the cold tile floor, mopping up water with paper towels. "Mr. President," the aide said, "what are you doing? Let the nurse clean that up!" And he said, "Oh, no. I made that mess, and I'd hate for the nurse to have to clean it up."

Many leaders are defined by moments of crisis or war or tragedy. But Ronald Reagan was defined beautifully and appropriately by a very small incident with profound implications: The president was a servant. He would much rather serve than be served.

Under the leadership of C. William Pollard, the ServiceMaster Company has become an eight-billion-dollar corporation with over 250,000 employees and over twelve million customers in thirty-one countries. In his book *The Soul of the Firm*, he says that ServiceMaster's success is built on four simple objectives: to honor God in all they do; to help people develop; to pursue excellence; and to grow profitably. Put simply, the leadership model at ServiceMaster is a model of servant leadership. Says Pollard:

> Will the real leader please stand up? Not the president or the person with the most distinguished title or the longest tenure, but the role model. Not the highest paid person in the group, but the risk taker. Not the person with the largest car or the

biggest home, but the servant. Not the person who promotes himself or herself, but the promoter of others. Not the administrator, but the initiator. Not the taker, but the giver. Not the talker, but the listener.

What then are the distinguishing characteristics of a servant leader? Here are a few ways you can spot a genuine servant leader—and know if you yourself are a servant leader.

### A servant leader has relinquished the right to control.

A servant, by definition, cannot control people or circumstances or events. A servant can only serve.

Herb Kelleher puts it this way:

> A financial analyst once asked me if I was afraid of losing control of our organization. I told him I've never had any control and I never wanted it. If you create an environment where the people truly participate, you don't need control. They know what needs to be done and they do it. The more that people will devote to your cause on a voluntary basis, a willing basis, the fewer hierarchies and control mechanisms you need . . . I have always believed that the best leader is the best server. If you're a servant, by definition, you are not controlling.

### A servant leader sees servanthood as an end, not a means to an end.

I've read books on servant leadership that seem to promote servanthood as just another tool or technique for manipulating people. This attitude says, "I want power, and servanthood is a good way to get it. If I serve people, they will respond by gratefully becoming my followers." Servanthood is just another worldly manipulation, a subtle means of controlling people. It can even become a form of arm-twisting and extortion: *I served you; now you owe me.*

But authentic servanthood is not a means to an end. It's an end in itself. You don't serve others expecting a *quid pro quo.* You serve others expecting nothing in return. You serve simply to serve, period. Even if no one responds, you serve. Even if no one follows, you serve. Even if no one shows gratitude, you serve.

"Some day, you may well be sitting here where I am, now, as President of the United States," Franklin Roosevelt said to Wendell Willkie in the Oval Office in 1941, a year after he had beaten him and won a third term. "And, when you are, you'll be looking at that door over there and knowing that practically everybody who walks through it wants something out of you. You'll learn what a lonely job this is and you'll discover the need for somebody like Harry Hopkins [FDR's trusted aide] who asks for nothing except to serve you."

In October 2001 on a trip to Southern California I visited John Wooden at his Encino apartment. The famous college basketball coach, ninety-one at the time, met me and escorted me up to his apartment. As I walked in the front door, I entered a hall of fame—a museum of photos, plaques, autographed books, and sports memorabilia. It was staggering and fascinating. Most interesting of all was an area of his front hallway that was a tribute to just two people. The left-hand side of the hallway was devoted to Abraham Lincoln; the right-hand side was a kind of shrine to Mother Teresa.

"Coach," I said, "tell me about this. Why have you devoted this portion of your home to Lincoln and Mother Teresa?"

"Well," he said, "they're my two heroes." And he told me what he admired about them: their courage, selflessness, humility, sacrifice, integrity, and servanthood—all the qualities that have marked these two people as heroes to so many. And I thought, *How cool is that! The great John Wooden, every basketball player's hero, has heroes, too!*

And why these two? Well, elsewhere in this book we have talked about the humble character and servant leadership of Lincoln. His generals frustrated and disobeyed him, his cabinet members undermined him, his critics assailed him, his chronically depressed wife robbed him of peace and happiness—yet all he did was serve them. Even those who snubbed him and mistreated him, he served. Lincoln was not a perfect man, but he truly had the heart of a servant.

But why Mother Teresa? As a young woman, Mother Teresa taught in a Catholic high school in an upper-middle-class part of Calcutta.

Whenever she went out into the streets of the city, she saw leprosy victims who received no medical care and had no hope. She felt God calling her out of the cloistered security of her convent and into a ministry among India's lepers. Over the years, her Missionaries of Charity medical outreach has helped 150,000 leprosy sufferers.

Some years ago, she came to New York City to address a session of the United Nations. While in New York, she visited Sing Sing Prison, where she met four inmates with AIDS. The scourge of AIDS reminded her of the awful suffering endured by people with leprosy. She left the prison and went to see New York City mayor Ed Koch. She asked for his help in setting up an AIDS center. For her first patients she wanted the four prisoners she had just met. Koch called New York's governor, Mario Cuomo, then put Mother Teresa on the phone. The governor offered her not only those four prisoners, but all forty-three AIDS patients in the state prison system.

"I'll start with the four," she said, "and work my way up. Now, Governor Cuomo, I have a building in mind for my AIDS center, and I would like the state of New York to pay for it."

"Okay," said Cuomo, approving hundreds of thousands of taxpayer dollars in the blink of an eye.

Mother Teresa turned to Mayor Koch. "Today is Monday," she said. "I need to have all the permits for the center cleared by Wednesday. Can you do it?"

Mayor Koch grinned. "As long as you don't make me scrub the floors," he said. And Mother Teresa had her AIDS center. That's powerful servant leadership—a ninety-eight-pound nun with the force of a bulldozer!

Coach Wooden's two heroes were people who served not as a means to an end, but as an end in itself. They were servants, pure and simple.

*A servant leader is often a reluctant draftee.*

Jesus once told his disciples, "You did not choose me, but I chose you and appointed you to go and bear fruit—fruit that will last" (John 15:16). The twelve whom Jesus trained for leadership were not eager applicants. They didn't sign up for Jesus' traveling leadership school. They were drafted. They grew into the roles that he foresaw for them.

Leaders are still often drafted into the job, not by being tapped on the shoulder by Jesus but by being nudged by a combination of external circumstances and an inner sense of God's calling. The gifted preacher and author, A. W. Tozer, put it this way:

> A true and safe leader is likely to be one who has no desire to lead, but is forced into a position of leadership by the inward pressure of the Holy Spirit and the press of external situation. Such were Moses and David and the Old Testament prophets. I think there was hardly a great leader from Paul to the present day but was drafted by the Holy Spirit for the task, and commissioned by the Lord of the Church to fill a position he had little heart for. I believe it might be accepted as a fairly reliable rule of thumb that the man who is ambitious to lead is disqualified as a leader. The true leader will have no desire to lord it over God's heritage, but will be humble, gentle, self-sacrificing and altogether as ready to follow as to lead.[1]

### A servant leader is found in the doggonedest places.

Bosses tend to be found only in "boss places" (the ivory tower private office, the board room, the halls of power, the country club), doing "boss stuff" (giving orders, threatening and intimidating underlings, being served by others). Servant leaders are often found where you would least expect to find a boss, doing things that are nothing short of shocking: taking out trash, setting up chairs, scrubbing toilets, helping and loving people, listening to people's problems, serving, serving, serving. "No leader is worth his salt who won't set up the chairs," wrote management expert Peter Drucker.

Author and speaker Dr. Charles Swindoll is the former president of Dallas Theological Seminary and executive editor of the twenty-five volume Swindoll Leadership Library. He tells a story of servant leadership from his first year as a student at Dallas. It was 1959 and Swindoll was studying Greek under Dr. Bert Siegle, a soft-spoken and kindly professor. "I did not know what it was that made such an impact on us as we sat in Dr. Siegle's classroom," Swindoll recalls, "but at times it was as though we had been lifted into the heavenlies. Somehow this professor held us in the palm of his hand."

Dr. Siegle died in 1963, and Charles Swindoll attended the funeral. Only then did he learn the true extent of Dr. Siegle's servant leadership. Dr. Siegle had been teaching at Dallas since the 1930s, when the country suffered from the Great Depression. There were times when the seminary was unable to meet its payroll. If Dr. Siegle and his fellow professors had not sacrificed, the school might not have survived those tough times. Dr. Siegle believed in the influence the school was having, and he wanted to keep teaching. So in addition to his duties as a professor, Dr. Siegle also hauled the school's trash and served on its maintenance crew. He emptied wastebaskets in the classrooms and dorms and he laid tile in the bathrooms.

"When I heard that," Dr. Swindoll concluded, "I realized what it was about the man that had endeared him to us: His heart of humility had won our respect."

*A servant leader exemplifies love and caring.*

Buck O'Neil, veteran Negro leagues baseball great, is ninety years old and still going strong. One of the reasons for his longevity and vitality is his outlook on life:

> One thing I always repeat—on purpose—is this: "Give it up." You got to give it up. You got to give people love. I can honestly say I love everybody and hate no one. I hate cancer, which has touched so many of our lives, and I hate AIDS, and I hate hatred—men remain in ignorance so long as they hate. But I hate no human being.
>
> Sometimes at the end of my speeches I ask the audience to join hands and sing a little song. It goes like this: "The greatest thing in all my life is loving you." At first, the audience is a little shy about holding hands and singing that corny song, but by

and by, they all clasp one another's hands and the voices get louder and louder. They give it up. Got to give it up.

Bosses prize control, aggression, combativeness, and intimidation. They consider love a sign of weakness. Servant leaders exemplify empathy, caring, and love. They know the power that is generated by authentic caring in the workplace. They know it is not the commanders and autocrats who have transformed the world, but the mentors, teachers, and servants—those who practiced caring and concern, not coercion.

In a column for *Industry Week*, Lance Secretan lamented the fact that so many leaders in the corporate world "remain oblivious to the increased leverage and potential available to them if they traded their aggression and testosterone-saturated posturing for empathy, compassion, and love."

Secretan, who logs four-hundred-plus flights a year on the job, often encounters delays and shutdowns and considers it a normal feature of frequent flying. When stranded, he amuses himself by watching other flyers lose their composure and make fools of themselves. When airports are socked in, he says, "executives switch to warrior mode, berating airline staff with abuse, anger, and bombast." These bosses, used to getting results by intimidation, are supremely frustrated when all their red-faced shouting and threatening gets them precisely nowhere.

Once, stranded for fourteen hours in the Pittsburgh airport by a rainstorm, he observed one boss who was clearly used to getting his way venting his frustration on an airline customer service rep. The man tried sarcasm, shouting, bullying, and insults. Finally, he tried to impress the reservation clerk with his alpha male importance: "Do you know who I am?" he snarled.

The airline representative calmly picked up a microphone and made an announcement that was heard all over the terminal. Heads turned in the direction of the self-important exec as the announcement went out: "Ladies and gentlemen, we have a man here who doesn't know who he is. If anyone can identify him . . ."

On another occasion, when Secretan was delayed for three hours in Toronto, he saw a customer service rep taking heat from one angry customer after another. So he went to her and said, "I can see you're having a stressful day, and I clearly have some time to spare. Is there anything I can do to make things easier for you—get you some water, coffee, anything?"

The clerk looked at Secretan in astonishment. "No—but thanks for asking. And I'll tell you what—I've got to bump some people from economy to first class, and one of them might as well be you."[2]

### *A servant leader exemplifies obedience.*

No leader automatically deserves to be followed. Followers must be earned. One way a leader earns the right to be followed is by demonstrating followership and obedience himself. A leader who can obey is a leader who has walked where his people walk. He views them as partners, not underlings. He listens and learns and allows people to teach him while he is teaching and leading them.

Solon, the great Athenian statesman, once said, "Learn to obey before you command." ServiceMaster's Bill Pollard says, "The leader must be prepared to serve. He must be willing to do what he asks others to do; to listen and to learn before he talks; to be a giver, not a taker; to be a role model."

Historian H. W. Crocker III says Robert E. Lee's success came from knowing that a good leader is a good subordinate. Crocker contrasts Lee with fellow general Joseph E. Johnston, described as "a man with a high and prickly regard for himself." Jefferson Davis, the egotistical president of the Confederacy, was constantly trying to micromanage his generals. Johnston responded by refusing to communicate with Davis except when it suited him. Lee chose the course of obedience. He showed deference to Jefferson Davis's status and position. The president responded to Johnston's disdain by reining him in; he responded to Lee's obedience by giving Lee more trust, latitude, and freedom of action.

As Sam Rayburn, former Speaker of the House, once observed, "You cannot be a leader and ask other people to follow you unless you know how to follow, too."

*A servant leader exemplifies humility.*

The great preacher D. L. Moody once said, "God sends no one away empty except those who are full of themselves." Bosses are full of themselves; servant leaders are full of humility.

We all know the attitudes of a typical boss. Bosses are smug and superior; they look down on others and demand to be looked up to because of their rank and accomplishments. They are arrogant and self-important; they are right and everyone else is wrong; they serve no one and expect everyone to serve them. They are presumptuous and vain; they can admit no flaw or error. Their egos seem brittle and fragile, for they continually need to be fed with applause and praise.

Ulysses S. Grant was not your typical boss. On his way to a reception held in his honor, Grant got caught in a shower and offered to share his umbrella with a stranger walking in the same direction. The man said he was going to Grant's reception out of curiosity; he had never seen the general. "I have always thought that Grant was a much overrated man," he said. "That's my view also," Grant replied.

One of the great keys to the transforming power of the leadership of Gandhi was his humility, rooted in a desire to be completely identified and one with the poor and oppressed people he served. When he traveled, he traveled by third-class passage on trains. Third class was roughly the equivalent of being treated as human freight. Third-class passengers were crammed together with farm animals in miserable conditions of heat, filth, and stench. Asked why he traveled third class, Gandhi replied, "Because there is no fourth class."

Gandhi once went to England to discuss the conditions of the Indian people with King George V. (At that time, of course, India was a British colony.) Lord Mountbatten offered to fly Gandhi to England in his private plane; Gandhi chose third-class rail. He made the final leg of the trip by steamship, and scandalized British society by coming down the gangplank dressed only in a white loincloth. He led a goat— its milk, plus vegetables and nuts, were Gandhi's only food. He refused offers of plush hotel rooms, choosing to stay in a slum in London's East End. Returning from Buckingham Palace in his loin cloth, Gandhi was asked by a reporter, "Is that all you wore when you met the king?" Gandhi's humble reply: "The king wore enough for both of us."

### *A servant leader has dirty shoulders.*

From my friend Gil McGregor, announcer for the Charlotte Hornets, I learned something called "The Dirty Shoulders Principle." You can tell servant leaders by looking at their shoulders. Why dirty shoulders? Because a person with figuratively dirty shoulders is always lifting up others and letting them stand tall. A servant leader doesn't care who gets the glory and recognition. A servant leader thinks *we*, not *me*. Michael Jordan said, "I built my talents on the shoulders of someone else's talent. Without Julius Erving, David Thompson, Walter Davis, and Elgin Baylor, there never would have been a Michael Jordan. I evolved from them."

In the old top-down, pyramidal leadership model, the leader says, "My people exist to make me successful." But in the servant leadership model, the servant leader says, "I exist to make my people successful. I lift people up." Now it's true that the people's success becomes the leader's success—but selfishness is never the servant leader's motive. She doesn't lift others up in order to receive from them. She lifts others up for their own sake. She serves others without expectation of anything in return.

One of the great leaders of the American revolution was the Marquis de Lafayette, a distinguished French general and political leader. Born of an aristocratic family, he was passionate about the American Revolution. Though the French government was officially neutral, he left France to join George Washington's army. Washington appointed him a major general, and the two men became close friends. Lafayette was wounded at Brandywine, endured the hard winter with Washington at Valley Forge, and led with distinction in the Yorktown campaign. After the war, he returned home to France.

Almost forty years later, Lafayette returned to America, a man in his late sixties. He was accorded a hero's welcome, with receptions and parties wherever he went. During one of these events, he was greeted by an old soldier in a faded uniform—the kind of uniform worn by the Continental Army during the Revolution. The old soldier carried an ancient musket and a tattered old blanket was wrapped around his shoulders. "Do you remember me?" asked the old soldier.

"I cannot say that I do," said Lafayette.

"You recall the hard winter at Valley Forge," said the soldier.

"Who could forget?" asked Lafayette. "So many men died from the bitter cold alone."

"Indeed," said the soldier. "One night, General, you were on rounds, and you came to a sentry who stood watch. He wore thin clothing, and was freezing to death. You told him, 'Go to my hut, and you will find woolen stockings, a blanket, and a fire. Warm yourself, then bring that blanket to me. I will man your post while you are gone.' The soldier did as you said. He returned with the blanket, and you took that blanket and tore it in half. You gave half of the blanket to the soldier."

Lafayette's eyes misted. "I remember."

"General Lafayette," said the old soldier, taking the tattered blanket off his shoulders, "this is that blanket, and I am the sentry whose life you saved."

That is the legacy of a leader who lifts others up: a tattered scrap of cloth and a grateful human soul. Servant leaders have dirty shoulders.

## A servant leader mirrors God.

Servant leaders exemplify godliness. When people look at the life of a servant leader, they should see qualities of love, caring, forgiveness, tolerance, understanding, justice, truth, and integrity—the character traits of God himself.

When I was general manager of the 76ers, I became friends with Dr. C. Everett Koop, about whom author Philip Yancy wrote: "One of Dr. Koop's closest aides explained, 'What people didn't understand about Dr. Koop is that he is pro-life in the purest sense of the word: not *anti-death,* but *pro-life.* I have seen him with thousands of people . . . malnourished children, Washington socialites, dying AIDS patients, abused wives, abortion rights activists . . . and he treats every one of them as if he truly believes, which he does, that they are created in the image of God. He'll interrupt his busy schedule to meet with some disturbed person who insists on talking to the 'top doc.' He truly does respect the value of all human life.'"

During World War II, the city of London was taking a daily pounding from the Luftwaffe. German bombers blackened the skies over the city on a nightly basis, converting entire districts into piles of rubble. During the time the D-Day invasion of Normandy was being planned, General Dwight D. Eisenhower took a walk in London, accompanied by two aides. He wanted to do some soul-searching regarding the upcoming decisions that had to be made, and he thought the walk would clear his thinking.

Eisenhower and his aides passed a bakery on the way and noticed two boys with their noses pressed against the bakery window. The two boys were hungry and recently orphaned by the bombing. The tantalizing fragrance of freshly baked bread and pastries wafted out of the shop. Eisenhower stopped—then he went inside and bought two sacks of the very items the boys were eyeing in the window: chocolate-glazed donuts. The general handed a sack to each boy.

The two boys stared up in disbelief at the tall man, the Supreme Commander of the Allied Forces. One of the boys asked him, "Sir, are you God?"

Servant leaders are like that. They take a caring and empathetic interest in the needs of people around them. And when people look at a servant leader, they see God.

## THE PARADOX OF POWER, THE POWER OF LOVE

Nelson Mandela is a servant leader.

For most of his life, Mandela quietly but firmly opposed the racist policies of apartheid in South Africa. In 1964 the white minority government condemned him to life in prison. He spent twenty-seven years in prison for the "crime" of speaking out against racism and oppression. Then in 1990, as South Africa came under increasing pressure from the international community, Mandela was released. In

1994 apartheid was formally abolished, South Africa held its first free elections, and Nelson Mandela was elected president.

In four years, he went from being a prisoner of his country to the leader of his country. Many people in his position would have seized the opportunity to turn the tables on those who had stolen almost three decades of his life. But Nelson Mandela chose to flex his *moral* authority rather than the power of the state. He demonstrated to the world that he was a new kind of leader, following a very old leadership model—the model of Jesus Christ.

A little over a year after Mandela came to power, South Africa agreed to host the Rugby World Cup Tournament in Johannesburg, the capital of this overwhelmingly black African nation. But the tournament inflamed a major national debate. Many black South Africans objected to the tournament, calling rugby a white man's game. They demanded the removal of the South African team emblem, the springbok. The springbok, said the blacks, was a reminder of South Africa's oppressive apartheid history.

White Afrikaners, however, demanded that the tradition of the springbok remain intact. The springbok had been the emblem of every rugby team South Africa had ever fielded. Tensions escalated.

That's when Nelson Mandela stepped in. He paid a visit to the South African rugby team and called a press conference. As the media cameras clicked away, he answered questions—and he was dressed in a Springbok rugby jersey and a Springbok cap. "Before democratic rule came to South Africa," he said, "we blacks supported anyone who was playing against the Springboks. We were a divided country then, and the Springboks represented oppression. But that is in the past. We are a united country now. Regardless of the past, the Springboks are our team now. They may all be white, but they're our boys. The people of South Africa will get behind them and support them in this tournament."

The following day, the white coach of the Springboks gathered his players together and said, "There's no practice today. I want everyone to assemble in street clothes—suits and ties."

"Why?" the players asked. "Where are we going?"

"You'll see," said the coach.

The coach put the team on a boat and took them out to Robben Island, to the prison where Nelson Mandela had spent so much of his life. The coach led his players into one of the cells and said, "This is the cell where Nelson Mandela was imprisoned. He was kept here for twenty-seven years by the racist policies of our government. We white Afrikaners tolerated Mandela's imprisonment for all those years—yet he came out yesterday and publicly supported all of us. We can't let him down."

The Springboks were considered underdogs in the tournament, but they went out and played like champions, stunning the world by winning their first match. They continued on through the tournament until they faced New Zealand—the perennial powerhouse in the world of international rugby. It was a tough game, and by the end of regulation time, the score was tied.

In the stands was Nelson Mandela, clad in a Springboks jersey. Also in the stands was a choir of black South African children. During the time-out before overtime, the children began singing an old miners' song, much like the Negro spirituals sung by slaves in the old American South. Mandela began singing with them. Soon, thousands of people in the stands joined in, and that old song of hope swelled throughout the stadium.

As the song ended, the Springboks took the field, and they seemed supernaturally energized and empowered. The New Zealanders couldn't stop them. At the end of the overtime period, the World Rugby Championship belonged to the Springboks of South Africa. The championship didn't belong only to the whites on the team, but to all of South Africa, white and black alike. That night, whites and blacks celebrated and danced together in the streets of a united South African nation.

Nelson Mandela understood the ultimate paradox of leadership: A leader is not truly a leader unless he is a *servant* leader, serving all the people as a force for change, a force for unity, and a force for love.

# Winning Is Everything

Looking back from the vantage point of half a century, the course of World War II seems almost foreordained. But to leaders like President Franklin D. Roosevelt, General Dwight D. Eisenhower, and Prime Minister Winston Churchill, the outcome of the war was a blood-stained question mark. In fact, the story of the early stages of World War II is a tale of setback after setback for the Allies. In the Pacific Theater, Imperial Japan relentlessly advanced across China and spread misery throughout the Pacific islands. In Europe the forces of Hitler and Mussolini rolled across a continent, seemingly impossible to stop. A Nazi conquest of Britain seemed just over the horizon.

On May 13, 1940, as the newly appointed prime minister, Churchill stood before the House of Commons and described the dark and uncertain path that lay ahead:

> We have before us an ordeal of the most grievous kind. We have before us many, many long months of struggle and of suffering. You ask, What is our policy? I will say: "It is to wage war, by sea, land and air, with all our might and with all the strength that God can give us: to wage war against a monstrous tyranny, never surpassed in the dark lamentable catalogue of human crime. That is our policy." You ask, What is our aim? I can answer with one word: "Victory—victory at all costs, victory

in spite of all terror, victory however long and hard the road may be; for without victory there is no survival."

Let that sink in for a moment: *Without victory—no survival.* Winning the war was everything. Defeat was not an option. It was all or nothing, victory or destruction, us or them.

There is undeniable defiance—but also a touch of grim fatalism—in the words Churchill spoke a month later in the same House of Commons, June 18, 1940:

> Upon this battle depends the survival of Christian civilization. Upon it depends our own British life and the long continuity of our institutions and our Empire. The whole fury and might of the enemy must very soon be turned on us now . . . If we fail, then the whole world, including the United States, including all that we have known and cared for, will sink into the abyss of a new Dark Age . . . Let us therefore brace ourselves to our duties, and so bear ourselves that, if the British Empire and its Commonwealth last for a thousand years, men will say, "This was their finest hour."

In 1940, if World War II had been the Super Bowl, the smart money would have been on Germany with a 14-point spread.

The paradox of Winston Churchill was this: Though a Nazi victory seemed inevitable, England's defeat was not even a remote possibility in Churchill's thinking. He thought only of victory—*victory at all costs.* He kept a reminder in his office at No. 10 Downing Street. Next to his desk blotter was a cardboard sign with the words of Queen Victoria: "There is no pessimism in this house, and we are not interested in possibilities of defeat. They do not exist."

In 1940 winning was everything. The same is true today. The morning of September 11, 2001, it became painfully, shockingly clear that winning is still everything. Civilization is again at war with chaos and evil, and if we do not win, we will sink into the abyss of a new Dark Age.

There are so many other arenas where winning also is everything. As a society, we are at war with poverty, racism, ignorance, corruption, injustice, intolerance, and much more. We are engaged in a war that is being waged on multiple fronts. There are times when it seems as though the possibility of defeat far outweighs the chances of victory.

But we must win. There is no room for pessimism in our human family, and we are not interested in the possibilities of defeat.

Winning is everything. And we, as leaders, must be committed to building winning players, winning organizations, and a victorious society. Jesus, the Master Leader, the Great Servant, has shown us the way. In fact, he has exemplified for us an astounding paradox: We can win by losing. We can win even by dying. And if we, as leaders, follow the pattern he has left us, how can we help but win?

# SIX STEPS TO WINNING

I have in my possession an NBA championship ring. I don't wear it—the doggone thing is so big I'd be constantly scraping my knuckles on the ground. But it's a brilliant, glittering reminder of what it feels like to win a championship.

In 1983 I was general manager of the Philadelphia 76ers. What a team that was: Moses Malone, Bobby Jones, Andrew Toney, Maurice Cheeks, and Julius Erving, the legendary Doctor J. We racked up an incredible sixty-five wins to seventeen losses for the season, then swept the Knicks in the quarterfinals, lost only one game to the Bucks in the semifinals, and swept the titanic L.A. Lakers for the NBA title.

Returning to Philly, we received a victory parade, complete with tons of confetti. A million fans lined the parade route, and another fifty-five thousand fans filled Veterans Stadium at the end of the route. As the stadium rocked with screams and applause, Doctor J lifted the championship trophy toward the sky. The emotions of that moment are etched in my memory—elation and an incredible joy. It all comes back to me whenever I look at that glittering ring. That's what winning is all about.

And, ultimately, that's what leadership is all about: Winning. Our goal as leaders is to lead our people to victory. As General Douglas MacArthur once said, "There is no substitute for victory."

So how does winning happen? From my own experience, I've determined that winning is a six-step process. Let's take a look at those six steps and see how the pieces all fit together to produce victory.

## Step 1: Respect

Leaders must begin by building organizations of mutual respect. Respect means being regarded by others with honor or esteem. You can't buy it. You can't command it. Respect must be earned. You, the leader, only receive respect from people when they are favorably impressed with the authentic reality of who you are.

People respect you when you respect them. It comes down to the golden rule: Treat others as you would wish to be treated. Every person is due respectful treatment unless they demonstrate otherwise. When you invest respect in people, you will get it back with interest. If you don't respect your people, they will not respect your leadership. They will challenge you and undermine you. NFL quarterback Doug Flutie says, "There's a common bond when you work hard together and earn each other's respect."

You earn respect by demanding as much or more of yourself as you demand of others. People respect you when they see you working hard, persevering long, and enduring much. They respect you when they know you are not in an ivory tower above them, but in the trenches alongside them.

Rich DeVos, the CEO of the Orlando Magic sports organization (RDV Sports), put it this way:

> I built my whole business on respect for people. I build them up, not chew them out. I always believe that if you show respect, you get respect. Every person is a human being created in the image of God, with a purpose and a place in life. If we operate by this standard, we dignify other human beings by treating them as we ourselves wish to be treated. Respect for others is the most essential trait a leader must possess.

Rich's attitude of respect for people attracts people of respect to our organization. One of our past head coaches, Chuck Daly, put it this way:

> I respect Rich DeVos, the CEO of the organization. I also respect the security guard who patrols the entrance to the Orlando Arena. I understand the status of people. I also understand that people are people. The same thing applies to the players. I think they want to be respected.

I've written a lot of books and I've been on a lot of book tours. As a result, I've had a chance to talk to many limousine drivers all around the country. In the process, I've collected some interesting stories about famous people they have chauffered. I always ask my drivers, "Who is the most memorable person you have met? And why?" The answers I get almost always focus on the way those people treated the driver. Did they talk to the driver or ignore him? Did they treat the driver as human beings or as furniture? Did they ask questions about the driver's family, interests, and life?

The memorable people did. The self-important, self-interested people tended to be forgotten or remembered only with distaste.

I was on a book tour in 1998, and the driver who picked me up at the Phoenix airport was Gary Jackson. His most memorable passenger? Michael Jordan. "Michael was with his wife and children," said Gary, "and he's just a regular guy. At one point, I called him Mr. Jordan and he said, 'Don't call me Mister. I'm Michael. I should be calling you Mr. Jackson.' Well, that impressed me! Michael has so much respect for other people."

Respect is the first step to winning. Respect leads to *trust*.

## Step 2: Trust

Ralph Waldo Emerson once said, "Trust men and they will be true to you; treat them greatly and they will show themselves great."

When your people know you respect them, they respond by trusting you. Trust is the glue that holds relationships and organizations together. If you want to make your vision a reality, then you must be able to trust people to achieve that vision—and they must be able to trust you to lead them. Without two-way trust, your vision will never be more than a daydream.

Trust, like respect, must be earned. It is earned slowly—and it can be broken quickly. A leader builds trust by being:

- *Trusting.* You must be able to give your trust freely in order to receive trust in return. You must trust others so that you can delegate to them and empower them to reach for your vision. Trust generates trust.
- *Caring.* You must be focused on the good of your people. They must know that you are concerned about them as individuals, not just as cogs in the organizational machine. People trust leaders who value them as human beings.
- *Authentic.* You must be real, you must demonstrate integrity. If you are transparent and allow people to see, touch, and know the real you, then they will trust you.
- *Believable.* You must demonstrate absolute honesty and deal squarely with people. Never lie to people. If people know that you say what you mean and mean what you say, they will trust you.
- *Dependable.* If your people know that you keep promises and commitments, they will reward you with their own dependability and trust.
- *Selfless.* Selfish people aren't to be trusted—their motives are always suspect. When your people know that you are focused on the team and the players and not on self, they will respond with selflessness and trust.

"You can't just stand there," says coach Bobby Bowden, "and order players to do what you say because you're the coach . . . You need them to believe and have faith in you and in one another, because you need their trust when it's time to act."

When you trust someone, you put yourself at risk. When you ask people to trust you, you ask them to take a chance on you, and you promise not to let them down. When trust has been built, teamwork becomes possible. When there is trust, there is freedom to risk and make mistakes. If you pass the ball to your teammate and he makes an error, well, mistakes happen. You have confidence that you can pass the ball the next time and he'll do his best to make a winning play. Trust enables people to operate freely and confidently, without the nerve-wracking fear that their next mistake could be their last.

Orlando Magic guard Tracy McGrady is a leader on the team, and he knows the importance of two-way trust. "I've learned how to trust my teammates," he says, "and I've learned how to keep them involved. The only way you become a great player is to make your team great." And Bob Ortegel, a former college coach and now an analyst for the Dallas Mavericks broadcasts, once told me, "At the age of sixty, I've finally figured out what chemistry on a team is. It's not some mysterious and vague mixture of molecules. It's simply trust. If I pass you the ball, then I trust you to pass it back to me if I'm open and have a better shot."

Trust is the second step to winning. When you build a solid foundation of trust in the organization, a bond develops between leader and players. This bond of trust is called *loyalty*.

## Step 3: Loyalty

Loyalty is the state of being devoted—heart, mind, and soul—to another person or organization. Loyalty is being true to ourselves by being true to others. It is defending others when they are attacked or maligned. Leaders should always defend their people, and the people should always defend their leader. When situations arise where a person's actions or motives are in question, loyalty demands that we give each other the benefit of the doubt.

I'm going to mention my mentor Mr. R. E. Littlejohn one more time. One thing that impressed me about Mr. R. E. was that during the four years I worked with him, I only saw him angry once—and it was a righteous anger, rooted in his intense loyalty.

After our 1965 season, our radio announcer, John Gordon, was unfairly fired by the radio station that broadcast our games. Mr. R. E. demanded a meeting with the station manager. I was at the meeting, and I saw Mr. R. E. go after that station manager in a way I had never seen before. Mr. R. E. ended up moving our game broadcasts to another station in town, and John Gordon, currently the radio voice of the Minnesota Twins, was back in action broadcasting our games. In that incident, as always, Mr. R. E. demonstrated intense loyalty to his people, and his people responded with love and loyalty in return.

In all too many organizations, leaders demand loyalty while giving none in return. People often give the best years of their lives to a company only to get laid off or forced out just before retirement so the company can save a few bucks. Loyalty is not a gold watch and a swift kick on your way out the door. Loyalty is authentic caring. When people know their leaders are loyal to them, they will repay loyalty with loyalty.

For three years in the early 1990s, our Magic organization owned and operated the Minnesota Twins AA farm club in Orlando. I became good friends with Terry Ryan, who was a Twins super scout and is now the club's general manager. In the fall of 2001, major league baseball attempted to eliminate two teams, including the Twins.

Terry had an opportunity at that point to get a big contract as the general manager of the Toronto Blue Jays. A move like that would have secured his future—but Terry never even went for the interview. Even though there was no assurance he would even have a team in Minnesota, let alone a job, Terry Ryan chose loyalty over opportunity. As a result of the example he set, not one Twins executive, scout, or manager left the organization. They saw Terry pass the ultimate loyalty test—and they decided to cast their lot with him.

In February of 2002, word came down that the Twins were still in business. (In fact, as I write these words, the Twins are in first place in their division!) In all my years in sports, I can't remember a more shining example of loyalty to an organization and the people who work with you. Join me in rooting for Terry Ryan and the Twins.

Some leaders mistake disagreement with disloyalty. But when a person in the organization disagrees with a leader, it is often an act of supreme loyalty. "Loyalty means giving me your honest opinion," Colin Powell once said, "whether you think I'll like it or not." In every organization, there are times when leaders and subordinates must thrash out issues, volley opinions, bandy facts back and forth before coming to a decision. During that give-and-take exchange, leaders need to hear the truth from their people, and that frank exchange must be surrounded by a deep commitment to one another.

"We may not agree about which action to take," says Powell, "but I'll stick by you as we're arguing, as long as you stick by me once a decision is made." Notice the two stages Powell describes: During the discussion phase, loyalty means that subordinates should be free to argue their position as forcefully as possible. Loyalty demands that subordinates speak up. But once the decision is made, we are in a new phase. Once the leader makes the decision, loyalty demands that everyone fall into line behind the decision. There must be no dissension, undermining, backbiting, or grumbling about the decision, for that would be disloyalty of the rankest kind. Once the decision is made, everybody supports it—or they are out.

This is the kind of loyalty Colin Powell has always given to the presidents he served. It is no secret that Powell, who was chairman of the Joint Chiefs of Staff during the Gulf War, often butted heads with then-Defense Secretary Richard Cheney in White House strategy sessions. But that, of course, was during the discussion phase. Once President Bush had made his decision, Powell supported it a thousand percent.

In May 1991 *Newsweek* and the *Washington Post* carried stories critical of Powell, calling him "the Reluctant Warrior" and accusing him of being disloyal to George H. W. Bush's prosecution of the Gulf War. Soon after these stories appeared, the president called Powell. "Colin," said President Bush, "I saw the stories in the paper. Don't pay any attention to that nonsense. Don't let 'em get under your skin."

"Thank you, Mr. President," Powell replied.

"Barbara says hello," added President Bush. "See ya."

Later that day, at a press conference, the president took a question on the subject. "Nobody's going to drive a wedge between me and General Powell," he said flatly. "I don't care how many unnamed sources they claim to have, General Powell is someone I can totally count on. Next question."

Colin Powell understands what loyalty is all about. His story demonstrates that loyalty is repaid with loyalty.

Loyalty is the third step to winning. When there is a bond of loyalty between the leader and the players, you have something called a *team*.

## Step 4: Team

Gordon Bethune, CEO of Continental Airlines, says, "You want your company to run well? Here's an ironclad rule: Get everyone on the same team. Get everyone working for the same goal; get them to win or lose together."

Individuals play the game. Teams win championships. In a team, nobody ever says, *That's not my job.* Team players are flexible and adaptable. Any job that needs doing is *my job.* The concept of team is made up of a number of ingredients:

- *Cohesion.* Teammates stick together, and put the interests of the team ahead of self-interest.
- *Morale.* Teammates lift each other up, cheer each other on, and believe in each other.
- *Synergy.* The team works together to magnify the strengths and minimize the weaknesses of each individual.
- *Caring.* Teammates love each other and take care of each other.
- *Pride.* Teammates derive competitive satisfaction from winning and find joy in being the best.
- *Responsibility.* Each individual teammate takes responsibility not just for his own part of the team but for the whole team.

The concept of team is expressed again and again in the Bible and in the words of Jesus. Another word for team is *unity.* In John 17:22–23 Jesus prays that all of his followers would be unified—that they would be a team. And the book of Ecclesiastes puts the concept of team this way:

> Two are better than one,
> because they have a good return for their work:
> If one falls down,
> his friend can help him up.

But pity the man who falls
and has no one to help him up! . . .
Though one may be overpowered,
two can defend themselves.
A cord of three strands is not quickly broken.
                    *(Ecclesiastes 4:9–10, 12)*


A big part of a leader's job is to build and mold a team. That means encouraging team members to trust each other, know each other, build cohesion around the vision and team goals, and build a sense of loyalty to one another. The vision is up there in lights where everyone can see it. Together, the team members move toward that vision, cheering each other on, encouraging each other, loving each other, remaining unified. Charles Lindbergh and his aircraft, *The Spirit of St. Louis,* were one. Together on May 21, 1927, they achieved what no one had ever accomplished. From that point on, Lindbergh always referred to the plane and himself as "we."

Coach John Wooden expressed the concept of team when he said, "The man who puts the ball through the hoop has ten hands." And Bill Russell, veteran of the Boston Celtics, said, "The most important measure of how good a game I played was how much better I made my teammates play."

When NASA was reaching for the moon, the organization posted this motto throughout its offices: "This is the team. We're trying to go to the moon. If you can't put someone up, please don't put them down." That team spirit was exemplified by the man who best represents NASA—the first man on the moon, Neil Armstrong. Historian Douglas Brinkley said this about Armstrong:


He didn't want to become a celebrity over his moon walk because he really did think it was a team effort. He thinks of it as thousands of people at NASA that put the first man on the moon. He was just the man in the suit, the man of the moment. He feels it could have been others, so the trappings of celebrity never held an allure for him.

Neil Armstrong went to the moon because of teamwork. NASA achieved its objective because of teamwork. The concept of team is the crucial fourth step on the way to victory. Once you have a team, you are ready to *compete*.

## Step 5: Competition

Competition is good for leaders and organizations. Baseball manager Tony LaRussa stated, "You don't manage for the money or the publicity. It's about the competition." Great competitors force you to:

- Improve quality and service.
- Think strategically about the marketplace.
- Balance pricing, costs, and profit margins.
- Pay attention to customers and clients.
- Work hard.
- Learn and grow.

Competition entails risk. If you compete, you might lose. If you don't want to risk, then don't compete. But if you don't compete, you can't win. If you avoid risk, you lose by forfeit. You can't achieve victory without risking defeat. Golfer Sam Snead said, "Quit competing and you dry up like a peach seed."

Competitors are actually our allies. Competition not only forces us to be better than our opponents. It forces us to be better than ourselves, better than we can imagine. Competitors call forth the height and depth of all your abilities, energies, and determination. Joe Paterno, head football coach at Penn State, put it this way: "I hope the other side plays well. I hope they play to their limit because if they don't, there's no fun beating them. We want opponents who make us play better than we think we can play."

Michael Jordan has always thrived on competition, even when he was at the top of his game. "When you get to this level," he once said, "it doesn't stop your learning process. It just doesn't stop because you're getting paid astronomical dollars. You have to continue to improve . . . I want my opponents to chase me, not the other way around. When I have to chase them, it's time to do something else."

Competitors find a way to win. They don't complain about bad breaks, bad weather, a bad playing field, or bad officiating. Those are just conditions of the game. Winners factor them into their game plan, then find a way to win.

Competition is the step to winning. Once you have become intensely competitive, you are poised to *win*.

## Step 6: Winning

Every year after the NFL season is over, at least five head coaches are fired, along with their assistants. The same thing happens at the end of the NBA season. And the NHL season. And the major league baseball season. Why do all of these coaches lose their jobs? The answer is simple: Too many L's, not enough W's. In professional sports, they pay off on one thing only: wins.

The same is just as true in every other business. Whether you are a heart surgeon, a lawyer, a corporate CEO, an insurance sales person, a Realtor, or a politician, it all comes down to producing wins. If you're not winning, you lose.

Winners hate to lose even more than they love to win. Losing is an agony, a bad taste in your mouth. If it's not, it should be. If losing isn't agony for you, you'll never be successful. Reggie White, probably the greatest defensive lineman in NFL history, once said:

> I hate losing. Losing a big game is like having a football stuck in your throat—sideways. It hurts, man. Losing eats at you. It makes you mad. It makes you cry. It follows you around and destroys your sleep. I let guys know, "If losing does not torment you, move on. Go play for somebody else."

Go into a locker room of a professional team that cares about winning, that is passionate about a championship. If they have just won a big playoff game, you'll see celebration such as the average person on the street never experiences short of winning the lottery. But if the team has just lost a playoff game, look out! You'll see screaming and crying, people kicking trashcans and ripping the doors off of lockers. You'll see guys standing in the showers with a dazed expression on their faces, unable to comprehend the fact that their dreams have been dashed for another year. "I've never figured out a way to deal with losing yet, so it doesn't sit well," says hockey coach Pat Quinn.

Winners don't make good losers. Winners passionately want to win. It's all that matters. And that is how it should be.

Robert A. Caro, the biographer of Lyndon Johnson, tells a story that illustrates the late president's passion for winning. While campaigning for governor of Texas, Johnson developed painful kidney stones. He would experience incredible attacks of pain, accompanied by fevers of up to 105 degrees. His doctors told him he needed to be hospitalized or risk losing kidney function. Though he literally took his life into his hands, he refused to stop campaigning.

A campaign worker drove him back and forth across the state while he lay in the back seat, writhing in pain, perspiring profusely, gagging and retching. When the car would pull into a town, he'd get out, put on a clean white shirt, paste a smile on his face, and be ready to go. With a spring in his step, he would greet the crowds, shake hands, and give a rousing speech. Then he'd get back in the car, collapse in pain, and go to the next stop.

What motivated Lyndon Johnson? Caro answers: "He simply had to win."

Winners are never satisfied unless they win. Winners never say, "We tried hard. That's what counts." Winners never say, "Well, second place isn't so bad." You get what you settle for. If you never settle for second place, you'll be a winner.

There are four components to a winning team or organization:

- a leader who wants to win and can't stand losing
- players who want to win and can't stand losing
- preparation, training, and tools so that the players are adequately equipped to win
- a game plan that covers every contingency, especially adversity

So we know what it takes to win. But what does winning look like in real-world terms? Simple: You win when your vision is realized.

# A WORLD TO BE WON

A visionary leader named Walt Disney envisioned glittering theme parks that put a fairyland castle, a starship, and a frontier fort all within walking distance. His vision is now a reality—and it keeps on expanding.

A business leader named Sam Walton envisioned a retail empire based on low prices, excellent service, enthusiastic employees, and great customer care. Wal-Mart is now a reality, and it, too, keeps expanding.

Another business leader, Herb Kelleher, envisioned an airline that offers good, consistent, on-time service, low fares, fun, and peanuts—lots and lots of peanuts. His vision for Southwest Airlines is still flying high, and still expanding.

A civil rights leader named Martin Luther King Jr. foresaw a world of fairness, justice, economic opportunity, and racial harmony. Much has been accomplished in bringing his vision to pass—though there is still much to be done.

Our president, George W. Bush, has pictured for us a vision of a world beyond terrorism. It will take a lot of time, money, and even blood to bring about the realization of his vision. But he has promised that we will not fail, we will not falter, we will *win*.

What is winning? Winning is making visions come true.

Winning is increasing profits, market share, return on investment, and shareholder value. And winning is also taking care of employee needs, creating more jobs, changing lives, and making life better for families. Winning is transforming neighborhoods and transforming the world. Winning is spreading a message of hope, peace, tolerance, faith, and love.

Leadership is all about winning, and through winning a leader obtains authority. And winning is about building a better world. This is true whether you are leading a business, a government, a church, a religious organization, a civic organization, a military unit, a family. It's all about winning, and transforming the world for the better.

You may think, *But I'm not a social do-gooder, and I'm not particularly religious. I just want to lead my company more effectively and make it more successful.*

Well, I certainly applaud and affirm success. But why should success be separated from transforming the world? There is only one planet Earth, and we all have to live in it together—so why not make it a better place? David Packard, cofounder of Hewlett-Packard, once said, "The company should be managed first and foremost to make a contribution to society." To which Peter Drucker adds, "Moral vision and commitment to social values are the foundation of enduring business success." You make a buck—and make the world a better place. That's what I call winning!

In their book *The Thing in the Bushes*, Kevin Ford and Jim Osterhaus cite a number of companies that are winning by earning big profits *and* changing the world for the better. For example, the pharmaceutical firm of Merck and Company spent millions of dollars developing a cure for a disease of the African tropics called *onchocerciasis* or "river blindness," caused by parasitic worms that invade the body and attack the eyes. Once the drug was developed, Merck provided more than one hundred million Mectizan tablets free of charge. Today, river blindness has been virtually eliminated in Africa. Winning is everything, and Merck is a winner.

Another company, Fel-Pro, manufactures gaskets for the automobile industry. Fel-Pro is a family-friendly company that offers its employees flexibility through onsite child care, college counseling, tuition scholarships, and more. Fel-Pro doesn't just care about making a profit. The company cares about making life better for its employees. Winning is everything, and Fel-Pro is a winner.

And let me tell you a story about winning from my own hometown of Orlando. It begins with a man named Harris Rosen, who grew up in New York City, then moved to Orlando in the early 1970s to work at Disney. As it turned out, Rosen didn't fit in with the Disney corporate philosophy, so he and Disney parted company. He stayed in Orlando, scraped together twenty-five thousand dollars to buy a motel, and a huge success story was launched.

As Orlando grew as a tourist and convention city, the hotel industry grew as well. Harris Rosen's motel became successful, and he kept building hotels to compete with all the giant hotel chains. As a result, he has had enormous success and has become a very wealthy man.

In 1994 Harris got a call from one of the Orange County commissioners concerning the plight of the Tangelo Park community. About five thousand African-Americans lived in an area that was drug-infested, vice-infested, and rundown. The people who lived there had no hope of a better future. So Harris Rosen got involved with the needs in Tangelo Park. He invested over $4 million of his own money to provide vocational training for moms and dads, early childcare for kids, and full college scholarships for any Tangelo Park student who finishes high school. The program is eight years old and has produced 250 college grads, with many more kids in the pipeline. Many of these graduates are coming back to motivate the younger kids and tell them about their success story.

Today, Tangelo Park is totally cleaned up. There's great pride in the look of the neighborhood among the people who live there. A YMCA has been built, many Orlando businesses (including Disney and Universal) are partnering and contributing to the community. And I'm proud to say that the Orlando Magic and Miracle have also contributed significantly, both as an organization and through the individual contributions and efforts of our players. It has become a model program for the rest of country.

Now, imagine five hundred Harris Rosens around the country, cleaning up scores and scores of Tangelo Parks, giving hope to thousands and thousands of people while inspiring many thousands of young people and giving them a future through education. Could you make that kind of commitment to your community? It's just a matter of seeing a need, then stepping up to meet it.

We must begin to see ourselves as servant leaders of the world. We must enlarge our vision, looking beyond balance sheets and stock prices, and begin to see our organizations as powerful engines for changing lives and transforming the world. Winning *is* everything, and there's a whole world to be won.

So what are we waiting for?

If we are going to call ourselves leaders, then let's lead. Let's lift our eyes and expand our vision.

Remember Paradox 1: *A visionary leader sees what is not there.* As a leader, you *must* have a vision. Your vision is your definition of winning. What does winning look like to you? Is your vision big enough, bold enough, and broad enough to embrace this hurting world we live in? Are there ways your organization could impact not just the marketplace, but human lives and human society? Can you see what is not there? Do you dare envision what *could* be?

Remember Paradox 2: *A wise leader dares to be a fool.* Once you have a vision of what could be, will you go to any lengths—and even sacrifice your dignity—to communicate that vision to your people?

Remember Paradox 3: *The strong leader dares to be weak.* You can't do it all. But if you are willing to trust other people, work through other people, and empower other people, you'll accomplish more than you could ever imagine! Take that bold vision of a better world, and hand it off to your people. Let them run with it! Watch in astonishment as they hammer that dream of yours into a reality!

And along the way, never forget the crucial importance of Paradox 4: *To live, you must die.* You must die to self, die to your baser impulses, die to your ego. In short, you must be a leader of character. Flaws in your character can be fatal to your vision. There's too much riding on that grand, wonderful, world-transforming vision of yours—so don't let character flaws become your fatal Achilles heel. Deal with hidden sins and flaws, ask close friends to hold you accountable for growth and change. Guard that vision with your life.

And remember Paradox 5: *The successful leader encourages failure.* Obviously, we want to be leaders of competence, leading organizations of competent people. But we sometimes forget that it takes failure to build competence. Failure is a great teacher—and the only real failure is the failure to learn from failure. You and your people are growing and learning together, even through failure, and that is as it should be.

And don't forget to be bold! Don't forget Paradox 6: *Your toughest crises are your best opportunities.* Opportunities are all around you—but they come disguised as problems and crises! So be bold and seize those opportunities. Use crises and problems as stepping stones to winning.

Above all else, remember Paradox 7: *The greatest leader is a servant.* Don't be a boss. Be a *real* leader, a *servant* leader. A servant leader is a winner. Even when he loses everything, even when he loses his life, a servant leader wins it all.

## LEAD WELL, THEN DEPART

I once had a speaking engagement in Kansas City, Missouri. Every day, wherever I am, I have always run to stay in shape. So I left my hotel and ran down Main Street in Kansas City. At the corner of 40th and Main I noticed a park—a tiny, well-tended square of grass and shrubs with a huge stone marker. People tend to pass such things without looking, but I am always curious; stone markers always have a story behind them. I veered over to that little park and jogged in place while reading the inscription on the marker.

It was a memorial erected in honor of a Kansas City native, Major Murray Davis. Major Davis had served in World War I. He was killed at Exermont, France, on September 28, 1918. On one side of the monument, chiseled into the stone, were these words:

> A kindly, just, and beloved officer,
> wise in counsel, resolute in action,
> courageous unto death.

Jogging around to the other side of the monument, I read further:

> Seriously wounded, he refused
> to relinquish his command until,
> mortally wounded, he fell,
> leading his comrades to victory.
> His last words were,
> "Take care of my men."

I read those words and thought, *I wish I could have met that man. Major Murray Davis must have been an awesome servant leader!*

No leader lives forever, but the words and deeds of servant leaders truly live on after they are gone. The greatest leader of all is not the boss, but the servant of all. It is a paradox, and hard for us to understand why it is so, but it is true: If anyone wants to be first, he must be the very last, and the servant of all.

Great leaders are like Major Murray Davis: Their only thoughts are for others, for the ones they lead, the ones they serve. "Take care of my people" is the last thing they think about when their eyes close in death.

Winning *is* everything. But winning can also cost you everything. It can even cost you your life. But a true servant leader willingly pays the price of victory. What was true of Major Murray Davis, and what was true of that Great Servant Leader who was nailed to a cross so long ago, is still true today: A true leader would rather die in victory than live in defeat, because "whoever wants to save his life will lose it."

How can you lose your life, yet win the battle? It's a deep paradox—perhaps the deepest of all. Only the mind of a servant leader can grasp it.

Tryon Edwards, in his *New Dictionary of Thoughts*, expressed the meaning of a servant leader's life and death in these words:

> The leaves in autumn do not change color from the blighting touch of frost, but from the process of natural decay. They fall when the fruit is ripened and their work is done. And their splendid coloring is but their graceful and beautiful surrender of life when they have finished their summer offering to service to God and man. One of the great lessons the fall of the leaf teaches us is this: "Do your work well, and then be ready to depart."

That is the legacy of a great leader. He gives his life to others and is satisfied with their fruitfulness. Their glory is his glory. And when his work is finished and the fruit is ripened, the servant leader falls gracefully to the earth.

Do your work well, servant leader. Lead by serving, serve by leading. Render your service to God and to others, and when your time is done, you will be ready to depart. If you give your life to serving others, then whatever you have done will be enough.

# Acknowledgments

With deep appreciation I acknowledge the support and guidance of the following people who helped make this book possible:

Special thanks to Bob Vander Weide and John Weisbrod of the RDV Sports family.

I owe deep gratitude to my assistant, Melinda Ethington, for all she does and continues to do for my family and me.

Hats off to three dependable associates—proofreader Ken Hussar, Hank Martens of the RDV Sports mail/copy room, and my ace typist, Fran Thomas.

Hearty thanks are also due to Rolf Zettersten and Leslie Peterson of Warner Books and to my partner in writing this book, Jim Denney. Thank you all for believing that I had something important to say and for providing the support and the forum to say it.

And finally, special thanks and appreciation go to my family, and particularly my wife, Ruth. They are truly the backbone of my life.

# Notes

Introduction
1. "Football's Funniest Stories: Curly Lambeau," electronically retrieved at http://library.thinkquest.org/12590/curly.htm.
2. Quoted in "Jesus' Effect on History," electronically retrieved at http://www.why-jesus.com/history.htm.
3. Ibid.George Bancroft (1800–1891) wrote the ten-volume *Bancroft's History*.
4. Ibid. Will Durant (1885–1981) was a Pulitzer-winning historian and philosopher and author of *The Story of Philosophy* and *Heroes of History*.
5. Often misattributed to "Anonymous" or "Author Unknown," the work was published by Dr. James Allen Francis in *The Real Jesus And Other Sermons* (Judson Press, 1926).
6. Electronically retrieved at http://admiralty.pacific.net.hk/~jeremiah/inspiration.html.
7. Quoted in "Jesus' Effect on History."

Paradox 1: A Visionary Leaders Sees What Is Not There
1. Destiny Law, "Interview with Art Linkletter," MousePlanet.com, electronically retrieved at http://www.mouseplanet.com/destiny/071700.htm.
2. Previously published in Pat Williams, *Go For the Magic* (Nashville: Thomas Nelson, 1995), 86.

3. Bruce Bickel and Stan Jantz, *Stories We Heard About Hope* (Nashville, J. Countryman, 2001), 22.

4. Quoted by Kevin Ford and James Osterhaus, *The Thing in the Bushes* (Colorado Springs: Piñon Press, 2001), 49.

5. Compiled from reports electronically retrieved at http://www.nycroads.com/crossings/brooklyn/.

## Paradox 2: A Wise Leader Dares to Be a Fool

1. Bert Decker, *You've Got to be Believed to be Heard* (New York: St. Martin's Press, 1992), 64–66.

2. Dave and Tom Gardner, "The 13 Steps to Investing Foolishly—Step 1: What Is Foolishness?," electronically retrieved at http://www.fool.com/school/13steps/stepone.htm.

3. Nancy Gibbs and John F. Dickerson, "The Power and the Story," *Time*, December 6, 1999, electronically retrieved at http://www.cnn.com/ALLPOLITICS/time/1999/12/06/mccain.html.

4. John Huey, "Discounting Dynamo Sam Walton," electronically retrieved at http://www.time.com/time/time100/builder/profile/walton1.html.

5. Quoted in *People*, 13 May 2002.

6. Bert Decker, *You've Got to be Believed to be Heard* (New York: St. Martin's Press, 1992), 36.

## Paradox 3: The Strong Leader Dares to Be Weak

1. Kevin Freiberg, "Go Nuts! Hire for Attitude, Train for Skill," electronically retrieved at http://sandiegoconsulting.com/bureau/lr_articles_hire_for.shtml.

## Paradox 4: To Live You Must Die

1. Father Martin Tierney, "The Messiahship of Jesus," sermon of Sunday, September 17, 2000, electronically retrieved at http://staudoens.dublindiocese.ie/frompulpit.asp?ID=73.

2. Dr. Michael O'Brien, "Leadership by Resolve," electronically retrieved from www.executiveleadershipsolutions.com/leadership_resolve.htm. O'Brien, "Leadership by Resolve."

3. Skip Wood, Morry Gash, "Favre is leader of the Pack," *USA Today*, 19 October 2001, electronically retrieved at www.usatoday.com/sports/ nfl/packers/2001–10–19-favre.htm.

4. Ibid.

5. First quoted in Pat Williams with Jim Denney, *Got Game?* (Nashville: J. Countryman, 2002), 67.

6. Story compiled from Eric Pooley, "*Time* Person of the Year: Mayor of the World," *Time*, 31 December 2001, electronically retrieved at http: //www.time.com/time/poy2001/poyprofile.html; and Amanda Ripley, "We're Under Attack: An Oral History of 9/11," *Time*, 31 December 2001, electronically retrieved at http://www.time.com/time/poy2001/ poyoral.html.

7. Jim Denney, *Answers to Satisfy the Soul* (Clovis, CA: Quill Driver Books, 2002), 11.

## Paradox 5: The Successful Leader Encourages Failures

1. Jon Krakauer, *Into Thin Air* (New York: Anchor Books, 1998).

2. Author and article title unknown, *Investors Business Daily*, Friday 3 May 2002, 3.

## Paradox 6: Your Toughest Crises Are Your Best Opportunities

1 A. W. Tozer, in *The Reaper*, February 1962, 459, electronically retrieved at http://www.geocities.com/webofrob/quotations/ SpirtualLeadershipSanders.html.

2. Lance Secretan, "Spirit At Work—Honey or Vinegar?," IndustryWeek.com, 17 August 2000, electronically retrieved at http: //www.industryweek.com/Columns/ASP/columns.asp?ColumnId=639.

You can contact Pat Williams directly at:
Pat Williams
c/o RDV Sports
8701 Maitland Summit Boulevard
Orlando FL 32810
(407) 916–2404
pwilliams@rdvsports.com

If you would like to set up a speaking engagement
for Pat Williams, please call or write his assistant,
Melinda Ethington, at the above address or call
her at (407) 916-2454. Requests can also be
faxed to (407) 916-2986 or e-mailed to
methington@rdvsports.com.